W9-CKE-361

China and the Transformation
of Global Capitalism

China and the Transformation of Global Capitalism

Edited by HO-FUNG HUNG

The Johns Hopkins University Press
Baltimore

© 2009 The Johns Hopkins University Press
All rights reserved. Published 2009
Printed in the United States of America on acid-free paper
2 4 6 8 9 7 5 3 1

The Johns Hopkins University Press
2715 North Charles Street
Baltimore, Maryland 21218-4363
www.press.jhu.edu

Library of Congress Cataloging-in-Publication Data

China and the transformation of global capitalism /
edited by Ho-fung Hung.
p. cm. — (Themes in global social change)
Includes bibliographical references and index.
ISBN-13: 978-0-8018-9307-0 (hardcover : alk. paper)
ISBN-10: 0-8018-9307-0 (hardcover : alk. paper)
ISBN-13: 978-0-8018-9308-7 (pbk. : alk. paper)
ISBN-10: 0-8018-9308-9 (pbk. : alk. paper)
1. China—Economic policy—2000– 2. China—Economic
conditions—2000– 3. Capitalism. 4. Economic
history—21st century. I. Hung, Ho-fung.
HC427.95.C4367 2009
337.51—dc22   2008044013

A catalog record for this book is available from the British Library.

*Special discounts are available for bulk purchases of this book.
For more information, please contact Special Sales
at 410-516-6936 or specialsales@press.jhu.edu.*

The Johns Hopkins University Press uses environmentally friendly
book materials, including recycled text paper that is composed of
at least 30 percent post-consumer waste, whenever possible.
All of our book papers are acid-free, and our jackets and
covers are printed on paper with recycled content.

Contents

Preface

About thirty years ago, in 1978, the Chinese Communist Party undertook a bold step to rejuvenate China's economy by shifting it from a centrally planned system to a market system as well as by opening China to foreign investment. This dramatic transition coincided with the beginning of the profound transformation of global capitalism, a transformation commonly known as "globalization," which helped unleash decades of rapid economic expansion in China.

After three whole decades of rapid growth, China is no longer an ordinary developing country or a formerly socialist economy struggling to *respond to* the challenge of global capitalism. It has become a geoeconomic and geopolitical heavyweight *reshaping* the structure of global capitalism. While an array of outstanding studies has informed us about the impact of China's global integration on Chinese society and politics, there is still a need for serious analysis of the impact of China's ascendancy on the world.

Today's mass media networks across the globe have produced plenty of commentaries on the rise of China as a global power, some of which are emotionally charged and politically biased. While some cheer China's rise as the death knell of an allegedly vicious Pax Americana, others lament China's looming threat and compare China's rise to that of authoritarian Germany in the early twentieth century. Some speak with certainty about the advent of a Chinese century, while others prophesize China's coming collapse. As a reaction to this profusion of opinion, this volume offers a more rigorous, nuanced, and scholarly assessment of the long-term global impact of China's ascendancy.

The idea for this volume originated in the panel "China and Global Capitalism" that I organized for the American Sociological Association annual meeting in 2006. I am most grateful to Christopher Chase-Dunn and Henry Tom for their support to include this volume in the Johns Hopkins University Press series on global social change. Their incisive advice at different stages of the project was invaluable. The critical comments of the anonymous reviewers helped sharpen and tighten the arguments of the book. The technical support offered by Suzanne Flinchbaugh and Deborah Bors at the JHU Press was seamless. Clem Brooks and Tim Hallett, my colleagues at Indiana University, as well as the participants of the Political Economy and Culture Workshop at the sociology department there, offered me insights into revising the introductory chapters to broaden the book's audience and make it more accessible to nonspecialists. Jason Smith helped format the manuscript. Amy Vanstee and Martin Schneider copyedited all chapters. Jaime Kucinskas helped prepare the index. Last but not least, I thank the department of sociology and the Research Center for Chinese Politics and Business at Indiana University for their financial support toward the production of the final manuscript. This project would never have come to fruition without the generosity of these individuals and institutions.

China and the Transformation
of Global Capitalism

CHAPTER ONE

Introduction

The Three Transformations of Global Capitalism

HO-FUNG HUNG

IN NOVEMBER 2007, a midlevel central government official in China made a casual remark in an international financial forum. He said that the Chinese government should consider reducing the portion of its assets denominated in U.S. dollars and diversifying the currency mix of its gigantic foreign exchange reserve, which exceeded 1.5 trillion in U.S. dollars and has been the biggest in the world since 2006. Within a few hours, the value of the dollar in the international currency market plunged by 1.2 percent against the euro and 1.7 percent against the yen. The power of this ordinary official from a developing country to talk down the value of the hegemonic currency in the world economy was simply unimaginable two decades ago, when currency values in the developing and non-Western world (mighty Japan included) were heavily dominated by the monetary policies of Washington, D.C. *The Economist* was not exaggerating when it remarked that "global monetary policy is increasingly being set in Beijing as well as Washington" (*The Economist*, July 28, 2005). China has also begun to be seen as the key player determining the fate of global free trade. As a *New York Times* article about the failure of WTO trade talks in the summer of 2008 remarked: "Not so long ago, global trade talks were steered largely by the United States, the European Union, Canada and Japan. . . . [But now,] the balance of power in global trade has shifted irrevocably with the rise of China" (July 29, 2008). China's increasing influence in the global economy is also shown in the more recent global financial crisis, during which the viability of the fiscal and monetary remedies that the United States employed to stabilize its economy and hence the global economy depended largely on the willingness of China to keep on purchasing U.S. Treasury bonds.

Politically, China, having bolstered its resource security by diverting a mammoth amount of investment and financial aid to resource-rich, authoritarian countries in the developing world, increasingly attracts criticism from human rights activists. They blame China for its complicity in human rights abuses from Sudan to Burma. Gone are the days when these activists attributed many of the developing world's social and political ills to Washington (for its support of right-wing dictators) or Washington-based international financial institutions such as the World Bank and the International Monetary Fund (for their structural adjustment programs that allegedly pauperized vast populations in the developing world). Governments in wealthy countries also increasingly call for the cooperation of China, given its rapidly expanding economic clout and its permanent seat in the UN Security Council, to help defuse potentially explosive conflicts involving North Korea, Iran, and other places.

These recent developments exemplify how China is rapidly becoming a geo-economic and geopolitical heavyweight capable of shaping the course of development of the world system. Media outlets in the Western world, dazzled by China's economic performance, are not short on optimists who see the dawn of a Chinese century à la the coming of the American century a hundred years ago. Many in the development policy circle are even hailing the rise of a "Beijing consensus," characterized by incremental and restrained market reform, as a model of development displacing the "Washington consensus," which espoused radical economic liberalization (Ramo 2004; Skenkar 2005). To transcend this frenzied cheer and develop a more profound understanding of the present and future trajectories of China's economic ascendancy as well as its long-term impact on the global capitalist system, we need to go beyond the observation of contingent short-term trends. We must examine how the rise of China has been embedded in the development of global capitalism in a longer-term historical perspective. This volume, then, offers contributions from prominent global political economists who have been studying the impact of China's rise in their respective fields.

In retrospect, the rise of China has been made possible by the structural transformations of the global capitalist system since the 1970s. The transformations are threefold, including (1) the advent of a new international division of labor, (2) the twin decline of U.S. hegemony and the Cold War order, and (3) the general decline of antisystemic movements in the form of working-class-based, state-power-oriented mass politics. The key questions that guide this volume's inquiry are as follows: What are the historical legacies that enable China to grasp the opportunities offered by these transformations to generate an economic miracle in world-historical proportion, as we are seeing today? How is the economic ascendancy of China in turn shaping the courses of these transformations? What kind of new global order is that ascendancy fostering in the twenty-first century? Before we answer these questions, we need to understand the nature of the late-twentieth-century transformations of global capitalism that prepared the stage for China's rise.

THE MAKING OF A U.S.-CENTERED GLOBAL CAPITALIST ORDER

According to Immanuel Wallerstein's classic formulation, the world capitalist system is constituted by a hierarchical international division of labor, which differentiates the system into core, periphery, and semiperiphery zones. These three zones are specialized in high-value-added products, low-value-added products, and a mix of the two, respectively. This division of labor is contained in an interstate system, which is governed by a hegemonic power that enjoys overwhelming economic competitiveness and legitimate political leadership over other core states (Wallerstein 1974, 1979, 1980, 1989). The pursuit of profit and the accumulation of capital are not always smooth. They are periodically interrupted by intracore conflicts, in which core powers vie for hegemonic status, and surges of antisystemic movements, through which the subaltern classes resist the polarization between the haves and have-nots within the system (Chase-Dunn 1998; Arrighi and Silver 1999).

Following the turbulent four decades of the early twentieth century marked by the decline of British hegemony; the collapse of the nineteenth-century global free-trade order; total war among hegemonic contenders including Germany, Britain, and the United States; and the offensives of labor, communist, and anticolonial movements covering all corners of the world, the world system came to stabilize under U.S. hegemony in the mid–twentieth century (Arrighi 1994: ch. 4). This mid-twentieth-century global capitalist order was first and foremost grounded in the overwhelming superiority of the U.S. economy over all other core countries in Western Europe plus Japan, which were devastated by the war. American competitiveness was based on the Fordist-Keynesian regime of capital accumulation that gestated in the Progressive Era and consolidated in the midst of New Deal reforms. On the one hand, vertically integrated, scientifically and bureaucratically managed corporations pioneered by the Ford Motor Company became efficient economic units geared toward mass production of goods and services. On the other hand, Keynesian expansion of government's social spending, in combination with stable and high-wage employment in Fordist enterprises, fostered the ceaseless growth of a mass-consumption market that guaranteed the sale of mass-manufactured products (Gramsci 1971; Chandler 1977; Aglietta 1979; Harvey 1989).

In the quarter century following the end of the Second World War, most other core countries replicated this regime of capital accumulation while recovering from the war. These economies became profitable sites of investment for American transnational corporations and viable markets for American products. In the periphery of the world system, newly decolonized countries, influenced by American aid and encouragement, adopted state-led industrialization programs as a variant of the Fordist-Keynesian regime of high government spending and interventionist economic planning. Despite some success with these programs, however, many periphery countries failed to escape from the colonial division of labor under which they exported primary goods to core countries in exchange for manufactured products. These countries became growing outlets for U.S. agribusiness investment and manufacturing exports. With its corporations enjoying an unmatched advantage in both core and periphery countries, the United States warranted the financial stability of the global economy by maintaining the fixed gold value of the dollar, to which all major currencies were pegged under the monetary regime instituted at the Bretton Woods Conference of 1944. The gold standard of the dollar was backed by the colossal gold repository in the U.S. Federal Reserve (Block 1977; Gilpin 1987: chs. 4–5; Arrighi 1994: ch. 4; McMichael 2008: chs. 2–3).

Accompanying the geoeconomic centrality of the United States was its leadership in the Cold War geopolitical architecture. With the real or imagined threat of the expansion of Soviet socialism, capitalist states in the developed and developing world depended on the United States for their security. Under the NATO framework, Western European countries left their defense to the U.S. war machine and counted on American military presence to deter the Soviet tanks and nuclear missiles amassing along the East-West border. In East Asia, Japan was reduced to a semisovereign state under the pacifist constitution conceived during the U.S. occupation. Stripped of the right to develop its own army, Japan became a large springboard for the United States to project its military prowess into the West Pacific, which was dotted with U.S. or U.S.-friendly military bases from South Korea to the Strait of Malacca as smaller springboards for U.S. power projection (Katzenstein and Shiraishi 1997; Gowan 1999: chs. 2–4). In the developing world, most capitalist countries were U.S. client states in one way or another. These states could hardly survive internal rebellion or invasion by neighboring communists without financial and military aid from the United States. Whenever U.S. allies lost control of state power, the CIA was always there to help, as the numerous right-wing coups, from Iran in 1953 to Chile in 1973, show all too well.

During the heyday of U.S. hegemony, even antisystemic movements were absorbed into the establishment. In the early twentieth century, labor movements in the core countries and socialist as well as national liberation movements in the semiperiphery (Russia, Central and Eastern Europe) and periphery (the colonized world) were on the offensive. These movements significantly shifted the capital-labor and colonizers-colonized balance of power in favor of labor and the colonized. Building on these gains, these movements became part of the status quo in the mid–twentieth century. In the core countries, working-class–based parties and labor unions became a constituent component of the welfare state through electoral victory and institutionalized bargaining between labor and capital. In Eastern Europe and in the periphery, communist and national liberation movements came to power. These once destabilizing antisystemic movements, however, were as much pacified as they were successful in the postwar decades, when they lost most of their militancy and mutated from challengers to conservative stakeholders in the U.S.-centered global order. While mainstream worker organizations in core countries turned away from disruptive labor activism, countries in the Soviet bloc were ever more keen to stabilize the Cold War order through formal or illicit diplomatic dealings with the West, even at the height of a Cold War confrontation as tense as the Cuban missile crisis in 1962 (Arrighi et al. 1989; Wallerstein 1990; Arrighi and Silver 1999: ch. 3).

Becoming victims of their own success, traditional working-class–based politics waned in core countries when they were seen as part of a corrupt establishment and rejected by a younger generation of radicals coming of age in the late 1960s. In the 1960s, student and worker revolts caused less damage to the capitalist order than to the legitimacy of traditional labor unions and left-wing parties, which came to be labeled derogatorily as the "Old Left." In the meantime, the international communist movement had been on the defensive under effective containment by capitalist countries and challengers from within, as shown by the backing down of the Soviets in the Cuban missile crisis, the Budapest uprising in 1956, and the Prague Spring in 1968 (Arrighi et al. 1989; Amin et al. 1990; Chase-Dunn and Boswell 2000). The successful offensive of the Viet Cong in the 1960s was the exception that proved the rule. Despite its triumph in bogging down the U.S. Marines in the jungles of Vietnam, it never managed to trigger the domino effect in Southeast Asia that the United States had so feared. In a similar vein, despite Che Guevara's cult status among First World youth and his publicized goal of "creating two, three, many more Vietnams," he never succeeded in exporting any viable revolution to other Third World countries. The antisystemic movements that sprang up in the early twentieth century, which contributed significantly to the labor and Third World friendliness of postwar global capitalism, had lost their legitimacy and vitality as a progressive force for change by the 1970s, a decade when the global capitalist order started to experience profound geoeconomic and geopolitical reconfigurations.

TRANSFORMATIONS OF GLOBAL CAPITALISM IN THE LATE TWENTIETH CENTURY

By the late 1960s, Germany, Japan, and other core countries had fully recovered from the Second World War and had developed efficient manufacturing systems that were as competitive as, if not more competitive than, U.S. manufacturers. The resulting overflow of manufactured products in the world market threatened manufacturing profitability and ushered in a prolonged period of general decline in the rate of profit across the capitalist system (Brenner 2002). This trend of falling profit rates was the origin of the protracted economic and fiscal malaises in many core countries in the 1970s. Having lost its economic competitiveness to other core powers and suffered from a depletion of gold reserve owing to its deteriorating fiscal crisis and current account deficit, the United States became incapable of shouldering the burden of holding up the financial stability of the global economy. Immediately after Nixon announced the dissolution of the gold standard of the dollar in 1971, the Bretton Woods regime of the fixed exchange rate collapsed, and the global economy entered a period of ever-increasing volatility (Block 1977; Gilpin 1987: ch. 4). The Fordist-Keynesian regime of capital accumulation, which accounted for the more than two decades of postwar prosperity in most core countries, ran into deep crisis. Fordist corporations became ailing dinosaurs, simply too big and too bureaucratic to adapt to the increasingly volatile and competitive world economy. Fiscal deterioration of core governments curtailed their capacity in continuing the Keynesian strategy of stimulating the economy through ever-enlarging public expenditures (Harvey 1990: 121–200).

Economic crises in the capitalist core induced a new international division of labor in the 1970s as the first transformation of global capitalism. To cope with falling profits and cut costs, core corporations shifted from a Fordist, vertically integrated mode of organization to a more flexible form of organization based on multilayered subcontracting. The networks of subcontracting soon transgressed national borders when more labor-intensive segments of production were outsourced to manufacturers in peripheral, low-wage countries. Replacing the old core-periphery division of labor based on the periphery's export of raw materials in exchange for manufactured products from the core, the new international division of labor turned part of the periphery into new manufacturing bases of the global system (Froebel et al. 1980; Harvey 1990: 121–200; McMichael 2008: chs. 5–7; Hung 2008).

The original East Asian Tigers, being South Korea, Taiwan, Hong Kong, and Singapore, became the prime destination of these shifting manufacturing activities (we will see the forces behind the rise of East Asia in the next section). Thanks to their success as new manufacturing hubs, the Tigers' structural position in the world system rapidly ascended from the periphery to the semiperiphery (in the cases of South Korea and Taiwan) or even to the core (in the case of Hong Kong and Singapore), as indicated by their great leap in per capita national income (Arrighi and Drangel 1986). The scale and scope of this new international division of labor expanded dramatically in the 1980s and 1990s in the wake of the collapse of most import-substitution regimes in other parts of the developing world, in addition to the world trade liberalization that had been aggressively promoted by the United States since the Reagan administration.

Concurrent with the advent of the new international division of labor was the erosion of the legitimate leadership of the United States over other core economies. When economic competition among the United States, Europe, and Japan intensified in the 1970s in the midst of protracted economic woes, the struggle for export markets developed into trade wars, and the ideological homogeneity within this triple alliance against the Soviet bloc began to unravel. Policy makers and academics in Japan and continental Europe started to emphasize that their distinct models of capitalist development, under the names of "Japanese developmental state" and "German corporatist capitalism," for example, were superior varieties of capitalism compared with the American model of liberal capitalism. Even if the distinctiveness of European and Japanese capitalism is exaggerated, what matters most is that Japan and Europe no longer saw the American model as a universal one to emulate. They became keen on asserting their own identities as a counterpoint to the United States (Stallings 1995; Hall and Soskice, eds. 2001).

This intracore rivalry escalated in the 1980s, when the common enemy that had been binding the core powers together—the communist world—weakened dramatically. We saw in the previous section that by the 1970s, revolutionary movements crystallizing into the actually existing socialist states had lost their appeal as progressive alternatives to the capitalist order. Worse still, these centrally planned economies had lost their growth momentum by the early 1980s, and major socialist states started experimenting on market-oriented reform to differ- ent extents to rejuvenate their stagnant economies. It became all too clear that the socialist bloc no longer constituted a threat to the capitalist core. With the be- ginning of the end of the Cold War, Japan and Western Europe stepped up their efforts to increase their economic competitiveness vis-à-vis the United States by consolidating their respective regional orders. While Japan carved out its sphere of influence in East and Southeast Asia by deepening its investment and trade links within the region, European integration accelerated and European econo- mies extended and deepened their reach to Africa. By the late 1980s, it appeared that the direct influence of the United States was ever more constricted to the Americas. Many anticipated the rise of a tripolar structure of global capitalism, with the United States leading the Americas, Germany leading Europe and Africa, and Japan leading East and Southeast Asia (Stallings 1990; Katzenstein and Shiraishi 1997; Katzenstein 2005, 1997).

These first two transformations of global capitalism, namely, the inception of a new international division of labor and the decline of U.S. hegemony among core powers, occurred in conjunction with and were reinforced by the third trans- formation: the implosion of most working-class–based, state-power–oriented mass movements that had once effectively constrained the class power of capital across the world system. Whence the decline of actually existing state socialism removed a common enemy of core capitalist powers, aggravated the intracore rivalry, and triggered the decline of U.S. hegemony, the losing momentum of working-class movements and parties within core countries and elsewhere cleared the way for the deepening and widening of the new international division of labor.

In the 1980s, when the Reagan administration in the United States and the Thatcher government in the United Kingdom moved in concert to dismantle the Keynesian welfare state, to reverse state protection of stable employment, and to promote free trade globally, they met considerable initial resistance from orga- nized labor and the social movement sector in general at home and abroad. But when Margaret Thatcher famously declared that "there is no alternative," she meant it. She seemed to realize the wane of antisystemic movements across the world system and anticipate the dissipation of resistance to her neoliberal on- slaught. And she was right. The labor movements, having been part of the estab- lishment for a long time, were proven to be too tamed to resist neoliberal reforms. The so-called New Left, originating in the rebellious 1960s, were too disorganized to respond as well (or too indulgent in cultural politics to notice any global polit- ical economic changes at all). Within a few years, capital was freed from the past constraints of the redistributive and relatively labor-friendly Fordist-Keynesian regime of capital accumulation, and class power of capital vis-à-vis labor was substantially elevated by the energetic neoliberal states in the name of the free market. In a matter of two decades, outsourcing, deindustrialization, and casualization of work swept through major cities in core countries. Developing countries, one after the other, opened their gates voluntarily or involuntarily to the influx of transnational capital. Export-processing zones populated by unregulated despotic regimes of factory production proliferated throughout the developing world (Harvey 2005).

The rise of the new international division of labor, the rise of multiple and rival capitalist centers among core countries, and the rollback of antisystemic movements in the last three decades of the twentieth century constituted the stage on which China fostered its miraculous economic expansion. But before we move from these three transformations to the rise of China, we must first examine the rise of an East Asian regional capitalist order as the intermediate step linking the two processes.

THE THREE TRANSFORMATIONS, EAST ASIAN CAPITALISM, AND THE RISE OF CHINA

At the height of the Cold War, in the 1950s and 1960s, East and Southeast Asia occupied a special place in the U.S.-centric global capitalist order. As the two most deadly conflicts of the Cold War—the Korean War and the Vietnam War—were fought in the region, Asia was always regarded as the most vulnerable link in the containment of communism. The U.S. client states in the region were therefore deemed too important to fail. Washington was exceptionally generous in creating favorable conditions for these states to prosper, including financial and military aid and openness of Western markets to East Asian exports. These conditions enabled the emergence of resourceful developmental states, which managed to stay away from the temptation of import-substitution industrialization prevailing in most other developing countries and took on the export-oriented industrialization strategy early on (Haggard 1990; Wade 1990; Evans 1995; So and Chiu 1995). Having established dense export links to Western consumer markets by the 1960s, East Asia became the primary destination of industrial outsourcing in the advent of the new international division of labor in the 1970s.

Besides Cold War geopolitics, the success of Japan and the Tigers as industrial exporters is also attributable to internal characteristics of the region. The legacy of a communal, patriarchal, agrarian social order based on labor-intensive wet-rice cultivation and the peasant origins of most women factory workers in East Asia contributed to the docility, discipline, and low reproduction cost of labor in these countries (Bray 1986; Sugihara 2003; see also chapter 2 of this volume). The conscious leadership of Japan in advancing the regional economy also helped. Under the domination of Japanese capital either through Japanese foreign direct investment or the multilayered subcontracting system centered on Japanese corporations, Japan maintained a stable division of labor along the value chain with other East and Southeast Asian economies. Japan always specialized in higher-value-added products, and the four original Tigers, together with other late-coming new Tigers such as Thailand and Malaysia, concentrated on lower-value-added ones. When individual economies in the region moved up the value chain, they did so in a coordinated manner so that the East Asian region would move up as a whole without disrupting the intraregional division of labor. This collective and hierarchical path of regional development is characterized metaphorically as the inverted V–shaped "flying geese" model (Akamatsu 1962; Ozawa 1979; see also chapter 2).

In the 1980s and the first half of the 1990s, when the rivalry among American, Japanese, and European capitalism intensified, Japan shored up its global competitiveness by stepping up its investment and development assistance to its Asian neighbors to expand and consolidate its leadership role in East Asia. This model of capitalist development through regionalization was so successful that many saw in the early 1990s the emergence of a Japan-centered Greater East Asian Co-Prosperity Sphere, a prospect for which Japan had longed since the early twentieth century but militarism in the 1930s and 1940s failed to achieve (Doner 1997; Shiraishi 1997; Pempel 1997; Koschmann 1997). With the whole East Asian region behind it, Japan posed an increasing threat to the global economic leadership of the United States. This dynamic of East Asian regionalism and Japan's leadership in it, nonetheless, has been increasingly in flux since the early 1990s as a result of China's accelerating market transition and opening.

To look back, China's reintegration with the capitalist economies in East Asia and beyond was part and parcel of the grand demise of antisystemic movements. The seizure of state power by the Chinese Communist Party (CCP) in 1949 constituted one of the most spectacular achievements of the socialist revolutionary and national liberation movements in the twentieth century. The CCP was heavily involved in the Korean War and the Vietnam War and supported leftist guerrilla movements in various Southeast and South Asian states. It was precisely the existence of such a formidable communist regime that caused East Asia to be perceived as the weakest link in the U.S. camp of the Cold War.

In the 1950s, the CCP was closely affined to the Soviet Union. But starting in the 1960s, it increasingly departed from the Soviet model of a highly centralized command economy and moved to a distinct development pattern that hinged more on mass mobilization (Schurmann 1966; Selden 1993). The conjunction of the CCP's internal factional struggle, the territorial dispute between China and Russia, and the enthusiasm of the CCP to expand its influence to other revolutionary movements in the developing world at the expense of Soviet influence eventually led to an all-out ideological split between the two socialist states. While the Soviets were on the irreversible road of bureaucratization and accommodation with core capitalist powers, Mao and his ultra-leftist allies were anxious to keep China's revolution fervent by denouncing "Soviet revisionism" and mobilizing students and workers to smash the Stalinist bureaucratic machine created by the CCP itself during the Cultural Revolution of 1966–69 (see Chan 1985; Perry and Xun 1997; Meisner 1999; Esherick, Pickowicz, and Walder 2006). But Mao's ardent efforts to keep the revolution alive did not last long. After his opponents within the party were cleansed and Red Guard factionalism pushed China to the brink of civil war, Mao put a brake on the Cultural Revolution in the Party Congress of 1969, bringing an effective end to the Revolution despite its nominal continuation. After the Congress, Red Guard organizations were disbanded and their participants banished to the countryside, the party-state was rebureaucratized, and, most important, the CCP started reconciling with the U.S. camp of the Cold War to countervail the mounting military pressure at the Sino-Soviet border. The CCP's conservative turn culminated in the resumption of China's diplomatic relations with the United States, Japan, and most other Western capitalist states in the early 1970s. It marked the transformation of Communist China from an antisystemic force to a status-quo power in the global capitalist order (Dirlik 1994; Selden 1997).

China's reengagement with core capitalist powers in the early 1970s was followed by its full-fledged geoeconomic reintegration with these powers in the late 1970s, when the central government, out of the desperate aspiration to revive a national economy in tatters, started to empower selective local states to initiate market reform and open their local economies to foreign investors, particularly export-oriented manufacturers from other East Asian states (see; Shirk 1993; Naughton 1995; Zweig 2002; Guthrie 2006). Ceasing to be an antisystemic champion of working-class interests, the CCP came to employ its repressive apparatus, which was originally intended for exercising the "dictatorship of the proletariat" against the bourgeoisie, to ensure the docility of its huge rural workforce migrating to coastal cities to work under the despotic factory regimes (Pun 1995; Lee 1998).

The opening of China to foreign direct investment was initially restricted in the 1980s to its southern coastal provinces. The inflow of export-oriented manufacturing investment from Japan and the Four Tigers led to the integration of South China into the East Asian regional economic order characterized by the Japan-led flying geese formation. The majority of foreign direct investment in China had been from other East Asian economies, with Hong Kong, Taiwan, and Japan topping the list. From the 1980s to the 1990s, many regarded South China as the "Fifth Tiger" or the latest goose to join the flying geese formation, assuming that the rise of China was no more than a simple extension of the Japan-led regional order. China benefited tremendously from the capital, marketing networks, and management as well as the technical know-how that capitalists from Japan and the Four Tigers brought with their investments, just as Southeast Asian countries such as Thailand benefited from their investments. But when China's opening deepened, widened, and accelerated during the 1990s, it turned out that this was no ordinary goose. Provided with its huge supply of low-wage labor, its vast pool of engineers and technicians originating from the state socialist sector, and its potential as a megamarket for manufactured goods, China is capable of absorbing not only low-value-added manufacturing activities but also manufacturing investments from all levels of the value chain. The anxiety that China's rise was at the expense of other East Asian economies is best described by the well-known article "A panda breaks the [flying geese] formation" in *The Economist*:

> Most of China's neighbors react to the mainland's industrial rise with a mix of alarm and despair. Japan, South Korea and Taiwan fear a "hollowing out" of their industries, as factories move to low-cost China. South-East Asia worries about "dislocation" in trade and investment flows. . . . China is no goose. It does not conform to the . . . stereotype [of a flying goose], because it makes simple goods and sophisticated ones at the same time, rag nappies and microchips. . . . China makes goods spanning the entire value chain, on a scale that determines world prices. Hence East Asia's anxiety. If China is more efficient at everything, what is there left for neighbors to do? (August 25, 2001)

In fact, some did attribute the Asian Financial Crisis of 1997–98 to the rise of China, the competitive pressure from which threw many other vibrant, export-oriented, industrial economies in the region into disarray (Krause 1998; cf. Pempel ed. 1999). While absorbing much of the capital, marketing networks, and know-how in export-oriented manufacturing that other East Asian states had accumulated in the previous phase of East Asia's rise, the dazzling economic expansion of China is turning the rise of East Asia into the rise of China. To be sure,

Japan and the original Tigers eventually may devise effective strategies to reinstate their unique competitive edges, as illustrated by the high-tech boom of South Korea after the Asian Financial Crisis, the booming export of Japanese capital goods to China, and Singapore's aggressive bid to become an interregional hub linking East, Southeast, and South Asia. But China is undoubtedly becoming the single most important source of economic dynamism in Asia. That China, unlike Japan and all the Tigers, is not a client state of the United States but is an independent geopolitical and military force capable of challenging the United States—at least within Asia—makes its rise even more distinct from the earlier rise of Japan and the Tigers.

ARGUMENTS OF THE BOOK

The triple transformations of global capitalism in the late twentieth century, that is, the rise of the new international division of labor, the decline of U.S. hegemony and the Cold War order, and the great retreat of antisystemic movements, made the rise of East Asia and the later rapid economic expansion of China possible. But possibility differs from inevitability, and it still cannot fully explain the rise of China. In chapters 2 and 3, Giovanni Arrighi and Alvin So fill this explanatory gap by detailing how China's historical legacies enabled it to grasp the opportunities generated by these transformations, with the former focusing on the legacies of early modern times and the latter focusing on the Mao period of the People's Republic of China. For Arrighi, Europe and China diverged in their paths of market development in the early modern era. While the Chinese path was labor-intensive, capital-saving, and introverted, the Western path was labor-saving, capital-intensive, and extroverted under the military patronage of the state. While the Western path eclipsed the Chinese path in the century and a half following the Opium War of 1839–42, the Western path attained its limits in the 1970s, when the Chinese path began to resurge. This resurgence manifested first in the form of the rise of Japan and the East Asian Tigers, which has promptly been followed by the rise of China itself. Viewed in this light, China's rise today is not so much a surprise as it is a restoration of the long-term advantage of the Chinese path of development over the Western path, after a fleeting triumph of the latter.

Focusing on the legacies of the Communist party-state instituted in the three decades of Maoist development prior to the reopening of China, So argues in chapter 3 that the Maoist legacy is more an advantage than a constraint to China's economic growth in the reform era. The party-state laid the solid foundation of a strong developmental state, which enabled China to depart from the typical neo-liberal path of market reform that made many other developing countries succumb to transnational capital. The ideology of national liberation on which the legitimacy of the Chinese communist revolution was grounded enabled China to mobilize the support of diasporic Chinese capital in East Asia and beyond. Had it not been for the long- and medium-term historical legacies outlined by Arrighi and So, China would have found it much more difficult to seize the chance of the global capitalist transformation as described above.

As a beneficiary of these transformations, China is also starting to shape their courses. In the arena of geoeconomics, China's rise is empowering peripheral manufacturers and may well improve their bargaining position in the new international division of labor. Geopolitically, China's rise is creating new sources of conflict with core powers, which adamantly defend their economic dominance and natural-resource supply over China. But China is also heralding new alliances that can bring the world's interstate system closer to a multipolar order. In the realm of antisystemic movement, the rapid formation of a new working class in China, their integration into the global supply chain, and their budding activism could help revive the class power of global labor.

In chapter 4, Richard Appelbaum argues that the rise of China is reshaping the distribution of power and profit in the global supply chain. In the existing supply chain, most manufacturing contractors are small businesses that are so numerous and diffused that the few monopoly chain retailers from the core could easily throw them into cutthroat competition for contracts that entail very slim profit margins. But Appelbaum finds that the increasing consolidation of production into a few giant transnational contractors, which are based mostly in the Greater China Region and have started extending their manufacturing activities to Central and South America and Africa, is tilting the balance of power between retailers and contractors in the latter's favor. Some of these giant contractors are even resourceful enough to generate links with other firms and sectors locally that can speed up industrial upgrading and thereby foster broader-based economic development in China and East Asia at large.

While the rise of China is reshaping the economic balance of power between core and periphery, it is also generating a myriad of possible sources of geopolitical strain and conflict. History shows that the dramatic rise of any new economic power in the world system always comes at the expense of preexisting leading powers. This can lead to large-scale conflict between the rising and falling powers, as the experience of Germany's rise at the turn of the twentieth century shows all too well. The rise of China and Asia at large in the last three decades has, fortunately, not yet generated such conflict. József Böröcz explains this in chapter 5 by arguing that the loss of geoeconomic and geopolitical influence wielded by the traditional core powers caused by Asia's rise has so far been compensated by their geoeconomic and geopolitical gains resulting from the peripheralization of the Eastern European states and Russia. Böröcz expects that when the decline of the former Soviet bloc bottoms out, the further rise of China will truly come at the expense of core powers, after which geopolitical conflicts between the two parties will escalate dramatically. The imminent trade war between China and the Western world, together with recently mounting rhetoric about the "China threat" in the United States, Europe, and Japan, seems to attest to this prediction.

From a more specific angle, Paul Ciccantell, armed with the natural re-source–centric perspective of new historical materialism, delineates in chapter 6 how China's aggressive move to secure its natural resource supply is becoming a new and increasingly heated source of geopolitical rivalry. The resource compe-tition between China and Japan is an illustrative case. Just as the United States ag-gressively took over Britain's resource peripheries in different parts of the world during the early twentieth century and Japan took over the resource peripheries of the United States in the second half of the twentieth century, China is seizing Japan's resource peripheries by offering what appear to be better deals to raw ma-terial–exporting states and firms. What is distinct about the current China-Japan competition for natural resources is that the two countries lack the cultural affinity and alliance relationship that underlined Britain-U.S. and U.S.-Japan re-lations in earlier times. This increases the likelihood that China's aggressive ap-propriation of Japan's channels of natural resources supply could lead to conflict between the two countries. Worse, China's aggressive search for new resource pe-ripheries is also exacerbating its economic and political tensions with the United States and Europe.

While China's aggressiveness in securing its resource supply is pushing it to-ward a plausible collision course with existing powers, it is also moving China to-ward a new alliance with other major geopolitical players. According to John Gulick in chapter 7, the possibility of a Sino-Russian alliance is growing. On the one hand, Russia's abundant hydrocarbon deposits are an attractive alternative source of energy for China, as they could safely be transferred to China across its northern border without going through any region under U.S. control (such as the Strait of Malacca is to Middle East oil). China also could benefit, or is already benefiting, from the transfer of military and space technology from Russia. At the same time, Russia, fretting over the tremendous loss of its geopolitical clout and national prestige following the collapse of the Soviet Union, is increasingly pressed by the expanding U.S. military presence in Eastern Europe and West Central Asia. This pressure helps push Russia toward a deeper partnership with China, which shares its vision for a multipolar world and commands sufficient financial power to purchase its natural resources at whatever high prices. This plausible partnership, sure to benefit Russia and China both, could constitute the base of a formidable semiperiphery power bloc across Eurasia that poses a serious challenge to the United States and other core powers.

Beside the possibility of bringing about profound geoeconomic and geopolitical realignment, the rise of China also generates new possibilities for the revival of the world labor movement that could be powerful enough to reverse the mounting class power of capital against labor. Deindustrialization in many core countries during the 1980s and 1990s was accelerated by the demise of traditional labor unionism, which turned to protectionist and xenophobic postures in a desperate and futile attempt to curtail industrial outsourcing. But as Stephanie Luce and Edna Bonacich point out in chapter 8, the integration of a huge number of Chinese laborers working under draconian conditions in the production end of the global supply chain, their incipient labor activism, and the increasing militancy among logistic and service workers on the wholesale and retail end of the global supply chain are enabling the rise of transnational supply chain organizing that could foment the solidarity of workers from Shenzhen, China, to Long Beach, California. The highly integrated nature of the supply chain and the just-in-time mode of production and distribution mean that coordinated action at strategic nodes of the chain could cause a large disruption to the capital accumulation process, hence increasing the bargaining power of global labor.

From a different perspective, Beverly Silver and Lu Zhang, grounded on ethnographic investigation of labor politics in today's China and historical observation of new labor activism in previous rising centers of capitalism, further attest in chapter 9 to the plausibility of the global labor movement's revival, with China as a prospective new center of labor unrest. They find that dislocating capitalist transition in China has already triggered both "Polanyi-type labor unrest" and "Marx-type labor unrest," which were also seen by other rising manufacturing centers such as the United States in the early twentieth century and South Korea in the late twentieth century. While the Polanyi-type unrest, which resists the threat posed by the expanding market economy to preexisting livelihoods and social ties, is proliferating in China's northern cities, where employment and benefits of state factory workers are decaying under the market transition, the Marx-type unrest, which features proactive activism undertaken by the nascent proletarians created by the expanding market, is blossoming in the export-oriented industrial boom towns, where migrant laborers have started to organize for wage increases and improved working conditions.

In sum, what the chapters of this book present is not a predetermined, unilinear path of global capitalist development in the twenty-first century but a cacophony of possible trajectories of global change that the rise of China entails. Despite the divergence in details, the chapters converge on the observation of three emergent trends that China's rise is enabling: increasing bargaining power of peripheral manufacturers in the global supply chain, movement toward a multipolar interstate system amid rising geopolitical tensions, and resurgence of global labor power. To be sure, whether these trends will materialize into lasting new structures of global capitalism in the new century hinges much on the uninterrupted economic ascendancy of China.

In the conclusion, I take on the question of the sustainability of China's economic expansion. The internal sociopolitical dynamics of the Chinese miracle resembles in many ways the rapid economic expansion of the United States in the 1920s. Similar to the Roaring Twenties, today's China witnesses an increasing concentration of wealth and power into monopoly capital and a marginalization of the vast population in the share of prosperity. The consequence is a deteriorating internal economic imbalance characterized by overinvestment and underconsumption as well as China's overreliance on rich countries' debt-financed consumption spree, which has started to collapse since 2008. In addition, China's reckless industrialization fosters a deepening environmental crisis that increasingly constitutes a hindrance to China's further development. The good news is that the Chinese government is aware of the risk of a prolonged economic crisis as well as of the severity of environmental degradation. Major players within the government have been attempting to reshape China's developmental model to bring about a more balanced and environment-friendly economy. If they succeed, China's economic expansion will find a more sustainable course in the long run. The bad news is that these rebalancing acts are so far not sufficiently deep and timely and that the vested interests in the current developmental path are adamantly resisting such rebalancing efforts. In early-twentieth-century America, the changes in the sociopolitical structure necessary for more balanced and sustainable growth eventually came via New Deal reforms during the Great Depression. To be more precise, it was the Great Depression (and the subsequent Second World War) that made possible those long-delayed reforms, which had been deemed too radical to be realistic during the Roaring Twenties. It remains to be seen whether the recent global economic crisis, which is bringing grave challenges to the Chinese economy, will play a similar role of speeding up the necessary rebalancing of the Chinese economy.

We have reasons to expect that the rise of China and the global transformations it brings can continue in the long run. But as it took a depression and a world war for the rise of the United States to come to fruition, it is certainly possible that the China's rise over the long term will be likewise interspersed with the throes of economic turbulence, geopolitical conflict, and social upheaval in the medium run. That medium run is a highly indeterminate arena where precise prediction is extremely difficult, if not impossible. It is an arena where the strategic and contingent actions of states, enterprises, social movements, and other human agents within and without China truly matter.

REFERENCES

Aglietta, Michel. 1979. A Theory of Capitalist Regulation: The U.S. Experience. London: Verso.

Akamatsu, Kaname. 1962. "A Historical Pattern of Economic Growth in Developing Countries." Journal of Developing Economies 1, no. 1: 3–25.

Amin, Samir, Giovanni Arrighi, Andre Gunder Frank, and Immanuel Wallerstein. 1990. Transforming the Revolution: Social Movements and the World-System. New York: Monthly Review Press.

Arrighi, Giovanni. 1994. The Long Twentieth Century: Money, Power, and the Origins of Our Times. London: Verso.

Arrighi, Giovanni, and Jessica Drangel. 1986. "The Stratification of the World-Economy: An Exploration of the Semiperipheral Zone." Review 10, no. 1: 9–74.

Arrighi, Giovanni, Terence K. Hopkins, and Immanuel Wallerstein. 1989. Antisystemic Movements. New York: Verso.

Arrighi, Giovanni, and Beverly J. Silver. 1999. Chaos and Governance in the Modern World System. Minneapolis: University of Minnesota Press.

Block, Fred L. 1977. The Origins of International Economic Disorder: A Study of United States International Monetary Policy from World War II to the Present. Berkeley: University of California Press.

Bray, Francesca. 1986. The Rice Economies: Technology and Development in Asian Societies. Berkeley: California University Press.

Chan, Anita. 1985. Children of Mao: Personality Development and Political Activism in the Red Guard Generation. New York: Macmillan.

Chandler, Alfred. 1977. The Visible Hand: The Managerial Revolution in American Business. Cambridge, MA: Harvard University Press.

Chase-Dunn, Christopher. 1998. Global Formation: Structures of the World-Economy. Lanham, MD: Rowman and Littlefield.

Chase-Dunn, Christopher, and Terry Boswell. 2000. *The Spiral of Capitalism and Socialism: Toward Global Democracy.* Boulder, CO: Lynne Rienner.

Dirlik, Arif. 1994. *After the Revolution: Waking to Global Capitalism.* Hanover, NH: University of New England Press.

Esherick, Joseph W., Paul G. Pickowicz, and Andrew G. Walder, eds. 2006. *Cultural Revolution as History.* Palo Alto, CA: Stanford University Press.

Evans, Peter. 1995. *Embedded Autonomy: States and Industrial Transformation.* Princeton: Princeton University Press.

Froebel, F., J. Heinrichs, and O. Krey. 1980. *The New International Division of Labor: Structural Unemployment in Industrialized Countries and Industrialization of Developing Countries.* Cambridge, UK: Cambridge University Press.

Gilpin, Robert. 1987. *The Political Economy of International Relations.* Princeton: Princeton University Press.

Gowan, Peter. 1999. *The Global Gamble: Washington's Faustian Bid for World Dominance.* London: Verso.

Gramsci, Antonio. 1971. "Americanism and Fordism." *Selections from the Prison Notebooks.* New York: International Publisher, 277–320.

Guthrie, Doug. 2006. *China and Globalization: The Social, Economic, and Political Transformation of Chinese Society.* New York: Routledge.

Hall, Peter A., and David Soskice, eds. 2001. *Varieties of Capitalism: The Institutional Foundations of Comparative Advantage.* Oxford, U.K.: Oxford University Press.

Harvey, David. 1990. *The Condition of Postmodernity.* Oxford, U.K.: Blackwell.

———. 2005. *A Brief History of Neoliberalism.* Oxford, U.K.: Oxford University Press.

Haggard, Stephan. 1990. *Pathways from the Periphery: The Politics of Growth in the Newly Industrializing Countries.* Ithaca: Cornell University Press.

Hung Ho-fung. 2008. "Rise of China and the Global Overaccumulation Crisis." *Review of International Political Economy* 15, no. 2.

Katzenstein, Peter J. 1997. "Asian Regionalism in Comparative Perspective." In *Network Power: Japan and Asia,* ed. Peter Katzenstein and Takashi Shiraishi, 1–46. Ithaca: Cornell University Press.

Katzenstein, Peter J., and Takashi Shiraishi. 1997. "Regions in World Politics, Japan and Asia—Germany in Europe." In *Network Power: Japan and Asia,* ed. Peter Katzenstein and Takashi Shiraishi, 341–82. Ithaca: Cornell University Press.

Koschmann, Victor J. 1997. "Asianism's Ambivalent Legacy." In *Network Power: Japan and Asia,* ed. Peter Katzenstein and Takashi Shiraishi, 83–112. Ithaca: Cornell University Press.

Krause, Lawrence B. 1998. *The Economics and Politics of the Asian Financial Crisis of 1997–98.* New York: Council on Foreign Relations.

Lee Ching-kwan. 1998. *Gender and the South China Miracle.* Berkeley: University of California Press.

McMichael, Philip. 2008. *Development and Social Change: A Global Perspective.* 2nd edition. Thousand Oaks, CA: Pine Forge.

Meisner, Maurice. 1999. *Mao's China and After: A History of The People's Republic.* New York: Free Press.

Naughton, Barry. 1995. *Growing Out of the Plan: Chinese Economic Reform, 1978–1993.* Cambridge, U.K.: Cambridge University Press.

Ozawa, Terutomo. 1979. *Multinationalism, Japanese Style: The Political Economy of Outward Dependency.* Princeton: Princeton University Press.

Pempel, T. J. 1997. "Transpacific Torii: Japan and the Emerging Asian Regionalism." In *Network Power: Japan and Asia*, ed. Peter Katzenstein and Takashi Shiraishi, 47–82. Ithaca: Cornell University Press.

Pempel, T. J., ed. 1999. *The Politics of Asian Economic Crisis.* Ithaca: Cornell University Press.

Perry, Elizabeth J., and Li Xun. 1997. *Proletarian Power: Shanghai in the Cultural Revolution.* Boulder, CO: Westview Press.

Pun Ngai. 2005. *Made in China: Women Factory Workers in a Global Workplace.* Durham, NC: Duke University Press.

Ramo, J. C. 2004. *The Beijing Consensus.* London: The Foreign Policy Centre.

Schurmann, Franz. 1966. *Ideology and Organization in Communist China.* Berkeley: University of California Press.

Selden, Mark. 1993. *The Political Economy of Chinese Development.* Armonk, NY: M. E. Sharpe.

———. 1997. "China, Japan, and the Regional Political Economy of East Asia, 1945–95." In *Network Power: Japan and Asia*, ed. Peter Katzenstein and Takashi Shiraishi. Ithaca: Cornell University Press.

Shenkar, O. 2004. *The Chinese Century: The Rising Chinese Economy and its Impact on the Global Economy, the Balance of Power, and Your Job.* Philadelphia: Wharton School Publishing / Cornell University Press.

Shiraishi Takashi. 1997. "Japan and Southeast Asia." In *Network Power: Japan and Asia*, ed. Peter Katzenstein and Takashi Shiraishi, 169–96. Ithaca: Cornell University Press.

Shirk, Susan L. 1993. *The Political Logic of Economic Reform in China.* Berkeley and Los Angeles: University of California Press.

So, Alvin Y., and Stephen W. Chiu. 1995. *East Asia and the World Economy.* Boulder, CO: Westview Press.

Stallings, Barbara, ed. 1995. *Global Change, Regional Response: The New International Context of Development.* New York: Cambridge University Press.

Sugihara, Karo. 2003. "The East Asian Path of Economic Development: A Long-term Perspective." In *Resurgence of East Asia: 500, 150, 50 Year Perspectives*, ed. Giovanni Arrighi, Takashi Hamashita, and Mark Selden. New York: Routledge.

Wade, Robert. 1990. *Governing the Market: Economic Theory and the Role of Government in East Asian Industrialization.* Princeton: Princeton University Press.

Wallerstein, Immanuel. 1974. *The Modern World-System I: Capitalist Agriculture and the Origins of the European World-Economy in the Sixteenth Century.* New York: Academic Press.

———. 1979. *The Capitalist World-Economy.* New York: Cambridge University Press.

———. 1980. *The Modern World-System II: Mercantilism and the Consolidation of the European World-Economy, 1600–1750.* New York: Academic Press.

——. 1989. *The Modern World-System III: The Second Era of Great Expansion of the Capitalist World-Economy, 1730–1840s.* New York: Academic Press.

——. 1990. "Antisystemic Movements: History and Dilemma." In *Transforming the Revolution: Social Movements and the World-System,* ed. Samir Amin, Giovanni Arrighi, Andre Gunder Frank, and Immanuel Wallerstein, 13–53. New York: Monthly Review Press.

Zweig, David. 2002. *Internationalizing China: Domestic Interests and Global Linkages.* Ithaca: Cornell University Press.

CHAPTER TWO

China's Market Economy in
the Long Run

GIOVANNI ARRIGHI

"The Chinese modernization effort of recent years," wrote John K. Fairbank on the eve of the 1989 Tiananmen crackdown, "is on so titanic a scale that it is hard to grasp." Economic activities typical of the nineteenth century mixed with a flowering of postindustrial technologies, while issues of the Renaissance and the Enlightenment in the West competed with a reappraisal of China's own traditions. "Change is headlong; China's development is stretched thin. . . . No wonder Deng Xiaoping's reforms confuse us as well as people in China" (Fairbank 1989: 17).

Subsequent developments have compounded the confusion as China came to play a leading role in an expansion of trade within an Asia that now seems poised to surpass in value trade NAFTA or the European Union. Not only did the expansion of trade within so-called emerging Asia account for roughly 40 percent of the total increase of world trade between 1990 and 2006, but what is equally significant, this expansion was driven primarily by China acting as a regional export platform, importing more from Asia and exporting more to the rest of the world (Gruenwald and Hori 2008).

Part of the confusion arises from the fact that the East Asian region, with China at its center, had been, in Gilbert Rozman's words, "in the forefront of world development for at least two thousand years, until the sixteenth, seventeenth, or even the eighteenth century, after which it suffered a relatively brief but deeply felt eclipse" (Rozman 1991: 6). One measure of this eclipse—which Kenneth Pomeranz has aptly called the Great Divergence—is the share of world GDP of the leading states of East Asia (China and Japan) in comparison with that of the

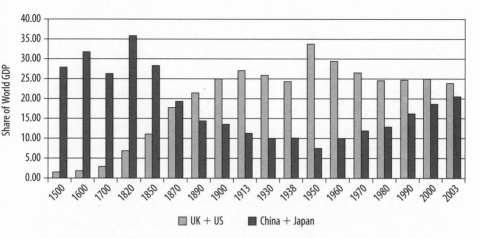

Figure 2.1. Combined GDP as a Percentage of World GDP: US + UK vs. China + Japan.
Source: Chart based on Maddison 2007
Note: GDP in millions of 1990 International Geary-Khamis Dollars

leading states of the West (Britain and the United States), shown in figure 2.1. But what made the eclipse especially disastrous is that by the end of the Second World War, China had become the world's poorest country; Japan had become a militarily occupied, semisovereign state; and most other countries in the region either were still struggling against colonial rule or were about to be torn asunder by the emerging Cold War divide.

This chapter seeks answers to three closely related questions. First, how and why did China and the surrounding region not only lose to the West its longstanding leadership in world development but also allow this loss to devastate it for more than a century? Second, what enabled the region to recover so quickly from this devastation after the Second World War? And finally, what is the relationship, if any, between the emerging centrality of East Asia and China in the contemporary global economy, on the one side, and the region's earlier leadership in world development, on the other?

THE GEOPOLITICS OF THE GREAT DIVERGENCE

In seeking answers to these questions, let us begin by noticing that the origins of the Great Divergence were primarily geopolitical rather than economic. Contrary to widespread belief, the *Communist Manifesto's* famous contention that the "cheap prices of commodities are the heavy artillery with which [the European bourgeoisie] batter[ed] down all Chinese walls," compelling "all nations, on pain of extinction, to adopt the bourgeois mode of production," as far China is concerned, does not stand up to historical scrutiny (Marx and Engels 1967: 83–84). Outside of cotton spinning (although not weaving), railways, and mines, there were very few economic activities in which Western merchants and producers could outcompete their Chinese counterparts (Feuerwerker 1970: 371–75; Esherick 1972: 10; Nathan 1972: 5; So 1986: 103–16; Kasaba 1993). As Marx himself later acknowledged in *Capital*, British gunboats rather than the metaphorical artillery of cheap prices were the true "midwife" of the subordination of China to the imperatives of the "endless" accumulation of Western capital (Marx 1959: 751).

As argued in detail elsewhere (Arrighi 2007: ch. 8), the forcible resolution in Europe's favor of the clash of civilizations that materialized in the Opium Wars of the mid–nineteenth century can be traced to a fundamental difference between the dynamics of the European and East Asian interstate systems during the preceding five centuries. Throughout this period, the dynamic of the European system was characterized by an incessant military competition among its main components and by a tendency toward the geographical expansion both of the system and of its shifting center. Long periods of peace among European powers were the exception rather than the rule. Thus, the "hundred years' peace" (1815–1914) that followed the Napoleonic Wars was "a phenomenon unheard of in the annals of Western civilization" (Polanyi 1957: 5). Moreover, even during this hundred years' peace, European states were involved in countless wars of conquest in the non-European world and in the escalating armament race that culminated in the industrialization of war. Although initially these involvements resulted in a new wave of geographical expansion that dampened conflicts within the European system, they eventually led to a new round of wars among European powers (1914–1945) of unprecedented destructiveness (Arrighi 2007: ch. 5).

In sharp contrast to this dynamic, the East Asian system of national states stood out for the near absence of intrasystemic military competition and extrasystemic geographical expansion. Thus, with the important exception of China's frontier wars, to be discussed presently, prior to their subordinate incorporation in the European system, the national states of East Asia were mostly at peace with one another, not for one hundred years but for three hundred (Arrighi 2007: 316). Moreover, they showed no tendency to build *overseas* empires in competition with one another and to engage in an armament race in any way comparable to the Europeans. East Asian states did compete with one another. Tokugawa Japan (1600–1868), for example, sought to create a tribute trade system centered on itself instead of China and to absorb technological and organizational know-how in agriculture, mining, and manufacturing from Korea and China (Kawakatsu 1994: 6–7; Sugihara 1996: 37–38). But this kind of competition tended to drive the East Asian system toward the making of a national economy rather than in the European direction of territorial expansion and the making of war.

The many wars that China fought on its frontiers in the first 150 years of Qing rule do not invalidate this contention, because they were aimed primarily at transforming a hard-to-defend frontier into a pacified periphery and a buffer against raiders and conquerors from inner Asia. Once that objective had been attained, as it was by the 1760s, territorial expansion ceased and military activities turned into police activities aimed at consolidating the monopoly of the Chinese state over the use of violence within the newly established boundaries. Although quite substantial, this territorial expansion paled in comparison with the successive waves of European expansion—the earlier Iberian expansion in the Americas and Southeast Asia, the contemporaneous Russian expansion in North Asia, and Dutch expansion in Southeast Asia, not to speak of the later expansion of Britain in South Asia and Africa and of its offspring in North America and Australia. The difference was not just quantitative but qualitative as well. The successive waves of European expansion were integral to a "self-reinforcing cycle" through which the competing military apparatuses of European states sustained, and were sustained by, expansion at the expense of other peoples and polities (McNeill 1982: 143). No self-reinforcing cycle of this kind could be observed in East Asia. Qing China's territorial expansion neither was driven by nor resulted in competition with other states in extracting resources from overseas peripheries. The logic of political economy associated with this kind of competition had little in common with China's practices. "Political expansion to incorporate new frontiers committed the government to a shift of resources to the peripheries, not extraction from them" (Wong 1997: 148).

These different dynamics of the European and East Asian systems can be traced in part to a difference in the distribution of power among the systems' units. Even before what Fernand Braudel has called the "extended" sixteenth century in European history (1350–1650)—which corresponds almost exactly to the Ming era in East Asian history (1368–1643)—political, economic, and cultural power in East Asia was far more concentrated in its center (China) than in Europe, where a center proper was hard to identify. But the difference became sharper with the thwarting in 1592–98 of Japan's attempt to militarily challenge Chinese centrality by conquest in Korea and with the institutionalization of the European balance of power by the Peace of Westphalia in 1648.

The balanced power structure of the European system in itself contributed to the disposition of European states to wage war on one another. As Karl Polanyi has underscored, balance-of-power mechanisms—the mechanisms, that is, whereby "three or more units capable of exerting power . . . behave in such a way as to combine the power of the weaker units against any increase in power of the strongest"—were a key ingredient in the organization of the hundred years' peace in the nineteenth century. Historically, however, balance-of-power mechanisms had always attained the objective of maintaining the independence of the partic-ipating units "only by continuous war between changing partners" (Polanyi 1957: 5–7). The main reason that in the nineteenth century those same mechanisms resulted in peace rather than war among European states is that political and eco-nomic power came to be so concentrated in the hands of Britain as to enable it to transform the balance of power from a mechanism that no individual state con-trolled and that functioned through wars into an instrument of informal British rule that promoted peace (Arrighi and Silver 1999: 59–64).

The nineteenth-century association between an increase in the imbalance of power and a decrease in the frequency of war among European states suggests that the imbalance of power typical of the East Asian system was a reason for the infrequency of wars among East Asian states. However, the previously noted fact that the nineteenth-century concentration of power in British hands was accom-panied by an escalation of interstate competition, both in the production of ever more destructive means of war and in the use of these means to gain access to ex-trasystemic resources, suggests that a greater imbalance of power cannot in itself explain the virtual absence of these two kinds of competition in the East Asian sys-tem. Some other ingredient had to be present in the European and absent in the East Asian "mix" to produce this difference in the pattern of interstate competition.

This other ingredient was the greater extroversion of the European develop-mental path in comparison with the East Asian path. Although trade within, be-tween, and across political jurisdictions was essential to the operations of both sys-tems, long-distance trade in general, and East-West trade in particular, was a far more important source of wealth and power for European than for East Asian states, especially China. It was this fundamental asymmetry that had made the fortunes of Venice and induced the Iberian states, instigated and assisted by Venice's Genoese rivals, to seek a direct link with the markets of the East (Arrighi 1994: ch. 2). Columbus's accidental "discovery" of the Americas, accomplished while seeking a shorter route to the wealth of Asia, changed the terms of the asym-metry by providing European states with new means to seek entry in Asian mar-kets as well as with a new source of wealth and power in the Atlantic. But even two centuries after the discovery, English economist Charles Davenant still claimed that whoever controlled the Asian trade was in a position to "give law to all the commercial world" (quoted in Wolf 1982: 125).

European rulers thus fought endless wars to establish an exclusive control over sea lanes linking West to East, because control over trade with the East was a critical resource in their pursuit of wealth and power. For the rulers of China, in contrast, control over these trade routes was far less important than peaceful relations with neighboring states and the integration of their populous domains into an agriculturally based national economy. This difference explains the low returns, relative to costs, of Admiral Zheng He's seven great voyages to Southeast Asia and across the Indian Ocean between 1405 and 1433. Given these low returns, it was eminently reasonable for the Ming not to waste resources in trying to control East-West sea lanes and concentrate instead on developing the national market, even though Zheng He's ships were perfectly capable to sail "around Africa and 'discover' Portugal several decades before Henry the Navigator's expeditions began earnestly to push south of Ceuta" (McNeill 1982: 44; Kennedy 1987: 7).

Indeed, even China's "tribute trade" had greater economic costs than benefits. Ever since the establishment of a unified taxation system under the Qin and Han dynasties, tributary relations between the Chinese imperial court and vassal states did not involve the collection of a tax. On the contrary, especially after the Tang dynasty—with the sole exception of the Yuan dynasty—vassal states offered the Chinese imperial court only symbolic gifts and received in return much more valuable gifts. Thus, what was nominally "tribute" was in fact a two-way transaction that enabled the Middle Kingdom to "buy" the allegiance of vassal states and, at the same time, to control flows of people and commodities across its far-flung frontiers (Arrighi et al. 2003: 241).

The sustainability of this practice depended on several conditions. The Chinese economy had to generate the resources necessary to buy the allegiance of the vassal states; the Chinese state had to be in a position to command these resources; and surrounding states had to be persuaded that attempts to seize resources from China by means that challenged the authority of the Chinese government (such as raids, conquest, war, and illegal trade) would not pay off. Despite, or possibly because of, their success in consolidating and expanding the national economy, by the early sixteenth century the Ming faced increasing difficulties in reproducing these conditions. Widespread corruption, mounting inflation, and increasing fiscal shortfalls on the domestic front were accompanied by growing external pressures from the expansion of the Jurchens in the north and from the expansion of illegal trade that bypassed Ming tax collectors along the southeastern coast. Internal degradation and external pressures reinforced one another, eventually leading to the collapse of the Ming in 1644 (Hung 2001a: 498–500l; 2001b: 12–18).

With the consolidation of Qing rule, the early Ming's policy privileging domestic over foreign trade resumed with greater vigor. While foreign trade was discouraged, the incorporation of borderlands on all sides increased the scale of the national market and reduced protection costs throughout the empire—a reduction that Qing rulers passed on to their subjects in the form of low and stable taxes. This low and stable taxation was accompanied by vigorous action aimed at stamping out bureaucratic corruption and tax evasion, through empire-wide land surveys, fiscal reforms, and a more effective system of gathering information. Moreover, in order to consolidate their power in relation to the Han landlords, the early Qing encouraged the ongoing partition of large estates into small plots and launched land-reclamation programs aimed at reestablishing the fiscal base without raising taxes (Jing 1982: 169–81; Huang 1985: 97–105; Perdue 1987: 78–79; Hung 2004: 482–83). This double "democratization" of land tenure—through the breakup of large estates and through land reclamation—called forth massive state action to maintain and expand the hydraulic infrastructure. Equally important, while relying on market mechanisms to feed China's huge and expanding population probably more than any of its predecessors, the Qing government surpassed them all in protecting the population from the vicissitudes of the grain market through a system of granaries that enabled it to buy and store grain at times of abundance and low prices and sell the grain back at submarket prices at times of scarcity and unusually high prices (Will and Wong 1991; Rowe 2001: 155–85).

The outcome of these policies was the remarkable peace, prosperity, and demographic growth that induced leading figures of the European Enlightenment to look to China "for moral instruction, guidance in institutional development, and supporting evidence for their advocacy of causes as varied as benevolent absolutism, meritocracy, and an agriculturally based national economy" (Adas 1989: 79; see also Hung 2003). And yet, neither the Chinese rulers nor their European admirers realized that the extroverted European developmental path was remaking the world through a process of creative destruction that would soon overshadow all of these achievements. "European ships"—in William McNeill's words—"had in effect turned Eurasia inside out. The sea frontier had superseded the steppe frontier as the critical meeting point with strangers, and the autonomy of Asian states and peoples began to crumble" (McNeill 1998: 231).

Crucial in this respect was the capitalist character of Europe's developmental path. This character was determined not by the mere presence of capitalist institutions and dispositions but by the relation of state power to capital. Braudel himself took imperial China as providing compelling evidence in favor of his distinction between *market economy* and *capitalism*. China did not just "have a solidly established market economy." It also had communities of merchants and bankers comparable to the business communities that constituted the preeminent capitalist organizations of sixteenth-century Europe. And yet, the state's "unmistakable hostility to any individual making himself 'abnormally' rich" meant that "there could be no capitalism, except within certain clearly defined groups . . . supervised by the state and always more or less at its mercy" (Braudel 1982: 153, 588–89).

Braudel exaggerates the extent to which under the Ming and the Qing—not to speak of earlier dynasties—capitalists were at the mercy of a hostile state. It remains nonetheless true that there is no parallel in East Asia for the *sequence* of ever more powerful states that in Europe identified themselves with capitalism—from the Italian city-states, through the Dutch proto–nation-state, to a state, Britain, in the process of becoming the center of a world-encircling maritime and territorial empire. It is this sequence more than anything else that marks the European developmental path as capitalist. And conversely, the absence of anything comparable to this sequence is the clearest sign that in the Ming and early Qing eras, market-based development in China and throughout East Asia remained noncapitalist. Closely related to this, in East Asia there was nothing resembling the incessant armament race and overseas territorial expansion typical of European states. "Much European commercial wealth," notes R. Bin Wong, "was tapped by needy governments anxious to expand their revenue bases to meet ever-escalating expenses of war. . . . Both European merchants and their governments benefited from their complex relationship." Since the late imperial Chinese state did not face the kind of financial difficulties encountered by European states between the sixteenth and eighteenth centuries, "Chinese officials had less reason to imagine new forms of finance, huge merchant loans, and the concept of public as well as private debt" (Wong 1997: 146).

Under these circumstances, the greatest opportunities for capitalism to develop in East Asia were not close to the centers but interstitially on the outer rims of the system's states. The most prominent embodiment of this development was the overseas Chinese diaspora, whose resilience and enduring economic importance has few parallels in world history. Despite periodic reverses and challenges from competitors, the overseas Chinese diaspora made extraordinary profits and provided a steady flow of revenue for local governments and remittances to China's coastal regions. It was nonetheless incapable of preventing European states, companies, and merchants from gradually filling the political void that the inward-looking policies of Qing China and Tokugawa Japan left in maritime East

Asia (Wang 1991: 85–86; Cushman 1993: 136; Hui 1995: 35–36, 79–80; Wang 1998: 320–23; Wills 1998: 333).

In short, the absence in East Asia of the synergy typical of the European developmental path among militarism, industrialism, and capitalism, which propelled, and was in turn sustained by, ceaseless overseas territorial expansion meant that East Asian states were at peace for much longer periods than European states and that China could consolidate its position as the world's largest market economy. But the lack of involvement in overseas expansion and in a European-style armament race eventually made China and the entire East Asian system vulnerable to the military onslaught of the expanding European powers. When Britain decided to force open the Chinese market to imports of Indian opium—a trade that was as baneful for China as it was beneficial for Britain—the Chinese government had no answer to the steam-powered warship that in a single day in February 1841 destroyed nine war junks, five forts, two military stations, and one shore battery (Parker 1989: 96). After a disastrous war, an explosion of major rebellions, and a second, equally disastrous war with Britain (now joined by France), China became a subordinate and increasingly peripheral member of the global capitalist system. This loss of status and power was a primary result of defeat in the Opium Wars. By revealing brutally the full implications of Western military superiority, the defeat awoke the ruling groups not just of China but of Japan as well to the imperatives of accelerated military modernization. It also drew them both into the kind of armament race that had long been a feature of the European system (cf. Tsiang 1967: 144; Fairbank 1983: 197–98; So and Chiu 1995: 49–50). Although industrialization efforts in China and Japan initially yielded similar economic results, Japan's victory in the Sino-Japanese War of 1894 was symptomatic of a fundamental difference between the two. In China, the main agency of the industrialization drive was provincial authorities, whose power in relation to the central government had increased considerably during the repression of the rebellions of the 1850s and whose adoption of industrialization consolidated their autonomy. In Japan, by contrast, the industrialization drive was integral to the Meiji Restoration, which centralized power in the hands of the national government at the expense of provincial authorities (So and Chiu 1995: 53, 68–72). The outcome of the Sino-Japanese War, in turn, deepened the underlying divergence in the trajectories of Japanese and Chinese industrialization. China's defeat further weakened an already fragile national cohesion, imposing further restrictions on sovereignty and crushing war indemnities, which led to the final collapse of the Qing regime and the growing autonomy of semisovereign warlords. This was followed by Japanese invasion and recurrent civil wars between the forces of nationalism and communism. Victory over China in 1894, followed by victory over Russia in the war of 1904–05, by contrast, established Japan—to paraphrase Akira Iriye—as "a respectable participant in the game of imperialist politics" (Iriye 1970: 552).

Major acquisitions of Chinese territory (including Taiwan in 1895) and the annexation of Korea as a colony in 1910 provided Japan with valuable outposts from which to launch future attacks on China as well as with secure overseas supplies of cheap food, raw materials, and markets. At the same time, Chinese indemnities amounting to more than one-third of Japan's national income helped Japan to finance the expansion of heavy industry and to tap additional funds in London for industrial expansion at home and imperialist expansion overseas (Feis 1965: 422–23; Peattie 1984: 16–18; Duus 1984: 143, 161–62). With the Japanese seizure of Manchuria in 1931, followed by the occupation of north China in 1935, the full-scale invasion of China starting in 1937, and the subsequent conquest of parts of inner Asia and much of Southeast Asia, Japan eclipsed Britain as the dominant power in the region. The bid for regional supremacy, however, could not be sustained. Stalemated in a fifteen-year war with China (1931–45) and facing the U.S.-led juggernaut unleashed in response to Japan's attack on Pearl Harbor, Japan succumbed in a classic example of imperial overreach. Once Japan had been defeated, the formation of the People's Republic of China (PRC) would contest Western hegemonic drives in a struggle for centrality in East Asia that has shaped trends and events in the region ever since.

THE U.S.-JAPANESE PHASE OF THE EAST ASIAN RENAISSANCE

In the hundred-odd years separating the Opium Wars and the Second World War, interstate relations in East Asia proved to be a combination of militarism, capitalism, and territorial expansionism that secured the fortunes of the West but brought great misfortune to East Asia, first and foremost to China and Korea but eventually to Japan as well. In the half-century following the end of the Second World War, in contrast, the process of hybridization of the Western and East Asian systems changed direction, gradually creating conditions favorable to the region's economic renaissance.

The U.S. military occupation of Japan in 1945 and the division of the region in the aftermath of the Korean War into two antagonistic blocs created, in Bruce Cumings's words (1997: 155), a U.S. "vertical regime solidified through bilateral defense treaties (with Japan, South Korea, Taiwan and the Philippines) and conducted by a State Department that towered over the foreign ministries of these four countries," all of which "became semisovereign states." The militaristic nature of this U.S. regime had no precedent in East Asia, with the partial exception of the Yuan regime in the late thirteenth and early fourteenth centuries and the aborted Japan-centered regime of the early twentieth century. Nevertheless, the U.S. regime presented three important similarities with the China-centered tribute trade system. First, the domestic market of the central state was incomparably larger than that of the vassal states. Second, in order to receive regime legitimation and to gain access to the central state's domestic market, vassal states had to accept a relationship of political subordination to the central state. And third, in exchange for political subordination, vassal states were granted "gifts" and highly advantageous trade relations with the central state. This was the "magnanimous" early postwar trade and aid regime of Pax Americana, which contributed decisively to the takeoff of the East Asian economic renaissance.

In light of these similarities, we may say that after the Second World War, the United States turned the periphery of the former China-centered tribute trade system into the periphery of a U.S.-centered tribute trade system. The U.S.-centered system, however, fostered a relationship of political exchange between the imperial and the vassal states that had no precedent in the old China-centered system. In this relationship, the United States specialized in the provision of protection and the pursuit of political power regionally and globally, while its East Asian vassal states specialized in trade and the pursuit of profit. This relationship of political exchange played a decisive role in promoting the spectacular Japanese economic expansion that initiated the regional renaissance. "Freed from the burden of defense spending," noted Franz Schurmann when the renaissance had just begun, "Japanese governments . . . funneled all their resources and energies into an economic expansionism that . . . brought affluence to Japan and [took] its business to the farthest reaches of the globe" (1974: 143).

U.S. "magnanimity" was rooted in, and conditioned by, U.S. Cold War objectives and financial capabilities. Crucial in this respect was George Kennan's policy of containment based on the idea, in the words of Cumings, "that four or five industrial structures existed in the world: the Soviets had one and the United States had four, and things should be kept that way" (1987: 60). Japan's industrial structure was one of the four; during and after the Korean War, it was accordingly buttressed by massive U.S. expenditures. Altogether, in the twenty-year period of 1950–1970, U.S. aid to Japan averaged $500 million a year (Borden 1984: 220). In spite of Kennan's exclusive interest in Japan, military and economic aid to South Korea and Taiwan combined was even more massive (Cumings 1987: 67).

Financial largesse of this order was hard to sustain and induced the United States to seek ways of harnessing Japanese economic power to U.S. political ends.

Already in 1949, the U.S. government had shown some awareness of the virtues of a "triangular" trade among the United States, Japan, and Southeast Asia, giving "certain advantages in production costs of various commodities" (first draft of NSC 48/1, quoted in Cumings 1987: 62). But it was only when the recovery of the Japanese economy had been consolidated and financial constraints on the United States began to tighten that the need to contain costs led to a redefinition of Japan's role in the East Asian regional economy. Thus, whereas in the 1950s the United States had promoted the *separate* integration of Japan and its former colonies within U.S. networks of trade, power, and patronage, in the 1960s it began promoting their *mutual* integration in regional trade networks centered on Japan. To this end, the U.S. government actively encouraged South Korea and Taiwan to overcome nationalist resentment against Japan's colonialist past and to open up their doors to Japanese trade and investment (Cumings 1993: 25).

Under the militaristic U.S. tribute trade regime, Japan thus got for "free" that economic hinterland it had fought so hard to obtain through territorial expansion in the first half of the twentieth century but had eventually lost in the catastrophe of the Second World War. Indeed, it got much more than that. Through the action of the U.S. government, it obtained admission to GATT and privileged access to the U.S. market and to U.S. overseas military expenditures. Moreover, the U.S. government tolerated an administrative closure of the Japanese economy to foreign capital that would have resulted in almost any other government being placed among the foes of the U.S. Cold War crusade.

In exchange for this special treatment, Japan became a highly effective "servant" of the U.S. warfare-welfare state. The cost advantages of incorporating Japanese business as an intermediary between U.S. purchasing power and cheap Asian labor—adumbrated in the first draft of NSC 48/1—began to be realized in the 1960s, when the tightening of financial constraints threatened a fiscal crisis of the U.S. state. The tripling of U.S. imports from Japan between 1964 and 1970 transformed the previous U.S. trade surplus with Japan into a $1.4 billion deficit. But in the absence of massive procurements of means of war and livelihood from Japanese sources at much lower costs than they could be obtained in the United States or elsewhere, the escalation of U.S. welfare expenditures at home and of warfare expenditures abroad in the 1960s would have been far more crippling financially for the United States than it already was.

Japanese assistance notwithstanding, the U.S.-centered Cold War regime in East Asia started breaking down soon after it was established. The Korean War had instituted that regime by excluding the PRC from normal commercial and diplomatic intercourse with the noncommunist part of the region through blockade and war threats backed by "an archipelago of American military installations" (Cumings 1997: 154–55). Defeat in the Vietnam War, by contrast, forced the United States to readmit China to normal commercial and diplomatic intercourse with the rest of East Asia. The scope of the region's economic integration and expansion was thereby broadened considerably, but the capacity of the United States to control the process was reduced correspondingly (Arrighi 1996; Selden 1997).

The crisis of the U.S. militaristic regime and the contemporaneous expansion of the Japanese national market and business networks in the region marked the reemergence of a pattern of interstate relations that resembled more closely the indigenous (East Asian) pattern—in which centrality was determined primarily by the relative size and sophistication of the system's national economies—than the transplanted (Western) pattern, in which centrality was determined primarily by the relative strength of the system's military-industrial complexes. While the defeat of the United States in Vietnam laid bare the limits of industrial militarism as a source of power, Japan's growing influence in world politics in the 1980s demonstrated the increasing effectiveness of economic relative to military sources of power.

This reversal of fortunes did not originate solely in the crisis of the U.S. military-industrial complex. It originated also in an incipient crisis of the vertically integrated, multinational corporations that had made the fortunes of U.S. capital since the 1870s. As the number and variety of these kinds of enterprises increased worldwide, the intensification of their mutual competition induced them to cut costs by subcontracting to small businesses activities previously carried out within their own organizations. The tendency toward the vertical integration and bureaucratization of business thus began to be superseded by a tendency toward informal networking and the subordinate revitalization of small business. This new tendency has been in evidence everywhere, but nowhere has it been pursued more successfully than in East Asia, where Japanese big business relied heavily on the assistance of multiple layers of formally independent subcontractors. Starting in the early 1970s, the scale and scope of this multilayered subcontracting system increased rapidly through a spillover into a growing number of East Asian states (Okimoto and Rohlen 1988: 83–88; Arrighi, Ikeda, and Irwan 1993: 55ff; Arrighi 2007: 167–72).

The spillover contributed decisively to the takeoff of the *regional* economic renaissance by promoting a massive transplant of labor-intensive industries such as textile, metal products, and electrical machinery to lower-income East Asian locations, first and foremost the emerging Four Tigers of South Korea, Taiwan,

Hong Kong, and Singapore. As rising wages undermined the comparative advantages of the Four Tigers in the lower value-added end of industrial production, enterprises from these states joined Japanese business in tapping the still abundant and cheap labor resources of a poorer and more populous group of neighboring (mostly ASEAN) countries. The result was a second round of labor-seeking regional expansion, which—like the first but on a larger scale—tended to undermine the competitiveness of the labor resources on which it was based. As soon as this happened, a third round took off on an even larger scale. Japanese and Four Tigers enterprises were joined by enterprises of second-round recipients of regional industrial expansion in transplanting lower-end, labor-intensive activities to even poorer and more populous countries (most notably, China and Vietnam) still endowed with large and competitive reserves of cheap labor (Ozawa 1993, 2003).

Japanese capital was the leading agency of this "snowballing" process of concatenated, labor-seeking rounds of investment that promoted and sustained the regional expansion of the 1970s and 1980s. From the start, however, the main intermediaries between Japanese and local business in most Southeast Asian countries were the overseas Chinese who had come to occupy a commanding position in local business networks in most Southeast Asian countries. The region-wide expansion of the Japanese multilayered subcontracting system was thus supported not just by U.S. political patronage from above but also by Chinese commercial and financial patronage from below (Hui 1995; Irwan 1995).

With time, however, patronage from above and below began to constrain the capacity of Japanese business to lead the process of regional economic integration and expansion. As a representative of Japanese big business lamented in the early 1990s, Japanese businessmen cannot influence policy decisions of other countries in the ways American business can, because Japan has no military power. "This is a difference . . . Japanese businessmen have to think about" (Friedland 1994). The difference was not just that Japan could not match the capacity of the United States to influence the policies of third countries. More important, Japan's dependence on U.S. military protection meant that its policies were far more susceptible to being shaped by U.S. interests than U.S. policies were to being shaped by Japanese interests.

This asymmetry was not a problem as long as the "magnanimous" postwar U.S. trade and aid regime was in place. But as soon as the United States decided to pull out of Vietnam and seek a rapprochement with China while financial constraints on U.S. largesse tightened, the supply "price" of U.S. protection for Japan began to rise steeply. Thus, during Reagan's escalation of the armament race with the

U.S.S.R. of the early and mid-1980s, Japan was asked to make major contributions to financing U.S. external account and internal fiscal deficits. In addition, when U.S. competition for funds in world financial markets provoked the near-bankruptcy of several Latin American countries, Japanese banks followed U.S. guidelines for handling the ensuing debt crisis—in the words of Barbara Stallings—"even more closely than the U.S. banks themselves" (1990: 19). And when the U.S. government decided to strengthen the IMF and the World Bank to handle the crisis, Japan readily agreed to increase its contributions to these organizations in ways that did not significantly alter their voting structure (Helleiner 1992: 425, 432–34). At the same time, the United States began strong-arming Japan into re-straining its competition through a massive revaluation of the yen and a stepping up of so-called voluntary restrictions on exports to the United States. All this cul-minated under George H. W. Bush in the extraction of a true "protection pay-ment" of $13 billion to pay for the Gulf War (Arrighi 2007: 257–58). Under these circumstances, the profitability of Japan's relation of political exchange with the United States began to wane. Worse still, U.S. business began restructuring itself to compete more effectively with Japanese business in the exploitation of East Asia's rich endowment of labor and entrepreneurial resources, not just through direct investment but also and especially through all kinds of subcontracting arrangements in loosely integrated organizational structures. The most spectacu-lar result of this tendency has been the displacement of vertically integrated cor-porations, such as General Motors, by subcontracting corporations, such as Wal-Mart, as the leading U.S. business organizations (Arrighi 2007: 171–72). As Gary Hamilton and Chang Wei-An have shown, "buyer-driven" subcontracting ar-rangements, like Wal-Mart's, were a distinctive feature of big business in late im-perial China and remained the dominant form of business organization in Tai-wan and Hong Kong up to the present (2003). We may therefore interpret the formation and expansion of U.S. subcontracting networks as another instance of Western convergence toward East Asian patterns.

Despite this convergence, the main beneficiary of the mobilization of East Asian subcontracting networks in the intensifying competitive struggle among the world's leading capitalist organizations was neither Japanese nor U.S. capital. Rather, it was another legacy of the East Asian developmental path: the overseas Chinese capitalist diaspora, which, as previously noted, had been for centuries the main locus of the seeds of capitalism that sprouted in the interstices of the China-centered tribute trade system. By generating a new spurt of Chinese migra-tion to Southeast Asia, the Communist victory over the Guomindang had replen-ished the entrepreneurial ranks of the diaspora. Shortly afterward, the Korean

War revived the flow of interregional trade and created new business opportunities for the overseas Chinese, as did the withdrawal of the European and U.S. colonial-era large-scale enterprises and the arrival of new multinational corporations seeking capable joint-venture partners. Although the U.S. embargo on trade with the PRC and the PRC's own restrictions on foreign trade stifled the role of the overseas Chinese as commercial intermediaries between mainland China and the surrounding maritime region, they nonetheless managed to consolidate their hold on the commanding heights of Southeast Asian economies (Wu and Wu 1980: 30–34; Baker 1981: 344–45; Wong 1988; Mackie 1992: 165; 1998: 142; Hui 1995: 184–85).

Overseas Chinese capital was thus eminently well positioned to profit from the transborder expansion of Japan's multilayered subcontracting system and the growing demand by U.S. corporations for business partners in the region. The more intense that competition over East Asian low-cost and high-quality human resources became, the more the overseas Chinese emerged as one of the most powerful capitalist networks in the region, in many ways overshadowing the networks of U.S. and Japanese multinationals (Ong and Nonini 1997; Arrighi et al. 2003: 316). But the greatest opportunities for their enrichment and empowerment came with the reintegration of mainland China in regional and global markets in the 1980s. Crucial in this respect was the opening of the PRC to foreign trade and investment, the success of which inaugurated an entirely new stage of the East Asian renaissance—the stage of the recentering of the regional economy on China.

THE CHINESE ASCENT AND THE LEGACY OF THE
EAST ASIAN INDUSTRIOUS REVOLUTION

The East Asian economic renaissance under U.S.-Japanese leadership was based on a snowballing process that mobilized on an ever-expanding scale the region's low-cost labor resources to supply the wealthy (and increasingly noncompetitive) producers and consumers of the West. Once the U.S.-centered militaristic regime in the region was forced to readmit the PRC to normal commercial and diplomatic intercourse with the rest of East Asia, China became the most likely ultimate destination of this labor-seeking snowballing process. But whether the process would enrich or impoverish China largely depended on the capacity of the Chinese government to ensure that Chinese subjects rather than foreign investors would be the main beneficiaries of the oncoming rush of labor-seeking investment.

Much of the success of Deng Xiaoping's reforms can be traced to the fulfillment of this condition through two key moves. One was the determination with which in the 1980s the PRC sought the assistance of the overseas Chinese in the pursuit of the double objective of reintegrating China in the regional and global economies and of seeking the recovery of Hong Kong, Macau, and, eventually, Taiwan in accordance with the "One Nation, Two Systems" model. This alliance proved far more fruitful than the Chinese government's open-door policy toward U.S., European, and Japanese corporations. Bothered by the regulations that restricted their freedom to hire and fire labor, to buy and sell commodities, and to remit profits out of China, these corporations tended to keep their investments to the bare minimum needed to gain a foothold in the PRC. The overseas Chinese, by contrast, were far less bothered by these regulations, which they could bypass or turn to their own advantage, thanks to familiarity with local customs, habits, and language; the manipulation of kinship and community ties; and the preferential treatment they received from Communist Party's CCP officials. Thus, while foreign corporations kept complaining about the "investment climate," Chinese entrepreneurs began moving from Hong Kong into Guandong almost as fast as (and far more massively than) they had moved from Shanghai to Hong Kong forty years earlier. Encouraged by the success, in 1988 the Chinese government redoubled its efforts to win the confidence and assistance of overseas Chinese capital by extending to Taiwan's residents many of the privileges previously granted to Hong Kong's residents (So and Chiu 1994: ch. 11).

Well before the Tiananmen Square crackdown, a political alliance was thus established between the CCP and overseas Chinese business. The cooling of U.S.-Chinese relations after Tiananmen Square dampened further Western enthusiasm for investment in China. But as soon as the Chinese ascent gained momentum under its own steam, Japanese, U.S., and European capital started investing ever more massively. Foreign direct investment, which had totaled only $20 billion for the whole decade of the 1980s, soared to $200 billion by 2000 and then more than doubled to $450 billion in the next three years. "But if the foreigners were investing," comments Clyde Prestowitz, "it was only because the Chinese were investing more" (Prestowitz 2005: 61; see also Arrighi et al. 2003: 316–17; Fishman 2005: 27).

Foreign capital, in other words, jumped on the bandwagon of an economic expansion that it neither started nor led. Foreign direct investment did play a major role in boosting Chinese exports, but the boom in Chinese exports was a late episode of the Chinese ascent, and even then, foreign (especially U.S.) capital needed China far more than China needed foreign capital. U.S. companies from Intel to General Motors faced the simple imperative of either investing in China to take advantage of the country's highly competitive labor supplies and fast-growing domestic market or losing out to rivals. Moreover, China quickly turned from a mere manufacturing center to a prime location in which to develop and sell high-tech goods. "There are few other countries that look like they could become this significant," noted the vice president of a high-tech U.S. corporation (Arrighi 2007: 353).

But how did China become this significant? In addition to the determination with which Deng sought the assistance of the overseas Chinese, the move that most decisively enabled Chinese producers to turn to their advantage the oncoming rush of labor-seeking investment from abroad was the revival of China's rural-based market economy tradition. With the introduction in 1978–1983 of the Household Responsibility System, decision making and control over agricultural surpluses was returned from communes to rural households. In combination with substantial increases in agricultural procurement prices in 1979 and in 1983, the system resulted in a major increase in returns to farm activity, which strengthened the earlier tendency of commune and brigade enterprises to produce nonagricultural goods. Although the government encouraged rural labor to "leave the land without leaving the village" through various barriers to spatial mobility, in 1983 it gave permission to rural residents to seek outlets for their products through long-distance transport and marketing. In 1984, it further relaxed regulations to allow farmers to work in nearby towns in the emerging collectively owned Township and Village Enterprises (TVEs; see Unger 2002; Cai, Park, and Zhao 2004).

Thanks to fiscal decentralization, which granted autonomy to local governments in the promotion of economic growth and in the use of fiscal residuals for bonuses, and to a new system of evaluating cadres on the basis of the economic performance of their localities, which provided local governments with strong incentives to support economic growth, TVEs became the primary loci of the reorientation of the entrepreneurial energies of party cadres and government officials toward developmental objectives. Mostly self-reliant financially, they also became the main agency of the reallocation of agricultural surpluses to the undertaking of labor-intensive industrial activities capable of absorbing productively rural surplus labor (Lin 1995; Walder 1995; Oi 1999; Whiting 2001; Tsai 2004; Wang 2005: 179; Lin and Yao, n.d.). The result was an explosive growth of the rural labor force engaged in nonagricultural activities, from 28 million in 1978 to 176 million in 2003. Most of the increase occurred in TVEs, which between 1980 and 2004 added almost four times as many jobs as were lost in state and collective urban employment. By the end of that period, TVEs employed more than twice as many workers as all foreign, private, and jointly owned urban enterprises combined (Arrighi and Zhang 2007).

As Deng Xiaoping himself admitted in 1993, the explosive growth of TVEs took Chinese leaders by surprise. Only in 1990 did the government step in to legalize and regulate them by assigning ownership collectively to all inhabitants of the town or village but empowering local governments to appoint and fire managers or to delegate this authority to a governmental agency. The allocation of TVE profits also was regulated, mandating the reinvestment of more than half within the enterprise to modernize, to expand production, and to increase welfare and bonus funds; most of what was left was dedicated to the construction of agricultural infrastructure, technology services, public welfare, and investment in new enterprises. In the late 1990s, attempts were made to transform vaguely defined property rights into some form of shareholding or purely private ownership. But since regulations were hard to enforce, TVEs had come to be characterized by such a variety of local arrangements that it proved difficult to categorize them (Woo 1999: 129–37; Hart-Landsberg and Burkett 2004: 35; Bouckaert 2005; Lin and Yao, n.d.).

And yet, despite or, perhaps, because of their organizational diversity, the TVEs made a decisive contribution to the success of the reforms. First, thanks to their labor-intensive orientation, they absorbed rural surplus labor and raised rural incomes without a massive increase in migration to urban areas. Indeed, most labor mobility in the 1980s saw farmers abandon farming to work in rural collective enterprises. Second, since TVEs were relatively unregulated, their entry into numerous markets increased competitive pressure across the board, forcing not just state-owned enterprises but all urban enterprises to improve their performance (Cai, Park, and Zhao 2004). Third, by becoming a major source of rural tax revenue, TVEs reduced the fiscal burden on peasants and thus contributed to social stability (Bernstein and Lu 2003; Wang 2005: 177–78). Fourth, and in key respects most important, by reinvesting profits and rents locally, TVEs expanded the size of the domestic market and created the conditions of new rounds of investment, job creation, and division of labor. As Lily Tsai has observed on the basis of extensive research in rural China, family lineage or affiliation with a particular temple are effective substitutes for formal democratic and bureaucratic institutions of accountability in subjecting local government officials to informal rules and norms that force them to provide the level of public goods needed to maintain social stability. In addition to social incentives, political rewards, such as becoming a member of the Communist Party, becoming a representative of People's Congress, or being appointed as a rural local cadre, constitute major incentives for TVE managers and entrepreneurs to reinvest surpluses in their local communities (Tsai 2007; Arrighi and Zhang 2007; Lin and Yao, n.d.).

In summing up the developmental advantages of China in comparison with South Africa—where the African peasantry has long been dispossessed from the land without a corresponding creation of the demand conditions for its absorption in wage employment—Gillian Hart has similarly underscored the contribution that TVEs have made to the reinvestment and redistribution of profits within local circuits and to their use in schools, clinics, and other forms of collective consumption. Moreover, a relatively egalitarian distribution of land among households enabled the residents of many TVEs to procure their livelihood through the intensive cultivation of tiny plots with industrial and other forms of nonagricultural work. Indeed, "a key force propelling [the TVEs'] growth is that, unlike their urban counterparts, they do not have to provide housing, health, retirement, and other benefits to workers. In effect, much of the cost of reproduction of labor has been deflected from the enterprise." This pattern, Hart goes on to suggest, could be observed not just in China but in Taiwan as well:

> What is distinctive about China and Taiwan—and dramatically different from South Africa—are the redistributive land reforms beginning in the late 1940s that effectively broke the power of the landlord class. The political forces that drove agrarian reforms in China and Taiwan were closely linked and precisely opposite. Yet in both socialist and post-socialist China, and in "capitalist" Taiwan, the redistributive reforms that defined agrarian transformations were marked by rapid, decentralized industrial accumulation *without* dispossession from the land. (Hart 2002: 199–200)

This observation raises the question of whether a large peasantry only partially separated from the means of producing its subsistence, as is the case in China, constitutes a greater competitive advantage in promoting economic growth than the urban and semiurban masses of unemployed and underemployed labor, more plentiful in sub-Saharan Africa and Latin America than in China. The answer that emerges from the foregoing analysis is that it does, provided that government policies succeed in mobilizing the peasantry as a source, not just of abundant supplies of cheap labor but also and especially of the entrepreneurial energies and managerial skills necessary to absorb those supplies in ways that expand the national market. While Deng's reforms were highly successful in this respect, the success depended critically not just on the tradition of socialist revolution discussed in Alvin So's contribution to this volume but also on an earlier and longer tradition of market-based development.

As Kaoru Sugihara has argued, in the eighteenth and early nineteenth centuries China experienced an "industrious revolution" that established a distinctive East Asian technological and institutional path. Particularly significant in this respect was the development of a labor-absorbing institutional framework centered on the household and, to a lesser extent, the village community. Contrary to the common view that small-scale production cannot sustain economic improvement, this institutional framework had important advantages over the class-based, large-scale production that was becoming dominant in England at about the same time. While in England workers were deprived of the opportunity to share in managerial concerns and to develop interpersonal skills needed for flexible specialization, in East Asia

> an ability to perform multiple tasks well, rather than specialization in a particular task, was preferred, and a will to cooperate with other members of the family rather than the furthering of individual talent was encouraged. Above all, it was important for every member of the family to try to fit into the work pattern of the farm, respond flexibly to extra or emergency needs, sympathize with the problems relating to the management of production, and anticipate and prevent potential problems. Managerial skill, with a general background of technical skill, was an ability which was actively sought after at the family level. (Sugihara 2003: 79–82, 87–90, 94, 117n2)

Although the East Asian institutional framework left little room for big innovations or for investment in fixed capital or long-distance trade, it provided excellent opportunities for the development of labor-intensive technologies that increased per capita *annual* income, even if they did not increase output *per day or per hour*. The difference between this kind of development and development along the Western path was a strong bias toward the use of human rather than nonhuman resources (Sugihara 2003: 87).

Hart's observation that in the TVEs intensive cultivation of small plots of land is combined with industrial and other forms of nonagricultural work and with investments in the improvement of labor quality supports Sugihara's contention of the persistence of the legacy of China's industrious revolution. Equally important in this respect is the tendency to use as fully as possible human resources and to endow such resources with managerial and general technical skills at the family level. Compounded by the educational achievements of the Chinese revolutionary tradition discussed in So's chapter, this tendency can be observed even in the practice of urban industries that substitute inexpensive educated labor for expensive machines and managers (Fishman 2004, 2005: 205–6; see also Taylor 2006).

The competitive advantages of this double substitution are obscured by statistics that show U.S. workers in capital-intensive factories to be several times more productive than their Chinese counterparts. But as a report in *The Wall Street Journal* has pointed out, these statistics do not show that the higher productivity of U.S. workers is associated with the replacement of many factory workers with complex flexible-automation and material-handling systems, which reduces labor costs but raises the costs of capital and support systems. By saving on capital (including management costs) and reintroducing a greater role for labor, Chinese factories reverse this process. The design of parts to be made, handled, and assembled manually, for example, can reduce the total capital required by as much as one-third (Hout and Lebretton 2003).

Recent reports suggest that this competitive advantage may be in the process of being jeopardized by the greater reliance of some Chinese industries on capital-intensive techniques of production. The true extent of the change for the Chinese economy as a whole is hard to assess; it is even harder to predict its impact on the Chinese ascent in the decades to come. But whatever its future, the legacy of China's eighteenth-century industrious revolution is the key to many of the puzzles that still surround China's precipitous economic rise during the last quarter-century.

CONCLUSIONS

If we now return to the questions raised at the beginning of the chapter, the foregoing analysis suggests three main answers. First, the century-long eclipse that China and the surrounding region suffered from the end of the Opium Wars to the end of Second World War can be traced to a fundamental asymmetry in East-West relations during the preceding five hundred years. Ming and early Qing China successfully created a self-centered market economy and a comparatively peaceful regional system of interstate relations. This made the entire region vulnerable to the inevitable clash with the globalizing tendencies of the extroverted European system driven by the synergy of a ceaseless armament race, capital accumulation, and territorial expansion. When the clash came, the convergence of the East Asian system toward the European pattern in response to China's defeat in the Opium Wars, far from mitigating an eclipse, made it all the more devastating.

Second, the quick recovery of the region after the Second World War was initiated by the peculiar militaristic order that the United States established in East Asia as an integral aspect of Cold War rivalries. This order created optimal conditions for the economic recovery of Japan. But more important, it created the conditions for the emergence of a Japanese-led snowballing process of labor-seeking investment that eventually became a powerful mechanism of regional economic integration and expansion. When the U.S. militaristic regime in the region broke down in the wake of U.S. defeat in Vietnam, the snowballing process gained new momentum through its extension to China, which soon emerged as the most powerful attractor of labor-seeking investment from the region and beyond.

Third and last, among the many ingredients that enabled the Chinese government to turn the oncoming rush of labor-seeking investment into an engine of national economic expansion, two legacies of the old China-centered regional system have played an especially crucial role. One is the overseas Chinese diaspora, which provided the PRC with a highly effective instrument of reintegration in the regional and global economies. The other is the high quality and low cost of the rural laboring masses that China inherited from its robust tradition of market-based, noncapitalist development. Although not the only ingredients in the Chinese economic "miracle," these two legacies have been among the most essential.

REFERENCES

Adas, Michael. 1989. *Machines as Measure of Men: Science, Technology and Ideologies of Western Dominance.* Ithaca: Cornell University Press.

Arrighi, Giovanni. 1994. *The Long Twentieth Century: Money, Power, and the Origins of Our Times.* London: Verso.

———. 1996. "The Rise of East Asia: World Systemic and Regional Aspects." *International Journal of Sociology and Social Policy* 16, no. 7: 6–44.

———. 2007. *Adam Smith in Beijing: Lineages of the Twenty-First Century.* London: Verso.

Arrighi, Giovanni, Po-keung Hui, Ho-fung Hung, and Mark Selden. 2003. "Historical Capitalism, East and West." In *The Resurgence of East Asia: 500, 150 and 50 Year Perspectives*, ed. Giovanni Arrighi, Takashi Hamashita, and Mark Selden, 259–333. London and New York: Routledge.

Arrighi, Giovanni, Satoshi Ikeda, and Alex Irwan. 1993. "The Rise of East Asia: One Miracle or Many?" In *Pacific Asia and the Future of the World-Economy*, ed. R. A. Palat, 42–65. Westport, CT: Greenwood Press.

Arrighi, Giovanni, and Beverly J. Silver. 1999. *Chaos and Governance in the Modern World System.* Minneapolis: University of Minnesota Press.

Arrighi, Giovanni, and Lu Zhang. 2007. "From the Washington to the Beijing Consensus and Beyond." Unpublished paper.

Baker, Christopher. 1981. "Economic Reorganization and the Slump in Southeast Asia." *Comparative Studies in Society and History* 23, no. 3: 325–49.

Bartlett, Beatrice S. 1991. *Monarchs and Ministers: The Grand Council in Mid-Ch'ing China, 1723–1820.* Berkeley: University of California Press.

Bernstein, Thomas P., and Xiaobo Lu. 2003. *Taxation without Representation in Contemporary Rural China.* New York: Cambridge University Press.

Borden, William S. 1984. *The Pacific Alliance: United States Foreign Economic Policy and Japanese Trade Recovery, 1947–1955*. Madison: University of Wisconsin Press.

Bouckaert, Boudewijn R. A. 2005. "Bureaupreneurs in China: We Did It Our Way—A Comparative Study of the Explanation of the Economic Successes of Town-Village-Enterprises in China." Paper presented at the EALE Conference, Ljubljana, Slovenia, September.

Braudel, Fernand. 1982. *Civilization and Capitalism, 15th–18th Century, II: The Wheels of Commerce*. New York: Harper and Row.

Cai Fang, Albert Park, and Yaohui Zhao. 2004. "The Chinese Labor Market." Paper presented at the Second Conference on China's Economic Transition: Origins, Mechanisms, and Consequences, University of Pittsburgh, Pittsburgh, Pennsylvania, November 5–7.

Cumings, Bruce. 1987. "The Origins and Development of the Northeast Asian Political Economy: Industrial Sectors, Product Cycles, and Political Consequences." In *The Political Economy of the New Asian Industrialism*, ed. F. C. Deyo, 44–83. Ithaca: Cornell University Press.

———. 1993. "The Political Economy of the Pacific Rim." In *Pacific-Asia and the Future of the World-System*, ed. R. A. Palat, 21–37. Westport, CT: Greenwood Press.

———. 1997. "Japan and Northeast Asia into the Twenty-first Century." In *Network Power: Japan and Asia*, ed. P. J. Katzenstein and T. Shiraishi, 136–68. Ithaca: Cornell University Press.

Cushman, Jennifer Wayne. 1993. *Fields from the Sea: Chinese Junk Trade with Siam during the Late Eighteenth and Early Nineteenth Centuries*. Studies on Southeast Asia, Southeast Asia Program, Cornell University, Ithaca, New York.

Duus, Peter. 1984. "Economic Dimensions of Meiji Imperialism: The Case of Korea, 1895–1910." *The Japanese Colonial Empire, 1895–1945*, ed. R. H. Myers and M. R. Peattie, 128–71. Princeton: Princeton University Press.

Esherick, Joseph. 1972. "Harvard on China: The Apologetics of Imperialism." *Bulletin of Concerned Asian Scholars* 4, no. 4: 9–16.

Fairbank, John K. 1983. *The United States and China*. Cambridge, U.K.: Harvard University Press.

———. 1989. "Keeping Up with the New China." *New York Review of Books*, March 16: 17–20.

Feis, Herbert. 1965. *Europe: The World's Banker, 1870–1914*. New York: Norton.

Feuerwerker, Albert. 1970. "Handicraft and Manufactured Cotton Textiles in China, 1871–1910." *Journal of Economic History* 30, no. 2: 338–78.

Fishman, Ted C. 2004. "The Chinese Century." *New York Times Magazine*, July 4.

———. 2005. *China, Inc.: How the Rise of the Next Superpower Challenges America and the World*. New York: Scribner.

Friedland, J. 1994. "The Regional Challenge." *Far Eastern Economic Review*, June 9.

Gruenwald, Paul, and Masahiro Hori. 2008. "Intra-regional Trade Key to Asia's Export Boom." *IMF Survey Magazine: Countries and Regions*, February 6.

Hamilton, Gary G., and Wei-An Chang. 2003. "The Importance of Commerce in the Organization of China's Late Imperial Economy." In *The Resurgence of East Asia:*

500, 150 and 50 Year Perspectives, ed. G. Arrighi, T. Hamashita, and M. Selden, 173–213. London and New York: Routledge.

Hart, Gillian. 2002. *Disabling Globalization: Places of Power in Post-Apartheid South Africa*. Berkeley: University of California Press.

Hart-Landsberg, Martin, and Paul Burkett. 2004. "China and Socialism: Market Reform and Class Struggle." *Monthly Review* 56, no. 3: 7–123.

Helleiner, Eric. 1992. "Japan and the Changing Global Financial Order." *International Journal* 47: 420–44.

Hout, T., and J. Lebretton. 2003. "The Real Contest between America and China." *Wall Street Journal*, September 16.

Huang, Philip C. C. 1985. *The Peasant Economy and Social Change in North China*. Stanford, CA: Stanford University Press.

Hui Po-keung. 1995. "Overseas Chinese Business Networks: East Asian Economic Development in Historical Perspective." Ph.D. diss., Department of Sociology, State University of New York at Binghamton.

Hung Ho-fung. 2001a. "Imperial China and Capitalist Europe in the Eighteenth-Century Global Economy." In *Review* (Fernand Braudel Center) 24, no. 4: 473–513.

———. 2001b. "Maritime Capitalism in Seventeenth-Century China: The Rise and Fall of Koxinga in Comparative Perspective." Unpublished manuscript. Department of Sociology, Johns Hopkins University.

———. 2003. "Orientalist Knowledge and Social Theories: China and European Conceptions of East-West Differences from 1600 to 1900." *Sociological Theory* 21, no. 3: 254–80.

———. 2004. "Early Modernities and Contentious Politics in Mid-Qing China, c. 1740–1839." *International Sociology* 19, no. 4: 478–503.

Iriye, Akira. 1970. "Imperialism in East Asia." *Modern East Asia*, ed. J. Crowley, 122–50. New York: Harcourt.

Irwan, Alex. 1995. "Japanese and Ethnic Chinese Business Networks in Indonesia and Malaysia." Ph.D. diss., Department of Sociology, State University of New York at Binghamton.

Jing Junjian. 1982. "Hierarchy in the Qing Dynasty." *Social Science in China: A Quarterly Journal* 3, no. 1: 156–92.

Kasaba, Resat. 1993. "Treaties and Friendships: British Imperialism, the Ottoman Empire, and China in the Nineteenth Century." *Journal of World History* 4, no. 2: 213–41.

Kawakatsu, Heita. 1994. "Historical Background." In *Japanese Industrialization and the Asian Economy*, ed. A. J. H. Lathan and H. Kawakatsu, 4–8. London and New York: Routledge.

Kennedy, Paul. 1987. *The Rise and Fall of the Great Powers: Economic Change and Military Conflict from 1500 to 2000*. New York: Random House.

Lin, Justin Yifu, and Yang Yao. n.d. "Chinese Rural Industrialization in the Context of the East Asian Miracle." China Center for Economic Research, Beijing University. Available at http://www.esocialsciences.com/articles/displayArticles.asp?Article_ID=647, accessed November 13, 2008.

Lin Nan. 1995. "Local Market Socialism: Local Corporatism in Action in Rural China." *Theory and Society* 24: 301–54.

Mackie, Jamie. 1992. "Changing Patterns of Chinese Big Business." *Southeast Asian Capitalists*, ed. R. McVey. Southeast Asian Program, Cornell University, Ithaca, New York.

———. 1998. "Business Success among Southeast Asian Chinese: The Role of Culture, Values, and Social Structures." In *Market Cultures: Society and Morality in the New Asian Capitalism*, ed. R. W. Hefner. Boulder, CO: Westview Press.

Maddison, Angus. 2007. *Contours of the World Economy, 1–2030 A.D.* New York: Oxford University Press.

Marx, Karl. 1959. *Capital*. Volume 1. Moscow: Foreign Languages Publishing House.

Marx, Karl, and Friedrich Engels. 1967. *The Communist Manifesto*. Harmondsworth: Penguin.

McNeill, William. 1982. *The Pursuit of Power: Technology, Armed Force, and Society since A.D. 1000*. Chicago: University of Chicago Press.

———. 1998. "World History and the Rise and Fall of the West." *Journal of World History* 9, no. 2: 215–37.

Nathan, Andrew J. 1972. "Imperialism's Effects on China." *Bulletin of Concerned Asian Scholars* 4, no. 4: 3–8.

Oi, Jean. 1999. *Rural China Takes Off: Institutional Foundations of Economic Reform.* Berkeley: University of California Press.

Okimoto, Daniel I., and Thomas P. Rohlen. 1988. *Inside the Japanese System: Readings on Contemporary Society and Political Economy*. Stanford: Stanford University Press.

Ong, Aihwa and Donald M. Nonini, eds. 1997. *Ungrounded Empires: The Cultural Politics of Modern Chinese Transnationalism*. New York: Routledge.

Ozawa, Terutomo. 1993. "Foreign Direct Investment and Structural Transformation: Japan as a Recycler of Market and Industry." *Business and the Contemporary World* 5, no. 2: 129–50.

———. 2003. "Pax Americana-Led Macro-Clustering and Flying-Geese-Style Catch-Up in East Asia: Mechanisms of Regionalized Endogenous Growth." *Journal of Asian Economics* 13: 699–713.

Parker, Geoffrey. 1989. "Taking Up the Gun." *MHQ: The Quarterly Journal of Military History* 1, no. 4: 88–101.

Peattie, Mark. 1984. "Introduction." In Ramon Myers and Mark Peattie, *The Japanese Colonial Empire, 1895–1945*, 3–26. Princeton: Princeton University Press.

Perdue, Peter C. 1987. *Exhausting the Earth: State and Peasant in Hunan, 1500–1850*. Cambridge, MA: Harvard University Press.

Polanyi, Karl. 1957. *The Great Transformation: The Political and Economic Origins of Our Time*. Boston: Beacon Press.

Pomeranz, Kenneth. 2000. *The Great Divergence: Europe, China, and the Making of the Modern World Economy*. Princeton: Princeton University Press.

Prestowitz, Clyde. 2005. *Three Billion New Capitalists. The Great Shift of Wealth and Power to the East*. New York: Basic Books.

Rowe, William. 2001. *Saving the World: Chen Hongmou and Elite Consciousness in Eighteenth-Century China.* Stanford, CA: Stanford University Press.

Rozman, Gilbert. 1991. *The East Asian Region: Confucian Heritage and its Modern Adaptation.* Princeton: Princeton University Press.

Schurmann, Franz. 1974. *The Logic of World Power: An Inquiry into the Origins, Currents, and Contradictions of World Politics.* New York: Pantheon.

Selden, Mark. 1997. "China, Japan, and the Regional Political Economy of East Asia, 1945–1995." In *Network Power: Japan and Asia,* ed. P. Katzenstein and T. Shiraishi, 306–40. Ithaca: Cornell University Press.

So, Alvin Y. 1986. *The South China Silk District.* Albany: State University of New York Press.

So, Alvin Y., and Stephen W. K. Chiu. 1995. *East Asia and the World-Economy.* Newbury Park, CA: Sage.

Stallings, Barbara. 1990. "The Reluctant Giant: Japan and the Latin American Debt Crisis." *Journal of Latin American Studies* 22: 1–30.

Sugihara, Kaoru. 1996. "The European Miracle and the East Asian Miracle: Towards a New Global Economic History." *Sangyo to keizai* 11, no. 12: 27–48.

———. 2003. "The East Asian Path of Economic Development: A Long-term Perspective." In *The Resurgence of East Asia: 500, 150 and 50 Year Perspectives,* ed. G. Arrighi, T. Hamashita and M. Selden, 78–123. London and New York: Routledge.

Taylor, A. 2006. "A Tale of Two Factories." *Fortune Magazine,* September 14.

Tsai, Kellee S. 2004. "Off Balance: The Unintended Consequences of Fiscal Federalism in China." *Journal of Chinese Political Science* 9, no. 2: 7–26.

Tsai, Lily. 2007. *Accountability without Democracy: Solidary Groups and Public Goods Provision in Rural China.* New York: Cambridge University Press.

Tsiang, Ting-fu. 1967. "The English and the Opium Trade." In *Imperial China,* ed. F. Schurmann and O. Schell, 132–45. New York: Vintage.

Unger, Jonathan. 2002. *The Transformation of Rural China.* Armonk, NY: M. E. Sharpe.

Walder, Andrew. 1995. "Local Governments as Industrial Firms: An Organizational Analysis of China's Transitional Economy." *American Journal of Sociology* 101, no. 2: 263–301.

Wang Gungwu. 1991. *China and the Chinese Overseas.* Singapore: Times Academic Press.

———. 1998. "Ming Foreign Relations: Southeast Asia." In *The Cambridge History of China Vol. 8 (2), The Ming Dynasty,* ed. D. Twitchett and F. Mote, 301–32. Cambridge, U.K.: Cambridge University Press.

Wang Juan. 2005. "Going Beyond Township and Village Enterprises in Rural China." *Journal of Contemporary China* 14, no. 42: 177–87.

Whiting, Susan H. 2001. *Power and Wealth in Rural China: The Political Economy of Institutional Change.* Cambridge, U.K.: Cambridge University Press.

Will, Pierre-Etienne, and R. Bin Wong. 1991. *Nourish the People: The State Civilian Granary System in China, 1650–1850.* Ann Arbor: University of Michigan Press.

Wills, John E. Jr. 1998. "Relations With Maritime Europeans." In *The Cambridge His-*

tory of China Vol. 8 (2), The Ming Dynasty, ed. D. Twitchett and F. Mote, 333–75. Cambridge, U.K.: Cambridge University Press.

Wolf, Eric. 1982. *Europe and the People without History*. Berkeley: California University Press.

Wong, R. Bin. 1997. *China Transformed: Historical Change and the Limits of European Experience*. Ithaca: Cornell University Press.

Wong Siu-lun. 1988. *Emigrant Entrepreneurs*. Hong Kong: Oxford University Press.

Woo, Wing Thye. 1999. "The Real Reasons for China's Growth." *China Journal* 41: 115–37.

Wu Yuan-li, and Chun-hsi Wu. 1980. *Economic Development in Southeast Asia: The Chinese Dimension*. Stanford: Hoover Institution Press.

CHAPTER THREE

Rethinking the Chinese Developmental Miracle

ALVIN Y. SO

During the Cold War era, China was generally seen by the Left in the West as a model of revolutionary socialism. The Left was especially attracted to the Maoist policies of public ownership, egalitarianism, mass mobilization, militant anti-imperialism, and the rejection of a reformist road to socialism (Halliday 1976). Nevertheless, in the late 1970s, when the advanced capitalist states lowered their hostility toward Communist China and welcomed China back to the world economy, China replaced Maoist policies with "market socialism." Since the late 1970s, China's economic development has stunned the world. The country has become one of the world's largest exporters of manufactured goods and sites for transnational investments while purportedly lifting hundreds of millions out of poverty.

In the West, the Left is divided on how to interpret China's transformation at the turn of twenty-first century. Some see China's market socialism as offering tremendous opportunities for achieving growth and poverty reduction, and they welcome China's regional and global emergence as it could serve as a counterweight to U.S.-style neoliberal and militarized capitalism (Silver and Arrighi 2000). Others denounce China's recent transformation as a move toward a neoliberal economy that contains the seeds for the reemergence of a foreign capitalist-dominated economy (Burkett and Hart-Landsberg 2005; Petras 2006).

This chapter argues that China's recent transformation actually is closer to the East Asian developmental state model than to the Western neoliberalism model. In the following sections, I first present the distinctive features of Chinese state developmentalism and explain how this model is different from that of neoliberalism. I then trace the transition from neoliberalism to state developmentalism in China during the past two decades and conclude by discussing the future trajectory of state developmentalism and its implication for the capitalist world economy.

NEOLIBERAL CAPITALISM

Up to the early 2000s, the Chinese state had been faithfully carrying out the policies of neoliberalism in its globalization drive (Harvey 2005). Since the Chinese economy was completely dominated by the state in the Maoist period, the aim of the post-Mao reforms was to liberate the market from the state in order to speed up capital accumulation. Thus, the Chinese states set up institutional frameworks to guarantee private-property rights and to promote free markets and free trade, with the hope that the Chinese economy would be invigorated and compete well in the capitalist world economy. It is with this neoliberal mindset that the Chinese state carried out the following policies during the last few decades:

- *Decollectivization and proletarianization of peasants.* Agricultural communes were dismantled in favor of an individualized "personal responsibility system." Township and village enterprises (TVEs) were created out of the former commune assets, and these became centers of entrepreneurialism, flexible labor practices, and open market competition. At the same time, the loss of collective social rights in the countryside meant that the peasants had to face burdensome user charges for schools, medical care, and other social services. Forced to seek work elsewhere after the end of collectivism, rural migrants flooded—illegally and without the right of residency—into the cities to form an immense labor reserve (a "floating population of indeterminate legal status"). China is now in the midst of the largest mass migration the world has ever seen. This rural "floating population" is vulnerable to superexploitation and puts downward pressure on the wages of urban workers (Pun 1999).
- *Marketization policy to restore/expand the market.* A new labor market was introduced to the Chinese economy in the late 1980s, creating a flexible labor force that is responsive to the ups and downs of the market. After a labor market is set up, state enterprises are no longer required to provide lifelong job security to their workers, and they are given the autonomy to hire and fire workers in the name of enhancing productivity and efficiency, as called upon by neoliberalism.
- *Fiscal decentralization and the weakening of the central state.* In the mid-

1980s, provincial, municipality, county, and township governments were subject to a bottom-up revenue-sharing system that required localities to submit only a portion of the revenues to the upper level. They were then allowed to retain most of the remainder. This fiscal-decentralization policy made local states into independent fiscal entities that had the unprecedented right to use the revenue they retained. The policy considerably weakened the central state's extractive capacity. The Chinese state is unable to control the extrabudgetary funds of the local governments, and its relative share of tax revenues has decreased to the extent that the central state has lost effective control over China's economic life (Oi 1992; Wang and Hu 2001).

- *Opening up and spatial differentiation.* The combination of decentralization and opening up has led to a very uneven pattern of spatial development in China, with rapid economic growth taking place mostly along the eastern coastal subregions. These subregions are characterized by an "extrovert" economy, that is, their economies are driven by foreign direct investment and export-led industrialization, and their economic growth has relied on their integration with the global commodity chains. For example, with regard to the commodity chain of athletic shoes, the 1990s observed the trend that transnationals (such as Nike and Reebok) moved their factories from their subcontractors in Taiwan to Guangdong and Fujian. Most of the raw materials were shipped from Taiwan, and the shoe factories in Guangdong were run by Taiwanese resident managers (Chen 2005).

- *Privatization and corporatization policy.* In the 1990s, the state enterprises (SOEs) underwent corporatization, so that they no longer depend on the state for funding and they must operate independently in the market. This was a conscious effort to cut the size of the state sector and to increase the size of the private sector. After corporatization, the SOEs were asked to operate like an independent, private, profit-making enterprises and to go bankrupt if they lose money (So 2006).

- *Commodification of social services.* Whereas the Maoist state provided social services (such as housing, health care, welfare, education, pension, and so on) based on need and free of charge to all citizens, the postreform state treats human services as a commodity to be distributed to people on market principles. Beneficiaries now must pay a part of the cost of these services in most welfare fields. Such changes can be seen in social insurance (pension, medical care, and the newly created unemployment insurance), higher education, and many personal services (Guan 2000).

- *Deepening of liberalization.* Petras points out that China's entry into the

World Trade Organization (WTO) is likely to lead to a further dismantling of the state sector, a dismantling of trade barriers, the removal of subsidies, the savaging of the countryside, the near unquestioning orientation toward the export market strategy, and the consolidation of foreign production as the leading force in the Chinese economy (2006: 424; see also Hart-Landsberg and Burkett 2004).

Through these processes, China has been moving toward the "neoliberal" capitalism model. On the one hand, the state is being downsized, state capacity is being weakened, the state's role in the economy is significantly reduced, and the state is offloading its welfare and human services onto the market and society. On the other hand, the private sector and the various labor, capital, and finance markets are expanding rapidly.

Like other neoliberal states, China suffered considerable costs during its march toward neoliberal capitalism, including rising unemployment, economic insecurity, class polarization, intensified exploitation, declining health and education conditions, exploding government debt, and unstable prices. Thus, Martin Hart-Landsberg and Paul Burkett point out that China's market reforms "have led not to socialist renewal but rather to full-fledged capitalist restoration, including growing foreign economic domination. The progressive community in the West is wrong to celebrate China as an economic success story" (2004: 9).

In response to these neoliberal policies, the Chinese working class has become restless. *China Labor Bulletin* reports that "almost every week in Hong Kong and mainland China, newspapers bring reports of some kind of labor action: a demonstration demanding pensions; a railway line being blocked by angry, unpaid workers; or collective legal action against illegal employer behavior such as body searches or forced overtime" (Pringle 2002). According to the official statistics, in 1998 there were 6,767 collective actions (usually strikes or go-slows with a minimum of three people taking part) involving 251,268 people. This represented an increase in collective actions of 900 percent from the early 1990s. In 2000, this figure was higher still, with 8,247 collective actions involving 259,445 workers. Given such widespread labor protests, no wonder that the Chinese government has identified labor problems as the biggest threat to social and political stability (So 2007).

DEPARTURE FROM NEOLIBERALISM

Even though neoliberalism has been a global trend since the 1970s, David Harvey points to the "uneven geographical development of neoliberalism" and "the complex ways in which political forces, historical traditions, and existing institutional arrangements all shaped why and how the process of neoliberalization actually occurred" (2005: 13).

Although the Chinese case fits nicely with the early stages of neoliberal market reforms, China's development since the mid-1990s has shown a departure from neoliberalism. First, in contrast to the image of a weakened state in neoliberalism literature, the Chinese state has considerably strengthened its managerial and fiscal capacity since the 1990s. The central party-state has instituted a new "cadre responsibility system" to strengthen its control over the evaluation and monitoring of local leaders. County party secretaries and township heads sign performance contracts, pledge to attain certain targets laid down by higher levels, and are held personally responsible for attaining those targets. There are different contracts for different fields, such as industrial development, agricultural development, tax collection, family planning, and social order. The Chinese party-state has the capacity to be selective, that is, to implement its priority policies, to control the appointment of its key local leaders, and to target strategically important areas (Oi 1989). Thus, Maria Edin argues that "state capacity, defined here as the capacity to control and monitor lower-level agents, has increased in China, and that the Chinese Communist Party is capable of greater institutional adaptability that it is usually given credit for" (2003: 36).

In addition, the state has strengthened its fiscal capacity. The central party-state introduced a "tax sharing scheme" (TSS) in 1994 to redress the center-local imbalance in fiscal matters (Yep 2007). TSS aims to improve the center's control over the economy by increasing "two ratios"—the share of budgetary revenue in GDP and the central share in total budgetary revenue. It seems that TSS did succeed in raising the two ratios, thus helping to arrest the decline of the fiscal foundation of the center and increase the extractive capacity of the central party-state (Loo and Chow 2006). Zheng argues that TSS has shifted fiscal power from the provinces to the center, so "now, it is the provinces that rely on the central government for revenue" (2004: 118–19).

Second, in contrast to the neoliberalism doctrine's call for less intervention, the Chinese state has intervened more deeply in the economy. The Chinese state engaged in debt-financed investments in huge megaprojects to transform physical infrastructures. Astonishing rates of urbanization (no fewer than forty-two cities have expanded beyond the one-million population mark since 1992) required huge investments of fixed capital. New subway systems and highways are being built in major cities, and 8,500 miles of new railroad have been proposed to link the interior to the economically dynamic coastal zone. China is also trying to build an interstate highway system more extensive than America's in just fifteen years, while practically every large city is building or has just completed a big new airport. These megaprojects have the potential to absorb surpluses of capital and labor for several years to come (Harvey 2005: 132). It is these massive debt-financing infrastructural and fixed-capital formation projects that suggest that the Chinese state has departed from the neoliberal orthodoxy and is acting like a Keynesian state.

Third, in contrast to the neoliberalism doctrine, which calls for the dismantling of the welfare state, the Chinese state presented in 2006 a new policy of "building a new socialist countryside" and a "harmonious society" (Saich 2007). This policy is significant because it could signal a change of ideological orientation in the Chinese state (Kahn 2006). Whereas the pre-2006 Chinese state endorsed a neoliberal orientation that could be called "GNPism," the Chinese state is now moving toward a more balanced orientation between economic growth and social development. While market reforms will continue, this new policy indicates that the state will take a more energetic role in moderating the negative impacts of marketization. In the new policy, the state should include "the people and environment" in its developmental plan and should not focus exclusively on GNP indicators and economic growth.

Thus, the new policy advocates a transfer of resources from the state to strengthen the fiscal foundation of the countryside. Not only was the agricultural tax abolished to help relieve the burden on farmers, there has also been a 15 percent boost in rural expenditure (to $15 billion) to bankroll guaranteed minimum-living allowances for farmers and an 87 percent hike (to $4 billion) for the health-care budget (Liu 2007). These policies indicate a massive infusion of funding from the state to the peasants and rural areas. In addition, there is a de-commodification of human services. Rural residents no longer have to pay the many miscellaneous charges levied by schools; fees at primary schools will be abolished as part of a nationwide campaign to eliminate them in the countryside for the first nine years of education. The state is also going to increase the subsidies for rural health cooperatives, which had been projected to be available in 80 percent of rural counties by 2008. For now, rural residents have to pay market rates at their village's private clinic. Most of them do not even have medical insurance and spend more than 80 percent of their cash on health care (Liu 2007). Furthermore, the new policy aims to reduce social inequality, especially the widening gap between the countryside and the city. Thus, pensions are to be made available for everyone, not just those enjoying the privileged status of registered urban residents. During the past two years, the state has also promoted the spread of the Minimum Living Standard Assistance plan for the rural population. This is potentially a highly significant development, opening up for the first time the real possibility of instituting a social safety net that covers the whole of the population, whether urban or rural (Hussain 2005; *The Economist* 2006).

Fourth, in contrast to the assumption that China is trapped in labor-intensive, low-tech, sweatshop export production, China has recently modernized its educational system, upgraded its science and research capabilities, and participated in high-tech production. In the 1990s, foreign corporations began to transfer a significant amount of their research and development activity to China. Microsoft, Oracle, Motorola, Siemens, IBM, and Intel have all set up research laboratories in China because of its "growing importance and sophistication as a market for technology" and "its large reservoir of skilled but inexperienced scientists, and its consumers, still relatively poor but growing richer and eager for new technology" (Buckley 2004). During the 1990s, China began to move up the value-added ladder of production and to compete with South Korea, Japan, Taiwan, and Singapore in spheres such as electronics and machine tools.

Fifth, whereas neoliberalism is seen as a project to restore/expand the power of the capitalist class, the capitalist class in China remains weak and dependent on the state for survival. Despite the rapid growth of the private sector, it has not severed its ties to the state sector. Instead, the private sector has numerous links with the state sector in terms of interlocking personnel and ownership. Many collective enterprises are owned and run by capitalists, while many private enterprises are spin-off state properties owned and run by state managers or their kin. This fusion makes it very difficult to distinguish what is owned by the state, by the collective, and by capitalists in the private sector because the boundaries of property relations are often blurred. In China, the capitalist class has responded to the challenges of globalization and the growing intensity of class conflict by reinventing itself as a class of nationalistic entrepreneurs and by undergoing political incorporation into the state (So 2003). Indeed, there is so much interpenetration that in 2001, the Chinese Communist Party finally accepted "progressive" people from the private sector into its own rank.

Sixth, whereas neoliberalism implies the loosening of national boundaries, in China nationalism is taken as a supreme value, and the Chinese state will try every means to preserve its national sovereignty. Thus, the Chinese state takes pains to emphasize its national humiliation in the nineteenth century and the first half of the twentieth century, is determined to pursue a national reunification project to recover the territory lost before the communist revolution (Hong Kong and Taiwan), and mobilizes its national sentiments through recent anti-Japanese protest and in international sports.

Finally, whereas neoliberalism perceives the triumph of transnational corporations and the loosening of national barriers to global production, marketing, and finance, in China the barriers erected to foreign portfolio investment, on top of the huge foreign-exchange reserve that the government has proactively accumulated for the last two decades, effectively limit the powers of international finance capital over the Chinese state. The reluctance to permit forms of financial intermediation other than state-owned banks—such as stock markets and capital markets—deprives capital of one of its key weapons against state power (Harvey 2005: 123).

In short, China has experienced a different pattern of development from neoliberal capitalism. During its initial phase of opening to the capitalist world economy, China did show traces of neoliberal capitalism, such as the dismantling of the welfare state, the weakening of state capacity, the expansion of a market economy and the private sector, a breakdown of national barriers to foreign investment, spatial differentiation, and the emergence of labor protests. However, within the past decade, China has moved beyond the neoliberal mode and closer to the pattern of state developmentalism in East Asia.

RISE OF STATE DEVELOPMENTALISM

Like other developmental states in East Asia, China has strong state machinery. The Chinese state is highly autonomous in the sense that it is not "captured" by vested economic interests. The old generation of the capitalists was largely destroyed in the communist revolution and the Cultural Revolution. The nascent capitalist class that emerged in the market reforms of the 1980s and 1990s is too weak and too dependent on the state to pose any challenge. In addition, the Chinese state has the capacity to carry out its developmental plans. Since the Chinese state owns the banks and controls the finance sector, it has powerful policy tools at its disposal that made the cooperation of indigenous business more likely: access to cheap credit, protection from external competition, and assisted access to export markets are all levers that the Chinese state can use to ensure business compliance with governmental goals. Since the Chinese corporations have a high debt/equity ratio, even the threat of withdrawal of state loans is a serious one.

Second, like other developmental states in East Asia, the Chinese state has actively intervened in the economy. The state has become the engine of powering capital accumulation. Aside from debt finance and infrastructure construction, the central Chinese state also develops plans for strategic development, decrees prices and regulates capital movement, shares risks, and underwrites research and development. At the local level, Jean Oi coined the phrase "local state corporatism" to describe how village, county, municipal, and provincial governments singlemindedly use their political authority to promote local capitalist development (1992). In Zouping, for example, local cadres raised the initial capital for new enterprises and closely supervised and assisted in their subsequent growth. Using their political authority, they mobilized capital for investment, arranged and allocated credit, and provided market information and technical expertise well in excess of what was initially present in the locality. Through this process, local states have taken on many characteristics of a business corporation, with local state officials acting as the equivalent of a board of directors.

Third, like other developmental states in East Asia, the Chinese state has actively mobilized the ideology of nationalism and defines itself as carrying out a national project to make China strong and powerful. In the postreform era, China experienced an ideological vacuum since the state could no longer be legitimized by Marxism or communism. Thus, nationalism became the state's only hope to gain the support of the Chinese people. The Chinese state seems to believe that the best approach is to build a strong sense of national cohesiveness based on cultural heritage and tradition, rather than to develop a nationalism based solely on hostility toward the outside world. Nationalism, however, can cut both ways. The Chinese state knows well that excessive nationalism might not only undercut the Communist Party's ability to rule but also disrupt China's paramount foreign-policy objective of creating a long-term peaceful environment for its modernization program. The Chinese state's concern is reflected in its rejection of more radical nationalism, such as that advocated by the authors of *The China that Can Say No*, as well as in its efforts to control anti-Japanese sentiment. Indeed, China's response to the Japanese provocation over the visit of the shrine was far more restrained than in Taiwan and Hong Kong. The Chinese state's attempt to control nationalism was also evident in its efforts to restrain anti-Americanism in the aftermath of the NATO bombing of the Chinese embassy in Yugoslavia (Ogden 2003).

Fourth, like other developmental states in East Asia, the Chinese state adopts authoritarian policies to discipline labor, suppress labor protests, and deactivate civil society in order to maintain a favorable environment for attracting foreign investment and facilitating capital accumulation. It seems that authoritarianism is unavoidable in export-led industrialization because labor subordination is an important means to cheapen labor and make the working class docile. Otherwise, the exports of the East Asian developmental states would not be competitive in the capitalist world economy, and transnational corporations would not relocate their labor-intensive production in East Asia. It is ironic that the Chinese state, with its tightly organized Leninist party-state machinery, has proven to be very effective in coopting labor activists, dividing the working class, and silencing labor protests.

Finally, like other developmental states in East Asia, China received an influx of capital during its initial phase of capitalist industrialization. During the Cold War era in the 1950s and 1960s, the massive influx of U.S. aids, loans, and contracts greatly helped East Asian states such as South Korea and Taiwan solve the problem of primitive accumulation and greatly enhanced their states' capacity to promote developmental policies. The United States, of course, did not provide similar aids, loans, and contracts to China to assist its developmental programs after the end of the Cold War in the late 1980s. Fortunately, there was a comparable influx of Chinese diaspora investment at the initial phase of transition to provide capital for primitive accumulation. Before 1978, Chinese diaspora capitalism thrived in Hong Kong, Taiwan, Singapore, and overseas Chinese communities. After the Chinese state adopted an open-door policy for foreign investment, Hong Kong accounted for the bulk of China's foreign investment and foreign trade. In the early 1990s, Hong Kong firms employed more than three million workers in the Pearl River Delta. By the end of the 1980s, Taiwan had become the second largest trading partner and investor for mainland China. In the 1990s, overseas Chinese entrepreneurs in Southeast Asia showed a visible interest in conducting trade and investment in China.

In short, China's latest developmental pattern is closer to that of the East Asian developmental state than to the neoliberal state. It has strong state machinery with a high degree of state autonomy and a strong capacity to carry out its goals. It greatly intervenes in the economy through developmental planning, deficit investment, export promotion, and strategic industrialization. It is also highly nationalistic and authoritarian, suppressing labor protests and limiting popular struggles. In addition, its capitalist industrialization greatly benefited from an influx of capital during the critical phase of primitive accumulation.

Nevertheless, China's state developmentalism has also shown some significant differences from that of other East Asian states. First, the Chinese developmental state has exhibited a strong tendency toward entrepreneurship. Although East Asian developmental state officials are promoting the hatching of capitalists, they seldom turn themselves into capitalists and become involved in running corporations. In China, however, not only were state officials asked to be good managers and turn state enterprises into profit-making businesses, but many state officials also informally turned public assets into quasi-public, quasi-private properties or simply into private companies. As is well documented, there is a fuzzy boundary between state enterprises and collective/private enterprises, and it is difficult to draw a clear boundary between state officials and private capitalists. Rather, the Chinese characteristic is a hybrid state-capitalist "walking on two legs" (*liangtiao-tui zoulu*) in both the state sector and the private sector.

Second, the Chinese developmental state has used a local, "bottom-up" strategy. East Asian developmental states adopted a centralized policy, and it was their central governments that played the most active role in development. However, in China, because of the legacy of communism, the policy of fiscal decentralization, and the country's vast territory, local officials in provincial, county, and village governments played a much more active role than their counterparts in East Asian developmental states. Instead of promoting the development of urban industrialization and megacities, Chinese local state officials have promoted the development of rural industrialization and small and medium-sized cities. In South China, for example, a new "bottom-up" development mechanism is taking shape, in which initiatives are made primarily by local states to solicit overseas Chinese and domestic capital, mobilize labor and land resources, and lead the local economy to enter the orbit of international division of labor and global competition.

Third, although the Chinese developmental state has relied on "GNPism" and nationalism as its bases of legitimacy, it has also paid more attention to egalitarianism than its East Asian counterparts during their industrial takeoff phase. Having gone through the legacy of revolutionary socialism under the Maoist regime and having as a constitutional tenet that workers and peasants are the masters of society, the Chinese "developmental" state was much more vulnerable to the charges of inequality, poverty, and exploitation than were its East Asian developmental-state counterparts. Thus, the Chinese state many times backed off from carrying out those policies that could lead to massive layoffs and the elimination of social safety nets. In its latest policy, in 2006, the Chinese state aims to build a new socialist countryside, abolish the agricultural tax, infuse the peasants and the rural areas with funding, and try out some decommodification policies of providing free education, subsidizing health care, guaranteeing a minimum living standard, and instituting a safety net that covers the whole of the population.

Given that China is moving in the direction of a developmental state, we must answer the following questions: What explains the transition from neoliberalism to state developmentalism in China? What is the future of this state developmentalism?

THE TRANSITION FROM NEOLIBERALISM
TO STATE DEVELOPMENTALISM

To begin with, this is a transition, not a rupture or a revolution. The transition from neoliberalism to state developmentalism took a fairly long time. It has been a gradual, adaptive process without a clear blueprint. The reforms have proceeded by trial and error, with frequent midcourse corrections and reversals of policy. In other words, the Chinese developmental policies have not been a complete project settled in "one bang" but an ongoing process with many midcourse adjustments.

When the Chinese state first tried out neoliberalism in the 1980s and 1990s, it found that it didn't work. The capitalist class was too small, too weak, and too dependent on the state to be the agent of historical transformation in China. But the transnational capitalist class was too strong, too greedy, and too eager to take advantage of Chinese capital and Chinese labor. If neoliberalism had its way, China would be totally dominated by foreign corporations and turn into a territorial outpost for transnational capital. Moreover, China observed that "shock therapy"— which called for the dismantling of the centrally planned economy as soon as possible—not only did not work but led to the downfall of the communist states in Eastern Europe.

Besides, the situation in China was not desperate. The Chinese state was not under any threat of foreign invasion, had not incurred any large amount of foreign debt, and faced no immediate threat of rebellion from within. As such, the Chinese state still had the autonomy and capacity to propose and implement various developmental policies "from above." For instance, the state could selectively introduce different types of developmental policies, vary the speed of market reforms, expand/limit the space of opening up to transnational capital, and most important, still have the freedom of adjusting (or even reversing) its policies if they did not work.

The asymmetrical power relationship between the state and other classes has given the state a free hand to try different developmental policies during the past few decades. The weak, dependent capitalist class is politically impotent to capture the state to carry out the neoliberal path of development. Facing growing labor unrest and popular struggle against such capitalist abuses as child labor in the coal mines, discrimination against immigrant workers, and environmental degradation, the capitalist class is powerless to reverse the policy toward state developmentalism.

Situated in East Asia, China has been long attracted to the developmental-state model and the remarkable postwar economic growth in South Korea, Taiwan, and Japan. Thus, Chang Kyung-Sup points out that there is a conscious process of learning and transplanting technologies, industrial organizations, and state policies among the East Asian states (2007).

FUTURE TRAJECTORY

If the Chinese experience is characterized by trial and error, midcourse corrections, and reversals of policy, what is the future trajectory of state developmentalism? Is it possible that this mode of state developmentalism will fade away in the near future?

One possible scenario is the return to neoliberalism, as in South Korea. In the 1990s, the Korean developmental state was dismantled when the *chaebols* (big business corporations) were empowered by their interlinkages with transnational corporations. This global reach has made the *chaebols* so powerful that they were able to dismantle the Economic Planning Board, set up nonstate financial institutions, and push for financial liberalization (Chiu and So 1996).

Although at present the Chinese capitalist class is small and weak, it could grow and become very powerful in a couple of decades. If this happens, the capitalist class will no longer be content to be a junior partner of the ruling coalition. Instead, it will expand its economic interest and impose its own class project on the state. Harvey points out that neoliberalism is the project of the capitalist class through which it has restored/expanded its power in advanced capitalist countries (2005).

Another possible scenario is the imperial path. State developmentalism has become so successful that it has greatly empowered the Chinese nation in the world economy. When China expands, it will inevitably run into conflict with other hegemonic states. In the "rise of China" scenario, the great powers in the world economy will fight with China over control of the market, resources (especially oil), technology, finance, and territory. History tells us that the existing hegemon will always want to hold onto its power and try every means to prevent other states from challenging its position. Unless China can win this battle of hegemonic transition, it will not emerge as the center of capital accumulation in the twenty-first century.

State developmentalism, by drawing upon the nation symbol and building up a strong state, does provide an impetus toward the above scenario of the rise of China and the hegemonic struggles in the world economy. While it is too optimistic, as Silver and Arrighi have claimed, to say that "China appears to be emerging as the only poor country that has any chance in the foreseeable future of subverting the Western-dominated global hierarchy of wealth," the issues concerning China's state developmentalism do require more in-depth analysis because of their global implications (2000: 69).

REFERENCES

Buckley, C. 2004. "Let a Thousand Ideas Flower: China Is a New Hotbed of Research." *New York Times*, September 13, C1, C4.

Burkett, Paul, and Martin Hart-Landsberg. 2005. "Thinking about China: Capitalism, Socialism, and Class Struggle." *Critical Asian Studies* 37: 433–40.

Chang Kyung-Sup. 2007. "Developmental Statism in the Post-Socialist Context: China's Reform Politics through a Korean Perspective." Paper presented to the conference "Chinese Society and China Studies," Nanjing, China, May 26–27, 2007.

Chen Xiangming. 2005. *As Borders Bend: Transnational Spaces on the Pacific Rim.* Lanham, MD: Rowman and Littlefield.

Chiu, Stephen, and Alvin Y. So. 2006. "State-Market Realignment in Post-Crisis East Asia: From GNP Developmentalism to Welfare Developmentalism?" Paper presented to the conference "The Role of Government in Hong Kong," Hong Kong, November 3, 2006.

The Economist. 2006. "Asia: Dreaming of Harmony; China." October 21, 76.

Edin, Maria. 2003. "State Capacity and Local Agent Control in China: CCP Cadre Management from a Township Perspective." *China Quarterly* 173: 35–42

Guan Xinping. 2000. "China's Social Policy: Reform and Development in the Context of Marketization and Globalization." *Social Policy and Administration* 34: 115–30.

Hart-Landsberg, Martin, and Paul Burkett. 2004. "China and Socialism: Market Reforms and Class Struggle." *Monthly Review* 56: 1–116.

Harvey, David. 2005. *A Brief History of Neoliberalism.* Oxford, U.K.: Oxford University Press.

Halliday, Fred. 1976. "Marxist Analysis and Post-Revolutionary China." *New Left Review* 100: 165–92.

Hussain, Athar. 2005. "Preparing China's Social Safety Net." *Current History* 104: 683–722.

Liu, Melinda. 2007. "Beijing's New Deal." *Newsweek*, March 26.

Loo Becky and Sin Yin Chow. 2006. "China's 1994 Tax Sharing Reforms: One System, Different Impact." *Asian Survey* 46: 215–37.

Ogden, Suzanne. 2003. "Chinese Nationalism: The Precedence of Community and

Identity over Individual Rights." In *China's Developmental Miracle: Origins, Transformations, and Challenges*, ed. Alvin Y. So. Armonk, NY: M. E. Sharpe.

Oi, Jean. 1989. *State and Peasant in Contemporary China: The Political Economy of Village Government*. Berkeley: University of California Press.

———. 1992. "Fiscal Reform and the Economic Foundations of Local State Corporatism in China" *World Politics* 45: 99–126.

Petras, James. 2006. "Past, Present, and Future of China: From Semi-Colony to World Power?" *Journal of Contemporary Asia* 36: 423–41.

Pringle, Tim. 2002. "Industrial Unrest in China: A Labour Movement in the Making?" *China Labour Bulletin*, January 31, 2002. Available at www.hartford-hwp.com/archives/55/294.html, accessed December 20, 2008.

Pun Ngai. 1999. "Becoming Dagongmei: The Politics of Identity and Difference in Reform China." *China Journal* 42: 1–19.

Saich, Tony. 2007. "Focus on Social Development." *Asian Survey* 47: 32–43.

Silver, Beverly J., and Giovanni Arrighi. 2000. "Workers North and South." In *2001 Socialist Register: Working Classes, Global Realities*, ed. Leo Panitch and Colin Leys. New York: Monthly Review Press.

So, Alvin Y. 2003. "The Making of a Cadre-Capitalist Class in China." In *China's Challenges in the Twenty-First Century*, ed. Joseph Cheng, 475–501. Hong Kong: City University of Hong Kong Press.

———. 2007. "The State and Labor Insurgency in Post-Socialist China." In *Challenges and Policy Programs of China's New Leadership*, 133–50. Hong Kong: City University of Hong Kong Press.

So, Bennis Wai Yip. 2005. "Privatization." In *Critical Issues in Contemporary China*, ed. Czeslaw Tubilewicz, 50–79. New York and London: Routledge.

Wang Shaoguang and Hu Angang. 2001. *The Chinese Economy in Crisis: State Capacity and Tax Reform*. Armonk, NY: M. E. Sharpe.

Zheng Yongnian. 2004. *Globalization and State Transformation in China*. New York: Cambridge University Press.

CHAPTER FOUR

Big Suppliers in Greater China

A Growing Counterweight to the Power of Giant Retailers

RICHARD P. APPELBAUM

The explosive globalization in the labor-intensive production of consumer goods is by now a well-known and well-documented phenomenon. Small firms as well as large ones have been able to access factories around the world. The global networks through which this international production is coordinated are typical buyer-driven global commodity chains in which "large retailers, marketers and branded manufacturers play the pivotal roles in setting up decentralized production networks in a variety of exporting countries," typically located in the developing world (Gereffi and Memedovic 2003: 3). While some of these factories have historically been large (for example, in the footwear industry), most contractors have been relatively small. This has reinforced their vulnerability to the big buyers: many factories have historically been part of "captive networks," limited to simple, low-value-added assembly operations that follow detailed instructions from their clients (Gereffi, Humphrey, and Sturgeon 2003: 12).

We are now entering an era in which a qualitatively higher degree of integration between production and distribution has begun to reshape the entire buyer-driven global commodity chain (Abernathy et al. 1999; Bonacich 2005; Bonacich and Wilson 2005). Two trends have emerged in the past decade, particularly in the Pacific Rim region, that are altering the boundary between "manufacturer" on the one hand and "retail buyer" on the other: the emergence of giant retailers and the emergence of the commensurately large factory contractors who serve them. Scholars have begun to study the first trend, which has been the subject of a Sloan Foundation Industry Studies workshop led by sociologist Gary Hamilton (see, for example, Hamilton and Petrovic 2006a, b). The second trend, however, remains understudied and, as a result, largely untheorized.

In the following discussion, I argue that the emergence of giant transnational contractors may alter the dynamic of global supply chains, including the current seemingly unstoppable dominance of giant U.S.- and EU-based retailers as market makers. At the very least, I will argue, the rise of China as an economic power will likely impact the current dynamic in several ways. At a minimum, giant contractors—"big suppliers"—are themselves market makers for their own suppliers, exerting increasing control over key aspects of the production supply chain. More speculatively, if the current trends continue, the giant contractors may come to challenge the power of all but the biggest "big buyers" they serve. This could alter the governance structure of some global supply chains, raising the possibility that Taiwanese- and Chinese-based multinational big suppliers may themselves someday morph into big buyers, challenging the firms they now serve. As the East Asian economies mature, moving from export-oriented industrialization to producing for their own internal markets, the dynamics that once favored the growing power of U.S.- and EU-based big buyers may also shift, eroding the market-making ability of the latter relative to multinationals based in the East Asian economies. China in particular has moved increasingly toward complementing export-oriented industrialization with an emphasis on "indigenous innovation" (*zizhu chuangxin*), now that a large and growing internal market has emerged. First announced as "The Decision on Accelerating Scientific and Technological Progress" at the Third National Conference on Science and Technology in 1995, this has become a central feature of China's economic strategy, emphasized both in the 11th Five-Year Plan (2006–2011) and in its Medium- and Long-Term Plan for the Development of Science and Technology.[1] As China's leaders see it, the country's development has reached a point where China can no longer depend exclusively on the uncertainties of technology transfer from foreign multinationals if it truly hopes to upgrade its economy. By investing heavily in basic and applied research, product development, and commercialization of what it sees as leading-edge technologies, China hopes to "leapfrog development," becoming a world-class producer of many of the products it now exports for foreign firms. Whether this will enable its increasingly big suppliers to morph into globally competitive big buyers remains an open question, although it is arguable that—given China's current growth trajectory and supporting government policies—such a transition may well occur sooner rather than later.

THE EMERGENCE OF GIANT TRANSNATIONAL CONTRACTORS

The appearance of giant factories as global suppliers for Wal-Mart and other large retailers is a largely unexpected development, since so many business and man-

agement theorists, emphasizing "flexible specialization," the "virtual corporation," and other forms of decentralized production and distribution, have argued
that the era of the gigantic production facility was over (see, for example, Piore
and Sabel 1986; Kapinsky 1993; Pine and Davis 1999). No longer would entrepreneurs assemble tens of thousands of workers at capital-intensive factory complexes such as River Rouge or Cannon Mills. But the past decade has in fact seen
the emergence of giant transnational corporations, mainly from Hong Kong, Taiwan, South Korea, and China, that operate massive factories under contract with
consumer-goods buyers—retailers and branded manufacturers—a trend that may
well portend a dramatic shift of organizational power within global supply chains.
The emergence of these giant transnational contractors has yet to be examined.

In the textile and apparel industries, for example, the consolidation of production, both at the factory and country level, is highly pronounced and will greatly
accelerate now that the thirty-year-old Multifiber Arrangement (MFA), whose
quota system resulted in the dispersal of clothing production to some 140 countries, expired on January 1, 2005. The end of the MFA is predicted to lead to a consolidation of production into larger companies and a smaller number of supplying countries because of the economies of scale that can be achieved (Speer
2002). Industry sources claim that large retailers and manufacturers such as
the Gap, JCPenney, Liz Claiborne, and Wal-Mart—which once sourced from
fifty or more countries—will source from ten to fifteen when quotas no longer
constrain their sourcing decisions (Malone 2002; Just-style.com 2003; McGrath
2003). A large body of research predicts that with the end of the MFA, China
alone may eventually claim as much as half of all export-oriented apparel production, with potentially devastating effects on those developing countries in South
Asia, Central America, the Caribbean, and Africa that have become highly dependent on textile and apparel exports (Nordås 2004). (For a detailed treatment,
see UNCTAD 2004, 2005.)[2]

Examples of giant East Asia–based contractors abound. In the textile and apparel industries, the Taiwanese multinational Nien Hsing Textile Company, "the
largest specialized denim fabric and garment in-one-stream manufacturer in the
world," boasts a "customer base from designer brands such as Calvin Klein,
DKNY, Tommy Hilfiger, Nautica, Mudd Jeans, GAP, Levis Japan to retail private
labels or importers such as JCPenney, Wal-Mart, Target, VF Jeanswear (Lee,
Wrangler), Sears, No Excuses etc."[3] Nien Hsing has factories in Taiwan, Mexico,
Nicaragua, and Lesotho. Yupoong, a Korean multinational that has become the
world's second largest cap manufacturer, has factories in the Dominican Republic, Vietnam, and Bangladesh. Yupoong's "flexfit" hats (motto: "worn by the world")

are exported to some sixty countries (Yupoong 2003). In consumer electronics, large contract factories also provide integrated production and final assembly of circuit boards, personal computers, cell phones, handheld digital devices, game consoles, and other IT devices for brand names such as Dell, Hewlett-Packard, Ericsson, and Siemens. Southeast Asia, and China in particular, have become the center of the most advanced consumer-electronics fabrication (UNCTAD 2002; Lüthje 2005). The world's largest electronics contract manufacturer, the U.S.-based Flextronics, employs nearly one hundred thousand workers worldwide, half of whom are in Asia, mainly southern Malaysia (close to its Asian headquarters in Singapore) and southern Guangdong Province in China (Flextronics 2003; Lüthje 2005).

A number of these large firms, particularly those from Taiwan, have set up operations in Latin America and Africa. By 2003, for example, Taiwanese firms had invested an estimated $2.1 billion in South Africa, Swaziland, and Lesotho, employing more than 110,000 workers, representing a fifth of the workforce in the latter country (Du Ling 2003).

SUPPLY-CHAIN MANAGEMENT IN CHINA'S APPAREL AND TEXTILE INDUSTRIES

China's textile and apparel production remains concentrated in small- and medium-sized firms in the coastal areas, although this is changing, both as firms move inland in search of cheaper labor and as larger firms—with advanced forms of supply-chain management—become more central. Cao Ning identifies three kinds of supply-chain management in China: vertical integration, traditional purchasing, and third-party coordinated (Cao 2005).

In *vertically integrated supply chains*, retailers have internalized the supply chain, at the least owning their own assembly plants and sometimes achieving additional backward integration through ownership of yarn and textile factories and even cotton farms. Hong Kong's Esquel Group, "one of the world's leading producers of premium cotton shirts," is an example. Esquel produces its own brand (the "Pye" label), although it primarily produces for other clients. Overall, the firm's forty-seven thousand employees manufacture sixty million garments annually, with seventeen factories in nine countries, including garment manufacturing facilities in China, Malaysia, Vietnam, Mauritius, and Sri Lanka, as well as cotton farms and yarn factories. Esquel's retail outlets in Beijing in 2000, which carry its "Pye" series, provide an example of vertical integration: "From the cotton field to the retail outlet, Esquel is the absolute coordinator" (Cao 2005). According to its Web site,

Esquel's vertically integrated operations ensure the highest quality in every step of the apparel manufacturing process. Production begins in Xinjiang province in northwestern China, where the Group grows its own Extra Long Staple (ELS) Cotton and Organic Cotton, continues through spinning, weaving, dyeing, manufacturing, packaging and retailing. Esquel's textile and apparel production is complemented by strong product development capabilities. The Group's design and merchandising team work closely with its research and development center to create unique finishings such as wrinkle-free and nano-technology performance qualities that consistently give Esquel the cutting edge in the apparel industry.

The degree to which such vertical integration signals a move from manufacturing to retailing is open to debate, however. While Esquel's high degree of vertical integration can be seen as a form of market-making in terms of control over suppliers, the company remains primarily a manufacturer for others. Its high-end Pye brand represents a small percentage of the company's total revenues.[4]

The second kind of supply-chain management is the familiar *traditional purchasing supply chain*, in which the retailer contracts with independent manufacturers to produce garments according to specification (Cao 2005). Either the retailer or the manufacturer can assume responsibility for supply-chain coordination. Manufacturer-coordinated supply chains are of special interest because they signal a possible shift in supply-chain control from retailer to manufacturer. One form of manufacturer coordination—"vendor managed inventory"—is illustrated by the Hong Kong–based TAL Group. TAL,* founded in 1947 as a single textile spinning mill in Hong Kong, has grown into one of the major apparel manufacturers, incorporating design, logistics, and fabrication.[5] Its global workforce of twenty-three thousand employees, producing annual sales of $600 million, are found in factories in Hong Kong, Thailand, Malaysia, Taiwan, China, Indonesia, Vietnam, Mexico, and the United States. TAL's clients include Brooks Brothers, L.L. Bean, JCPenney, Giordano, Lands' End, Liz Claiborne, Nautica, and Tommy Hilfiger, with retailers acquiring the majority of its sales. TAL accounts for one out of every eight dress shirts sold in the United States. Its success is attributed to its ability to manage its supply chain efficiently:

> Today, TAL boasts that it is one of the few Asian suppliers capable of handling a variety of EDI documents, such as purchase order (PO), advance ship notice (ASN), invoice, point-of-sales (POS) data, order status, etc. . . . From the late 1990s to today, the hurdle has once again been raised: Firms are now being asked to synchronize their supply and demand activities far more effectively

and this means ensuring that far-flung product development, marketing/sales, and supply chains are in close coordination. TAL responded by enabling vendor managed inventory with customers such as J.C. Penney. In doing so, TAL was able to link its designers and its factory floors half a world away to the points of sale in the U.S., resulting in ever greater efficiencies for its customers and expanded business opportunities for TAL. . . . Now as an integrated synchronization services provider with manufacturing capabilities, TAL not only has visibility into demand at the retailer's point of sale, i.e. to demand from the final consumer, but can link this information back directly to production operations on the factory floor as well as to product development and R&D activities. (Koudal and Long 2005)

By relying on TAL as its principal supplier, JCPenney is able virtually to eliminate inventory of its private label dress shirts. TAL runs point-of-sale data from JCPenney's North American stores through its proprietary software to determine the quantity of different styles, colors, and sizes of shirts to make—all without the need to consult with JCPenney itself. TAL even designs and test-markets JCPenney's new shirts. As Kahn writes, "The new process is one from which Penney is conspicuously absent. The entire program is designed and operated by TAL Apparel Ltd. . . . TAL collects point-of-sale data for Penney's shirts directly from its stores in North America, then runs the numbers through a computer model it designed. The Hong Kong company then decides how many shirts to make, and in what styles, colors and sizes. The manufacturer sends the shirts directly to each Penney store, bypassing the retailer's warehouses—and corporate decision makers" (Kahn 2003: A1).

TAL provides similar services to Brooks Brothers and Lands' End. Vendor-managed inventory gives the manufacturer increased market-making power over its suppliers, thereby signaling a shift in power from retailer to contractor: it is now the contractor, rather than the retailer, who manages the supply chain (Kahn 2003). TAL's New York City–based design team develops the style, TAL analyzes sales data to determine the quantity to produce for JCPenney stores, and TAL's Asian factories turn out the product. According to one management consultant who has studied the industry, "You are giving away a pretty important function when you outsource your inventory management. That's something that not a lot of retailers want to part with" (cited in Kahn 2003: A1).

The third kind of supply-chain management is the *third-party coordinated supply chain*, in which garment trading companies provide the coordination, oversee quality control, and sometimes provide fashion design (Cao 2005). The prime example of this form of supplier market making is the Li & Fung Group, the giant multinational trading company based in Hong Kong, with a staff of twenty-five thousand distributed across more than seventy offices in forty countries and territories, with 2006 revenues of $10.4 billion (Li & Fung 2007). In addition to garments and footwear, Li & Fung export management includes furnishings, toys, stationery, home products, sporting goods, and travel goods. Trading companies such as Li & Fung have reportedly become more powerful, taking the lead in supply-chain management (Kahn 2004b; Pun 2005). Li & Fung is organized into three core businesses: exporting services, value chain logistics, and retailing.

1. Li & Fung Ltd. manages the export supply chain for a variety of consumer goods, "work[ing] together to find the best source for different components or processes, and drawing on a global network of some 10,000 factories. Activities span the supply chain, including initial product development and design, raw material sourcing, production planning, factory sourcing, manufacturing control, quality assurance, export documentation, and shipping consolidation. Its venture capital fund invests in consumer products companies in Europe and the United States. By way of example (this from an interview with Li & Fung CEO Victor Fung in the *Harvard Business Review*), the company might fill a large order by sourcing its yarn from Korea, doing the dying in Taiwan, purchasing buttons and zippers in China, and assembling the final product in Thailand" (Magretta 2002).

2. Integrated-Distribution Services (IDS Group) provides "value-chain logistics" throughout Asia in "three core business areas": marketing (sales, billing, and collection), logistics (shipping, warehousing, and delivery), and manufacturing (fabrication, testing, and packaging).

3. Li & Fung Retailing Ltd. operates more than 950 retail outlets, with 11,500 employees, in Greater China, Singapore, Malaysia, Thailand, Indonesia, the Philippines, and South Korea for Toys"R"Us, Circle K, and Branded Lifestyle. Toys"R"Us is a joint venture with the U.S.-based parent company (in 1999, Li & Fung acquired 100 percent ownership of the business in Hong Kong, Taiwan, Singapore, and Malaysia). Branded Lifestyle represents major European and U.S. brands in Asia seeking to establish a consciousness of "brand values" for its clients (these include Salvatore Ferragamo and Calvin Klein, among others).

RETAILERS MOVE CLOSER TO THEIR SUPPLIERS

The emergence of large contract factory suppliers alters the power dynamics of global manufacturing, as lean retailing, with its associated cost-cutting and quick

response, compels retailers to shift such critical functions as inventory management and sales forecasting to giant contract suppliers (Kahn 2003: A1). The example of TAL provides one illustration of this trend. In some cases, this shifting
of key functions has even meant the migration of many pre- and postproduction
functions, including design, warehousing, and control over logistics, to Asia—as
is seen with Luen Thai in China (Kahn 2004b).

Luen Thai Holdings is a leading apparel supplier, with more than twenty-five
thousand employees and twelve manufacturing facilities and fourteen offices in
nine countries, and with 2006 revenues of $662 million (Luen Thai 2006, 2007).
The company produces more than eighty million pieces of garments annually,
including sleepwear, pants and shorts, sports and active wear, ladies' fashion,
intimate wear, and children's wear (Luen Thai 2006). Luen Thai is rapidly
expanding, having recently acquired GJM from Warnaco, Tomwell Ltd. from the
Jones Apparel Group, and a 50 percent stake in On Time and embarked on a 50–
50 joint venture with Guangzhou Huasheng Garment Company. In addition, it
has formed a joint venture with Yue Yuen for its sports and active wear.[6] The company, pursuing a "design to store" business model, has created a "supply-chain city"
in Dongguan—a two-million-square-foot factory, a three-hundred-room hotel, a
dormitory for the factory's four thousand workers, and product-development centers.[7] The factory permits apparel manufacturer Liz Claiborne and other Luen
Thai customers to work in a single location, their designers meeting directly with
technicians from the factory and fabric mills to plan production far more
efficiently.[8] The consolidated supply chain is projected to reduce Liz Claiborne
and Luen Thai staff by 40 percent, cutting costs and improving turnaround by
providing tight coordination over logistics. Liz Claiborne, which currently sources
from some 250 suppliers in thirty-five countries, plans to consolidate sourcing in
a handful of places, using facilities such as the Luen Thai complex; it has already
begun to relocate staff from its Hong Kong and New York City offices. This process of consolidation has been reinforced by the end of the MFA, which has encouraged major apparel countries to concentrate production in a smaller number
of much larger facilities in a relative handful of countries. In addition to the labor
cost savings that would result from concentrating production in China, Liz Claiborne and Luen Thai executives believe that "the real gains would come by re-
organizing their entire production process so as to be able to cut down on turnaround times for new clothes and coordinate logistics." Having everyone in a
single location—designers, fabric and raw-material suppliers, sewers—is viewed
as significantly cutting costs and improving turnaround time, "getting new styles
into stores faster": "Instead of having 100 people spread between New York and

Asia doing the same job, the new supply-chain city will enable the two companies to reduce staff to 60 people in China, concentrating all functions closer to the factory floor. . . . By moving all but the most critical designers and trend spotters to Asia, the company can dispense with the tedious back and forth, slashing precious weeks off production times and getting up-to-minute fashions into stores sooner. . . . In the new supply-chain city, everyone from the fabric mill to the store will use the same scan-and-track inventory system. Goods can roll off the factory floor and go straight to a store" (Khan 2004a: B1).

THE WORLD'S LARGEST FOOTWEAR SUPPLER:
A COUNTERWEIGHT TO NIKE?

Yue Yuen/Pou Chen Industrial Holdings, based in Hong Kong, is the world's largest maker of branded athletic and casual footwear, with $3.7 billion in revenues during FY 2006 (Yue Yuen 2007b).[9] The company produced nearly two hundred million pairs of branded athletic shoes for export in 2006, an increase of nearly three-quarters over the previous five years, representing 17 percent of the world total (Yue Yuen 2007a; Merk 2008). The company is Nike's biggest supplier, providing 15 to 30 percent of its shoes (estimates vary widely), with one Indonesian factory reportedly turning out a million shoes a month for Nike; other major footwear clients include Reebok, Adidas, Asics, New Balance, Puma, Timberland, and Rockport (owned by Reebok). While most of its shoes are made in factories throughout southern China (four out of six are in Dongguan Province), the company also has factories in Vietnam and Indonesia.[10] Overall, it operated 373 production lines as of 2006 (Yue Yuen 2007a). Yue Yuen is also expanding its sports apparel production, having acquired Pro Kingtex, invested in Eagle Nice, and formed a joint manufacturing venture with Luen Thai, among other activities, although this segment contributes less than 2 percent of the company's total revenues (Yue Yuen 2006, 2007b).

Yue Yuen's global workforce of 280,000 people in 2006 has grown by half in the past five years, primarily as a result of its steady growth as the leading manufacturer of athletic shoes but also because of the growth of its Greater China (China, Taiwan, and Hong Kong) wholesale and retail operations. In terms of its manufacturing capabilities, Yue Yuen boasts what are likely the world's largest footwear manufacturing plants in Dongguan, China (with 1.4 million square meters of manufacturing floorspace), and Ho Chi Minh City, Vietnam (1.3 million square meters; see Yue Yuen 2007a). Its sprawling factory complex in Dongguan alone reportedly employs some 110,000 workers, including twenty-one thousand for

Nike and thirteen thousand for Adidas. The Nike production sector includes recently renovated dormitories for its workers (eight women to a spartan room, in two rows of bunk beds), a cafeteria, and a recently constructed "activities center" that includes a library and reading room, a karaoke and dancing facility, a chess room, and meeting rooms and classrooms. Nike reportedly invested some $4.5 million in these renovations; it uses the new facilities to offer workers courses in personal finance, computers, and counseling.[11]

As of September 2006, Yue Yuen's expansion into wholesale and retail sales boasts a network of more than 2,100 wholesale distributors in the greater China region, operating 640 retail outlets, distributing products from the major brands made in its factories (Merk 2003; Yue Yuen 2007b).[12] Revenues from the company's wholesale and retail operations in Greater China grew by four-fifths during the previous year — although they still represented only a small percentage of total revenues (5.4 percent). As of FY 2006, Asian markets accounted for 30 percent of Yue Yuen's total turnover — second only to the United States (38 percent; see Yue Yuen 2007b). The company is bullish about its wholesale and retail operations and claims to be "on track" in terms of its goal of opening one thousand additional stores or counters by 2008 (Yue Yuen 2007b): "China domestic consumption will continue to be robust and . . . the 2008 Beijing Olympics will be a catalyst for increased sporting goods sales in China. The Group will earmark more resources to expand its market share in the Greater China region" (Yue Yuen 2007b).[13] As it turns out, Yue Yuen profit surged 56 percent in the first nine months of 2008, largely thanks to the Beijing Olympics (Hong Kong Trade and Development Council 2008).

Yue Yuen is also engaged in the upstream production of raw materials, shoe components, and even production tools — affording a high degree of vertical integration over its supply chain. In 2002, for example, it acquired Pou Chen's interest in sixty-seven upstream footwear-material providers, including raw materials, equipment, and shoe components (Yue Yuen 2006). It is also seeking downstream integration as a way of exerting tighter control over its logistics. As the company reports, "To accelerate its downstream vertical integration, SupplyLINE Ltd, a joint venture between Yue Yuen and Logistics Information Network Enterprise ("LINE"), a wholly-owned subsidiary of Hutchison Port Holdings, was formed to act as a Lead Logistics Provider, offering fully integrated supply chain and logistics solutions that shorten lead times for inbound materials and outbound products" (Yue Yuen 2006). The company is clearly emerging as a market maker with regard to its own suppliers. Yet how much of a market maker is Yue Yuen in the retail sector, in its dealings with major brands such as Nike or Reebok? When Yue

Yuen's costs rose sharply in 2004, it was able to pass on less than a third of the cost increase to its customers, forcing the company to post a 1.6 percent year-to-year decline in profits, the first such decline in twelve years.[14] While some analysts regard this as an indication of the relatively weak bargaining power of even the largest contractors in relation to the brands that rely on them (Fong 2005), others disagree (Hermanson 2005). Moreover, the company reported that in 2006, "the average selling price continued its upward trend, reflecting the product mix change and the increase in underlying material costs," suggesting that it was in fact able to pass on some of its cost increases to its buyers (Yue Yuen 2007b).

Whereas Wal-Mart's relationship with its suppliers is famously fleeting, determined purely by price considerations, the athletic-footwear industry requires close cooperation between buyer and supplier, achieved through stable, ongoing relationships. Yue Yuen, for example, began as a suppler for Wal-Mart in the 1970s but eventually developed the know-how, technological capacity, and size to move up to high-end brands such as Nike. Because the major brands require a highly diversified product mix and flexible production systems, Yue Yuen's high degree of vertical integration (including control over inputs and logistics) enables it to work with customers that require rapid market response. These same requirements afford the company a fair amount of bargaining power with even its largest customers (Ho 2005).

Yue Yuen is already engaged in a limited way in original brand manufacturing; is it likely to "learn through doing" and eventually replace Nike and its other clients as a leading designer and retailer of athletic shoes? Nike and Yue Yuen depend highly on one another, reducing the probability that Nike will cut production if Yue Yuen begins to market its own low-cost brands in China (Ho 2005). However, Yue Yuen is a highly profitable business, thanks to its broad and loyal client base; it is unlikely to threaten those relationships by creating potentially competing brands (Chan 2005; Pun 2005).

At the present time, it is clear that while Yue Yuen is a powerful market maker with regard to its own suppliers, it remains subordinate to its buyers, particularly the largest ones, such as Nike. Beginning with design and throughout the complex process of manufacturing athletic footwear (which involves as many as two hundred different steps), Nike's hand is felt—as is evidenced by the thousand production specialists Nike employs to work closely with its suppliers (Merk 2008). Yue Yuen depends more on Nike than the reverse; moreover, it has carved out a highly profitable niche as the world's leading supplier, a niche it would not want to jeopardize.[15] Jeroen Merk, who has conducted a detailed study of Nike's relationship with Yue Yuen, concludes that "even though Yue Yuen has enough skills and cash to launch their own brand, they deliberately decided not to do so because that would make them a direct competitor of many of their customers. In fact, Yue Yuen is very concerned with protecting brand secrets. The company makes sure that its R&D centre never puts competing brands in the same place. This also implies that Yue Yuen cannot break into end-markets directly" (Merk 2008).

Although Yue Yuen had eyed the 2008 Beijing Olympics as a significant opportunity for expansion into retailing, the company did not develop and market its own brands for the occasion. According to one newspaper account, "The company will make the most of the 2008 Beijing Olympics to gain market share in the mainland. . . . Pou Chen executives emphasized that their company would never develop own-branded shoes to rival its customers including Nike. Yue Yuen has long promoted Nike, adidas and Reebok sport shoes at its stores" (*Taiwan Headlines* 2007).

CHINA'S RAPID GROWTH AND THE PROSPECTS FOR UPGRADING

China's rapid economic growth has averaged around 9 percent annually for the past two decades; it exceeded 10 percent in 2007, although it fell below 10 percent in 2008. Even allowing for exaggerated claims and poor governmental statistics, China's growth is explosive by any standard. Bear in mind that these are average figures; the growth poles of China—south China in Guangdong Province around the Pearl River Delta, Shanghai, and the Yangtze River Delta—are growing at much greater rates. The lion's share of growth is concentrated in south China, which accounts for nearly half the country's exports. The region boasts the highest concentrations of manufacturing, the largest factories, the greatest influx of labor from rural areas, the world's third and fourth busiest ports (Hong Kong and Shenzhen), and the world's largest freight facility (*IAM Journal* 2005: 17).

A wide range of consumer-goods industries have contributed to this growth. As already noted, China is predicted to account for as much as half of world textile exports once the full effects of the end of the MFA are realized. In 2004, China accounted for 45.1 million computers (an increase of 39 percent from just one year earlier), 70.5 million air conditioners (an increase of 43 percent), 30.3 million refrigerators (30 percent), and 23.5 million washing machines (19 percent). Similar yearly increases were posted in metal-cutting machinery (36 percent), cement equipment (63 percent), metal-rolling equipment (60 percent), and tractors (84 percent). China has plans to export to the United States a million automobiles from its Chery Automobile Company by 2010. "Morgan Stanley . . . says that China now absorbs half of the world's cement production, a fourth of its copper, and a fifth of its aluminium" (*IAM Journal* 2005: 15). This accelerated growth has created enormous energy needs; the International Energy Agency reports that China accounted for a third of the increase in global demand for oil between 2002 and 2004 (*IAM Journal* 2005: 13–14).

Government policy in China has fostered the creation of vibrant industrial districts composed of clusters of suppliers, manufacturers, and contractors that specialize in a single product, fostering economies of scale, lowering transaction costs, and cutting prices. It has opened land for the development of industrial parks, given tax benefits to businesses, built transportation networks and other infrastructure, and subsidized utilities. Private companies, with government support, build factory complexes that include dormitories and hospitals. The resulting clusters create synergies that foster technological development (Barboza 2004). According to Ruizhe Sun, president of the China Textile Information Center, "In terms of vertical supply chain, China has no competition. We have button makers, fabric makers, thread makers, zipper makers, you name it" (cited in Barboza 2004).

At the high end of the technology spectrum, the Shenzhen campus of Huawei Technologies, manufacturer of globally competitive telecommunication equipment, boasts a research center, football fields, swimming pools, and housing for three thousand families. Baosteel, based in Shanghai, is projected to be the third largest producer of steel in the world by 2010. The Lenovo Group, amid much fanfare, bought IBM's ailing PC business in December 2004. The Haier Group, China's leading maker of home appliances, has offices in one hundred countries. And TCL Electronics, China's most profitable maker of televisions, acquired the TV business of France's Thomson in 2004; its website claims TCL-Thomson Electronics to be "the largest color television enterprise in the world." More than ten Chinese companies number among the Fortune 500 (see table 4.1).

And China is investing heavily in the next generation of technologies. As noted in the introduction to this chapter, China is investing heavily in science and technology in the hopes of becoming an "innovative society" within the next decade or so. Its plans to double the percentage of GDP that goes into research and development (to 2.5 percent) by the year 2020, and—thanks to its export-oriented industrialization surpluses— the existence of extensive foreign-currency reserves to bankroll its high-tech ambitions promise to transform China's role in global supply chains in the coming years (Appelbaum and Parker, forthcoming). All of this suggests a strong future counterweight to the power of Wal-Mart and other "big buyers," as China moves rapidly from being an export platform to becoming a technology and industrial power in its own right.

TABLE 4.1.

Top Chinese Companies in the Fortune 500 (as of 2003, in billions of US$)

	Sector	Revenue	Net income
PetroChina	Oil/gas	36.60	8.39
Sinopec	Oil/gas	51.10	2.60
CNOOC	Oil/gas	4.93	1.39
Baosteel	Steel	5.31	0.84
Chalco	Aluminum	2.80	0.43
Lenovo[†]	PCs	2.97	0.14
SAIC	Cars	0.83	0.18
TCL	TVs/electronics	3.40	0.07
Haier	White/brown goods	9.70	n/a
Wanxiang	Car parts	2.00	n/a
Huawei	Telecom equipment	5.00[‡]	0.30[‡]

Source: *The Economist*, January 6, 2005
[†]To March 2004
[‡]2004 estimate

The economic power of giant retailers remains limited in China, which initially regulated the expansion of foreign retailers (for example, requiring substantial local partnerships). Wal-Mart may account for some 3 percent of China's total exports, but in terms of retail presence, by 2008 the company had only one hundred "hypermarkets" in China, accounting for a small percentage of its international sales.[16] Since joining the World Trade Organization, China has eased its restrictions on foreign retailers, and Wal-Mart planned to open another fifteen stores in 2005, including supercenters in Beijing and Shanghai, the first in those cities (Wal-Mart already has a supercenter in Shenzhen), with talk of increasing its floor space in China by as much as half in the near future (Chandler 2005). Former Wal-Mart CEO David Glass views China as one place where continued expansion is possible: "If you look at Europe, it's difficult to green-field or grow a company of much size. But you can build an enormous-sized company in China if you make some fairly aggressive assumptions about what's going to happen to it. It's the one place in the world where you could replicate Wal-Mart's success in the U.S." (Gilman 2004).[17]

Yet even Wal-Mart may face an uphill battle in China. China's state-run Shanghai Brilliance Group, its largest retailer, claims sales of $8.1 billion in 3,300 stores. And Wal-Mart is also competing with France's Carrefour, which has more than one hundred "hypermarkets" (Rigby 2008). Yet the biggest challenge to retail expansion in China may be cultural: with small apartments and limited space for consumer items, the growing number of middle-class Chinese shoppers are accustomed to shopping on foot, making frequent trips for small-volume purchases.

DIRECTIONS FOR FUTURE RESEARCH

There is growing evidence that consolidation in consumer-goods industries, with increasingly integrated production and distribution systems between giant retailers and equally giant contractors, may be replicating the vertical-integration characteristic of the earlier Fordist mode of organizing production. These dynamics remain poorly understood. What is needed is a long-term project that will chart the impact of changes in retailing and contracting. In particular, I suggest a number of interrelated questions that could guide systematic, long-term investigations, focusing principally on China but also on East Asia generally—bearing in mind that the present moment is but a snapshot within the changing dynamics of the world economy:

1. How does the trend toward concentration of production in large transnational contractors impact the relative power of contractors vis-à-vis retailers in supply-chain networks—for example, the ability of contractors to negotiate production costs or "move up" into such higher-value-added activities as designing and marketing their own labels?

2. How do recent innovations in supply-chain management influence the relationship between big buyers and their suppliers—for example, when the largest suppliers take over many of the functions of supply-chain management from retailers? What is the role of giant trading companies, such as Li & Fung, which appear to be becoming increasingly central in supply-chain management?

3. What happens if a growing number of retailers move geographically closer to their principal suppliers, for example, in the form of Luen Thai's "supply-chain city," a move that also undoubtedly signals a desire to be closer to China's rapidly emerging markets?

4. How does the rise of China as an industrial power change the dynamics of the global supply chains in which Chinese firms are involved? Will China's largest suppliers move increasingly into retailing, first locally, then regionally: How will this affect the dominance of the world's current retail giants? And how will China's growth in capital-intensive industries (such as shipbuilding, automotive, aircraft, construction, and so on) affect the relative power of retail-controlled supply chains?

5. To what extent will the emergence of large contractors generate links with other firms and sectors that contribute to industrial upgrading and more broadly based economic development? Does their vertical integration re-

strict the formation of local economic links that might stimulate more broad-based economic growth?

6. Finally, what will be the impact of China's move into advanced technologies on the dynamics of global supply chains? As China increasingly bases its economic policies on technology-driven growth rather than on low-cost exports, how will this affect those firms that have emerged as the principal low-cost suppliers of foreign big buyers? Will they use their supply-chain networks, technical knowledge, and foreign-currency reserves to transition into something else—perhaps multinational big buyers in their own right, beginning by serving China's growing consumer class?

NOTES

1. China's Medium- and Long-Term Plan calls for increasing funding for four "mega science projects" (nanotechnology, development and reproductive biology, protein science, and quantum research), as well as "mega engineering projects" in sixteen key areas (for a detailed discussion, see Bai 2005; Suttmeier, Cao, and Simon 2006; Appelbaum and Parker, forthcoming).

2. See also Malone (2002), Speer (2002), Kearney (2003), Just-style.com (2003), McGrath (2003), and Nordås (2004).

3. See www.nht.com.tw/en/about-2.htm, accessed November 9, 2008.

4. The foregoing information comes from Esquel's Web site, www.esquel.com/en/index.html. Esquel's client list includes Banana Republic, Brooks Brothers, Hugo Boss, J.Crew, JCPenney, Marks and Spencer, Nike, Nordstom, Polo Ralph Lauren, and some fifteen other leading brands. Esquel's Gaoming factory complex (Guangdong Province) does the weaving, dying, and assembly. The firm's recently opened weaving mill occupies twenty-nine acres and is described as "China's most advanced woven fabric manufacturing facility," an environmentally friendly facility featuring "the textile industry's most advanced machinery and advanced computer control systems to reduce operational errors, ensure quality and shorten production time"; see www.esquel.com/en/index7.html; accessed November 9, 2008.

5. The information about TAL comes from the company's Web site, www.talgroup .com/en/index.html, accessed November 9, 2008. The company was originally called South China, then—through a collaboration with Jardine Matheson—became the textile Alliance Group (TAL). See www.vendormanagedinventory.com for more information about that business model.

6. Yue Yuen, the world's leading manufacturer of footwear, became a "strategic shareholder" in Luen Thai when it acquired a 9.9 percent stake in 2004.

7. A second supply-chain city is being developed in Qing Yuan, also in Guangdong Province; in addition, Luen Thai maintains supply-chain centers in the United States and the Philippines (Luen Thai 2006).

8. Luen Thai's principal customers also include Polo Ralph Lauren, Limited Brands, adidas, Dillard's, Nike, and Fast Retailing (Luen Thai 2006).

9. Yue Yuen Industrial Holdings is the principal source of Pou Chen's shoe production; as of June 2004, Pou Chen held 50.1 percent of the stock in Yue Yuen. Yue Yuen's fiscal year ends on September 30.

10. China, Indonesia, and Vietnam together account for 90 percent of all athletic-footwear production (Merk 2006).

11. I visited the Nike/YY factory in Dongguan in September 2005, as a guest of Nike. The immaculate and ultramodern activities center, newly opened, showed no sign of having been used; even the polished glass tables had no smudges or fingerprints.

12. Other clients include Polo Ralph Lauren, Kenneth Cole, Calvin Klein, and NBA Properties. Yue Yuen is the exclusive China licensee for Converse, Wolverine, and Hush Puppies (Xinhua 2007). About 60 percent of Yue Yuen's footwear production is for Nike, Reebok, and Adidas-Saloman (Merk 2003).

13. Judging by its Interim Report for the first six months of FY 2007 (ending March 31), the company's growth trajectory appears to be continuing, despite rising wage pressures and continuing cost of the petroleum-based imports that constitute a major part of the company's costs. Yue Yuen added fourteen additional production lines, bringing its total to 387; its year-to-year production of shoes increased 15 percent (111 million pairs for the six-month period); and wholesale/retail sales grew by 37 percent, accounting for 8 percent of total revenues (in comparison with 5.4 percent for FY 2006; see Yue Yuen 2007c). However, on July 26, 2007, Credit Suisse initiated coverage on Yue Yuen with an "underperform" call because of what it regarded as the company's "decreasing exposure to the retail business sector," claiming that "Yue Yuen is actively considering spinning off its retail business arm in China" (Xinhua 2007).

14. The cost of the petrochemicals that comprise a significant portion of the raw materials used in making shoes increased 50 to 60 percent (Fong 2005).

15. In 2002, 28 percent of Yue Yuen's athletic-shoe production was for Nike, yet it supplied only 15 percent of Nike's total demand (Merk 2006: 16). Yue Yuen's net profit rate in 2002 (11.9 percent) was higher than that of Nike (6.2 percent), Reebok (2.9 percent), or Adidas (3.4 percent; see Merk 2006: 17). The company has continued to post nearly double-digit profits (10.02 percent in 2006; see http://finance.google.com/finance?q=HKG:0551).

16. According to one frequently cited statistic, "If Wal-Mart were a country, it would be China's sixth-largest export market." Wal-Mart executives talk of doubling their purchases from Chinese suppliers (Chandler 2005). Regarding Wal-Mart's presence in China, the company has recently acquired a 35 percent interest in the Taiwanese Trust-Mart chain, which gives it partial ownership of another 102 Trust-Mart stores in China (Rigby 2008).

17. With the exception of Mexico and a few other developing economies, Wal-Mart has generally not fared well in securing significant market share; see Chandler (2005).

REFERENCES

Abernathy, Frederick H., John T. Dunlop, Janice H. Hammond, and David Weil. 1999. *A Stitch in Time: Lean Retailing and the Transformation of Manufacturing—Lessons from the Apparel and Textile Industry.* Oxford, U.K.: Oxford University Press.

Appelbaum, Richard P., and Rachel A. Parker. 2008 (forthcoming). "China's Bid to Become a Global Nanotech Leader: Advancing Technology through State-Led Programs and International Collaborations." *Science and Public Policy.*

Bai Chunli. 2005. "Ascent of Nanoscience in China," *Science* 309, no. 1: 61–63.

Bonacich, Edna. 2005. "Wal-Mart and the Logistics Revolution." In *Wal-Mart: Template for 21st Century Capitalism?*, ed. Nelson Lichtenstein. New York: New Press.

Bonacich, Edna, and Jake Wilson. 2005. "Wal-Mart's Global Production and Distribution System." *New Labor Forum.*

Cao Ning. 2005. "Different Structures in the Textile Industry's Supply Chain." *Peking University Luen Thai Center for Supply Chain System R&D Bulletin,* April 30. Available at www.pkultc.com/englishindex.asp.

Chan Kai-wah. 2005. Associate Director, Hong Kong Christian Industrial Committee. Interview, September 15.

Chandler, Clay. 2005. "The Great Wal-Mart of China." *Fortune,* July 25.

Du Ling. 2003. "Taiwanese Investment in South Africa, Swaziland, and Lesotho: A Case Study by Ambassador Du Ling." Statement by Representative Du Ling, Taipei Liaison Office in the Republic of South Africa at the African-Asian Society, Balalaika Hotel, Sandton, June 12. Available at www.roc-taiwan.org.za/press/ ~~~~~~~~/~~~~~~~~~ html.

Fong Mei. 2005. "Why Yuan Revaluation May Not Be a Cure-All." *Wall Street Journal,* February 1, A11.

Flextronics. 2003. Corporate Fact Sheet Asia. CD-ROM files. Singapore.

Gereffi, Gary, John Humphrey, and Timothy Sturgeon. 2005. "The Governance of Global Value Chains." *Review of International Political Economy* 12, no. 1: 78–104.

Gereffi, Gary, and Olga Memodovic. 2003. "The Global Apparel Value Chain: What Prospects for Upgrading by Developing Countries?" Sectoral Studies Series, United Nations Industrial Development Organization, Vienna, Austria. Available at www.unido.org/index.php?id=012218, accessed November 15, 2008.

Gilman, Hank. 2004. "The Most Underrated CEO Ever." *Fortune Magazine,* March 21. Available at http://money.cnn.com/magazines/fortune/fortune_archive/2004/04/05/366366/index.htm, accessed November 15, 2008.

Hamilton, Gary, and Misha Petrovic. 2006a. "Global Retailers and Asian Manufacturers." In *Handbook of Research on Asian Business,* ed. Henry Wai chung Yeung, 208–20. Cheltenham, UK: Edward Elgar.

———. 2006b. "Making Global Markets: Wal-Mart and Its Suppliers." In *Wal-Mart: The Face of Twenty-first Century Capitalism,* ed. Nelson Lichtenstein, 107–52. New York: New Press.

Hermanson, Jeff. 2005. Personal communication. February 7.

Ho, Clare Tsai-man. 2005. Personal communication. April 25.

Hong Kong Trade and Development Council. 2008. "Yue Yuen Net Industrial Profit Up 56% During Jan-Sep." September 26, 2008. Available at http://garments .hktdc.com/content.aspx?data=garments_content_en&contentid=1054462, accessed December 20, 2008.

IAM Journal. 2005. "China Dolls." International Association of Machinists and Aerospace Workers, AFL-CIO. Spring.

Just-style.com. 2003. "Garment Industries in Bangladesh and Mexico Face an Uncertain Future." October 20. Available at www.sweatshopwatch.org/global/articles/ jsmexbang_oct03.html.

Kahn, Gabriel. 2003. "Made to Measure: Invisible Supplier Has Penney's Shirts All Buttoned Up." *Wall Street Journal,* September 11, A1.

———. 2004a. "Making Labels for Less: Supply-Chain City Transforms Far-Flung Apparel Industry." *Wall Street Journal,* August 13, B1.

———. 2004b. Personal communication. September 1.

Kapinsky, Raphie. 1993. *From Mass Production to Flexible Specialization: Micro-Level Restructuring in a British Engineering Firm.* London: Institute of Development Studies.

Kearney, Neil. 2003. "Trade in Textiles and Clothing after 2005." Presentation to the EU Directorate General on Trade, Conference on "The Future of Textiles and Clothing Trade After 2005," Brussels, Belgium, May 5–6. Available at http://trade-info.cec.eu.int/textiles/documents/153.doc.

Koudal, Peter, and Victor Wel-teh Long. 2005. "The Power of Synchronization: The Case of TAL Apparel Group." Deloitte Research Case Study (May). Available at www.deloitte.com/dtt/cda/doc/content/DTT_DR_TAL_May2005Web.pdf.

Li and Fung. 2007. Li and Fung Group website. Available at www.lifunggroup.com/ front.html, accessed August 30, 2007.

Luen Thai. 2006. "Investor Relations: About Us." Available at http://luenthai.quamnet .com/luenthai/IR-index.htm.

———. 2007. *Luenthai Holdings Limited Annual Report 2006.* April 20. Available at http://www2.luenthai.com/files/LTN20070419219.pdf, accessed November 15, 2008.

Lüthje, Boy. 2005. "Global Production, Industrial Development, and New Labor Regimes in China: The Case of Electronics Contract Manufacturing." In *China: The Labor of Reform,* ed. Mary Gallagher, Ching Kwan Lee, and Albert Park. London: Routledge.

Magretta, Joan. 2002. "Fast, Global, and Entrepreneurial: Supply Chain Management, Hong Kong Style." *Harvard Business Review,* OnPoint enhanced edition. October. (Original article: *Harvard Business Review,* September-October 1998, 103–14.)

Malone, Scott. 2002. "Who Loses to China?" *Women's Wear Daily,* November 26.

McGrath, Peter. 2003. Testimony before the United States International Trade Commission. Investigation 332–448, "Competitiveness of the Textile and Apparel Industries Investigation," January 22.

Merk, Jeroen. 2003. "The International Production of Branded Athletic Footwear."

Unpublished paper written for the International Conference on Global Regulation, Centre for Global Political Economy. Brighton: University of Sussex.

———. 2008. "Restructuring and Conflict in the Global Athletic Footwear Industry: Nike, Yue Yuen, and Labour Codes of Conduct." In *Global Economy Contested: Finance, Production and the International Division of Labour*, ed. Marcus Taylor. London: Routledge.

Nordås, Hildegunn Kyvik. 2004. *The Global Textile and Clothing Industry post the Agreement on Textiles and Clothing*. Geneva: World Trade Organization.

Pine, B. Joseph II, and Stan Davis. 1999. *Mass Customization: The New Frontier in Business Competition*. Boston: Harvard Business School Press

Piore, Michael, and Charles Sabel. 1986. *The Second Industrial Divide: Possibilities for Prosperity*. New York: Basic Books.

Pun Ngai. 2005. Interview with author. September 15.

Rigby, Elizabeth. 2008. "Tesco in New Drive on China." *Financial Times*, January 28. Available at www.ft.com/cms/s/0/45643bec-cd41–11dc-9b2b-000077b07658.html, accessed November 15, 2008.

Speer, Jordan K. 2002. "Sourcing in China: Firms Discuss Advantages, Issues." *Bobbin*, January 1. Available at www.apparelmag.com/bobbin/search/search_display.jsp?vnu_content_ id=1431921.

Suttmeier, Richard P., Cong Cao, and Denis Fred Simon. 2006. "China's Innovation Challenge and the Remaking of the Chinese Academy of Sciences." *Innovations* (Summer): 78–97.

Taiwan Headlines. 2007. "Yue Yuen Industrial Makes Bold Outlet Expansion in China." August 30. Available at http://english.www.gov.tw//TaiwanHeadlines/index.jsp?categid=8&recordid=79153.

UNCTAD (United Nations Conference on Trade and Development). 2002. *World Investment Report 2002: Transnational Corporations and Export Competitiveness*. New York and Geneva: UNCTAD.

———. 2004. *Assuring Development Gains from the International Trading System and Trade Negotiations: Implications of ATC Termination on 31 December 2004*. Note by the UNCTAD Secretariat, TD/B/51/CRP.1

———. 2005. *Impacts of the Agreement on Textiles and Clothing on FDI in and Exports from Developing Countries*. Geneva, Switzerland: UNCTAD Report.

Xinhua. 2007. "China's Yue Yuen 'Underperform' on Low Retail Exposure: Credit Suisse." July 26. Available at www.quamnet.com/fcgi-bin/news.fpl?par2=2&par3=02&par4=20070726121705361886einens, accessed November 15, 2008.

Yue Yuen. 2006. "Factsheet." Available at http://202.66.146.82/listco/hk/yueyuen/factsheet/fs060206.pdf, accessed November 15, 2008.

———. 2007a. "Production Faculties." Available at www.yueyuen.com/bOverview_productionFacilities.htm, accessed November 15, 2008.

———. 2007b. "Press Release: Yue Yuen Announces FY 2006 Results." January 18. Available at www.yueyuen.com/press_file/4Q2006-press.pdf, accessed November 15, 2008.

———. 2007c. "Press Release: Yue Yuen Announces 2007 Interim Results." June 21. Available at www.yueyuen.com/press_file/2QFY2007-English.pdf, accessed November 15, 2008.

Yupoong. 2003. "Company Overview." Available at www.yupoong.co.kr/company/index.jsp, accessed November 15, 2008.

CHAPTER FIVE

The "Rise of China" and the Changing World Income Distribution

JÓZSEF BÖRÖCZ

Geopolitics is the study of the ways in which organizations project their power into the world outside their boundaries. A key component of that power is the volume of economic resources available to any actor, especially as they compare to the resources of others—cooperative partners, competitors, and adversaries. This chapter analyzes changes in the geopolitics of the wealth and economic weight of states between the collapse of the Soviet bloc and 2001, the year in which the dynamics of global geopolitics was redefined by the reaction of the United States government to the 9/11 terrorist attacks.

The thirty-four-month period between February 4, 1989 (when the "round-table" negotiations between the Polish United Workers' Party and the opposition intellectuals began), and December 26, 1991 (when the Supreme Soviet repealed the 1922 Constitution, pronouncing the dissolution of the Soviet Union), saw a geopolitical transformation whose significance for the history of humankind we are only beginning to comprehend. Often referred to—erroneously—as "the end of socialism" or the "end of history," as well as—only a tiny bit more correctly, as the recent experiences of North Korea and Cuba suggest—"the end of the Cold War," the politico-economic essence of this geopolitical shift was the removal of a set of institutions that had placed constitutional-legal constraints on the operation of private capital for seventy-two years in the former USSR and forty-one years in Eastern Europe.

In 1917, the Russian revolution removed approximately 9.5 percent of the total global productive capacity and 8.6 percent of the world's population from direct control by private capital. This removal was imperfect and incomplete, and the state socialist economies never fully exited from the circulatory flows of global capitalism; yet it was significant enough to elicit a global strategic response from forces interested in the preservation of capitalism. The state socialist transformations in Asia and Eastern Europe, taking place in the aftermath of World War II, raised the proportion to approximately 18 percent of the gross world product and the number of people involved to just below one-third of the world's population. As a consequence of the collapse of state socialism in Europe, the total productive capacity of the former Soviet-bloc states of Eastern Europe and Northern Eurasia—with approximately 10.7 percent of the gross world product and 7.9 percent of the world's population in 1989—was once again subjected to the rules and dynamics of the capitalist world system.[1] The time elapsed since 1989 allows all analysts an opportunity to observe the processes of transformation that have taken place since the collapse of the Soviet geopolitical project quite clearly—and they are rather surprising.

I describe some of those processes in the general spirit of world-systems analysis.[2] The empirical basis for this study is provided by a *longue-durée* survey of global economic history, compiled by Angus Maddison (2001, 2003): The useful online supplement of Maddison's work provides appropriate data for the post-1989 period (1989 to 2001, to be more precise) for all states of the world. The cutoff point of 2001—a feature of Maddison's data—fortuitously allows my analysis to estimate the first effects of the collapse of the Soviet bloc without the confounding effects of the "war on terror" and the related hydrocarbon bump in the incomes of energy-producing states.

The world is a tightly organized, singular social fact, proponents of the world-systems perspective argue very forcefully. The fate of each actor (in this analysis, the global trajectory of each state) is linked to the fate of all other actors (all other states). Enrichment and attainment of global power by some actors is, hence, causally tied—if not always in a strictly zero-sum process, certainly through the capillaries of an intricately interwoven, multidimensional, historically formed, and slowly but resolutely shifting global web of network ties—to the impoverishment and loss of global influence by others. In order to gain a geopolitical understanding of the process through which states experience movement toward the core of the world system (centripetal mobility) or out of it (centrifugal movement), it is crucial to comprehend the trajectories of each state *with respect to all other states*.

Since the capitalist world system is a hierarchically organized whole containing extremely rich and wretchedly poor, very powerful and desperately powerless societies, in order to understand its basic dynamics, it is crucial to keep asking two fairly elementary questions: Can we see any shifts in the overall *logic* of centripetal and centrifugal mobility in the global system? What can the most outstanding cases of state mobility tell us about the directions of change in the world?

However significant, the end of the previous period's bipolar standoff was only one of the multiple, parallel processes of transformation taking place in the world in the twelve years that followed. The collapse of the Soviet project occurred in the context of the following additional large-scale historic shifts:

1. The internal integration of the West European states' suprastate organization of public authority, known today as the European Union, acquired unprecedented dimensions and intensity. That this large and increasingly influential public authority has steadfastly avoided becoming a state creates an entirely new dynamic in global geopolitics—a dynamic that requires creative responses from all other actors.[3]

2. As one pole (the Soviet side) withdrew from contention and dismantled its institutions designed to serve the bipolar standoff, the opposite side, with its institutions growing unhindered by the threat of mutual destruction, acquired unique dimensions in global power. As the various instruments of the Soviet state's global strategy were disassembled, there emerged a new strategic system—we could describe it as "post-bipolar"—whose key characteristic is an upsurge in the global military significance of one single state, the leading force of the "western" side of the bipolar standoff. Today, this state wields a military capacity that is unprecedented in the modern history of humankind, in terms of both its relative size and its lack of viable military rivals.

3. Meanwhile, the recent decades have witnessed a noticeable acceleration in the speed at which industrial production is moving away from the core areas of the world economy. To some extent in conjunction with this centrifugal displacement of manufacturing, the volume of foreign direct investment is higher than ever.

4. New kinds of global institutions are emerging whose sole purpose is to circumvent the regulatory and protective capacities of states. These institutions are increasingly acquiring the character of public authority; that is, they wield executive, "law-like" institutional powers on an unprecedented scale. As a result, states themselves increasingly can be subject to transnational, global quasi-legal processes and enforcement. The emergence of what is often referred to as the new, post-bipolar structures of "global governance" erodes the Westphalian principle of state sovereignty—always questionable in a global system created by colonialism and definitely shaken by the end of the 1980s by the very logic of the bipolar standoff anyway—making the sovereignty of even the hitherto most powerful

states increasingly subject to explicit, global bargaining. This phenomenon is to a large extent at the heart of popular discontent in Germany, and it partly explains the widespread hostility toward the EU constitution as well as the related upsurge in xenophobic, racist politics in France, the Netherlands, Austria, and Belgium today.

5. A very large part of industrial production has lost its previous significance as the leading sector of economic change. "Flexible accumulation," associated with high profits and requiring high levels of labor, knowledge, and constant structural adjustment, is often seen as a more attractive option than conventional, highly standardized, industrial production regimes. As a result, the power of conventional labor organizations—rooted in precisely those large-scale industrial mass-production systems—is also eroding, especially in the core and semiperipheral areas of the world economy. There is a boom in business services—especially legal, political, and financial services—that provide previously unimaginable levels of profitability for highly specific, or "niche," enterprises.

6. The global volume of speculative financial transactions—that is, deals without any solid "real-economic" basis—has increased exponentially.

7. The wealthiest, core societies of the world are aging rapidly, a fact that presents those states with new kinds of risks and challenges, such as new, intergenerational imbalances in their national accounts.

8. The states of the world's most impoverished societies have become completely dysfunctional with respect to their populations at large and/or predatory vis-à-vis indigenous capital.

9. Related to the previous point, we are seeing the appearance of new epidemics and other diseases (including some that we thought had been eradicated from the world), the proliferation of production systems that destroy the environment at a hitherto unknown speed, and the appearance and rapid spread of new techniques of global violence.

10. Finally, and perhaps most pervasively, the world has been integrated into a singular entity through political, cultural, linguistic, and moral practices that are profoundly Eurocentric and racist.

When one attempts to understand transformations in the overall logic of the global system of the mobility of states as well as the ability of specific states to improve their "standing" in the world, one observes a complex combination of these factors. Hence, it is impossible to separate the "net effects" of any individual factor. Yet, as my analysis suggests, if one considers some basic structures of global power and pays close attention to regional patterns, it is possible to derive some fairly powerful indirect inference.

ENRICHMENT VERSUS WEIGHT GAIN

Imagine that we place the states of the world in a two-dimensional analytical space. Figure 5.1 will help in orientation. In it, we combine two important measures: change in a state's per capita gross domestic product and change in the share of a country's GDP in the gross world product. The purpose is to portray the collective influence of a national economy and the average level of accumulation, two measures that often do not run in tandem, in the same figure. We use the vertical axis to plot each state of the world according to how its per capita gross domestic product has changed in the given period. In order to make the analysis comparable over time, we express these state-to-state figures as percentages of the world mean GDP per capita. Those states whose per capita GDP, measured in terms of the world average, has increased during the given period (that is, where the result of the subtraction is a positive number) are placed along the upper part of the vertical axis; those whose figure has decreased (where the subtraction returned a negative number) are placed in the bottom half of figure 5.1.

A useful gauge of the global geopolitical aspects of economic performance, the horizontal dimension indicates changes in the given state's economic weight in the world economy.[4] This we measure by observing the percentage share of the given state's GDP in the gross world product for the given year. As before, we subtract this value for the earlier time point from the later one. Those states whose global weight has increased—and have, hence, a greater economic basis on which to exert greater influence on the world system—are on the right-hand side of the figure; those that have lost economic weight (and, hence, some of their geopolitical significance) are on the left.

Economic weight is, of course, only one—and not necessarily, in every context, the only—important requirement for geopolitical power: the availability of key military, cognitive, moral, organizational, or natural resources may turn out to be more important determinants of an organization's ability to project its power to the outside world in particular situations, as the overwhelming evidence of the Vietnam War suggests, for instance. Yet, economic weight is, without doubt, a fundamental component of global power without which it appears to be quite difficult for a state to make a lasting and meaningful impact on today's economically integrated, tightly interwoven global system.

For illustration's sake, figure 5.1 indicates some of the geopolitically most interesting possible trajectories in terms of global economic weight. One possible path involves a process whereby a state is enriched in terms of its per capita GDP with respect to the world mean GDP per capita, while its global weight does not in-

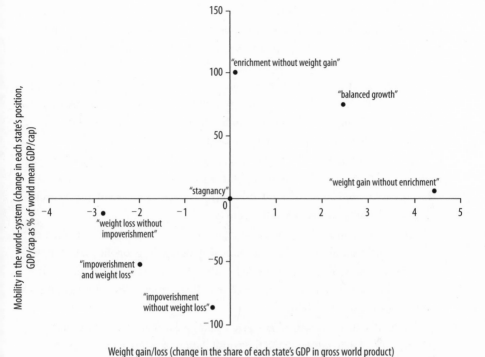

Figure 5.1. Two-Dimensional Model for Analyzing the Global Trajectories of States

crease perceptibly. This type of change appears in the top third of the graph, on the right side of the vertical axis, marked by the words "enrichment without weight gain." We can also imagine a different process of economic change, one in which a given state acquires significant global weight without experiencing much enrichment. Again, the backdrop to this process is a peculiar demographic pattern, namely, one in which a state's population growth is steeper than the world average population growth. This path, labeled "weight gain without enrichment," is found on the right-hand side of the graph above the horizontal axis. It is easy to see that, from the perspective of a state that strives to pursue the collective interests of its citizenry within the overall logic of global capitalism, the optimal pattern of change would be a combination of the two kinds of positive change. This pattern is included in figure 5.1 in the middle of the upper-right quadrant, marked "balanced growth." Obviously there exist the negative counterpoints to all these positive patterns: labeled appropriately as "impoverishment without weight loss," "weight loss without impoverishment," and "impoverishment with weight loss"; those are found in the bottom-left quadrant of figure 5.1.

The realization that states are not "free" to determine their mobility paths is a fundamental principle of all scholarly approaches to the global system: a host of macroeconomic, historical, geopolitical, geographical, demographic, social, cultural, and moral circumstances and events influence what global mobility paths are available to, and taken by, a given state. It would be quite a challenge to find any example of a state that "freely" chose its mobility path in this two-dimensional system of wealth and global influence in the five centuries of the modern, capitalist world system on record. Three general principles follow from this.

First, the various mobility paths indicated in figure 5.1 may result from extremely variegated, often outright opposite social, economic, political, and cultural conditions and opportunities for change. To a very large extent, the diversity of human global history is due to this very fact.

Second, the maneuvering room available to states can be, and most often is, varied across time and space, due to historical, geographic, geopolitical factors, to name just a few. As a result, it is extremely difficult to create a singular moral basis on which to compare the performance of actually existing states in terms of their ability to affect global mobility.

And, finally, the "success" of any given state's centripetal/influence-hoarding mobility project depends partly on the constellation of external factors, partly on the given society's internal resource structures, and partly on the quality of the collective responses to those external and internal conditions, as devised by the economic, political, and cultural elites who occupy the leadership positions in the given society.

At this point we are ready to examine the patterns in the global mobility of states since the collapse of the Soviet pole. Figure 5.2 models the mobility paths taken by all the world's states for which Maddison (2003) provides data regarding the 1989–2001 period.[5]

First, let us examine the contours of the distribution in figure 5.2. The middle portion of the upper-right quadrant of the graph is entirely empty. This signals nothing less than the fact that the—in many ways optimal—mobility path labeled earlier as "balanced growth" appears to have barely existed in reality during the twelve years on which this study focuses, except perhaps for the clearly decipherable growth achieved by Indonesia and Vietnam (marked in figure 5.2 as Indo and VN). It is safe to conclude, however, that *"balanced growth" was far from the dominant pattern* of the world system in the post–Cold War geopolitical transformation of the world economy. This simple observation lends some powerful support to those perspectives that argue that patterns of "economic development" under global capitalism are inherently uneven.

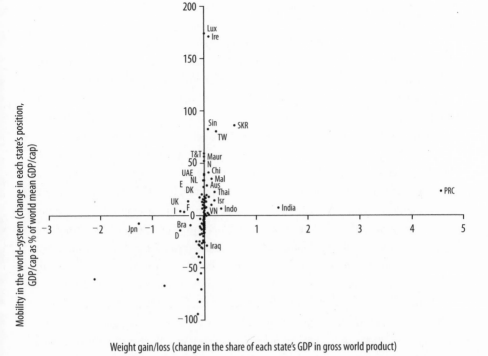

Figure 5.2. Global Trajectories of States, 1989–2001

What we do see, instead, are two extreme patterns of mobility, each constitut-
ing the other's perfect opposite. One can be described unambiguously as "weight
gain" without any comparable amount of "enrichment" on a per capita basis.
There have been two extremely important examples of this type in the world
economy during our period: the world's two most populous states. The People's
Republic of China has increased its global weight by a massive 4.6 percent of the
gross world product during the twelve years under study here, and India has
gained a global weight of about 1.5 percent. To put the two figures in perspective,
Maddison estimates the global weight of the two states at the data point closest to
China's socialist revolution and India's independence (1950) as 4.5 percent and
4.17 percent, respectively. For 2001, Maddison puts them at the level of 11.9 percent and 5.3 percent. Particular significance is lent to this by the *simultaneity* of
the two cases—that the two true giants of the world have come to motion at the
same time and more or less *on the same path*, even if at a different speed. China's
upswing—or "peaceful rise," in the official terminology of the Chinese Communist Party—has been in effect for more than twenty years now, and it has been,

perhaps even more remarkable, basically unaffected by the cyclical patterns of the capitalist world economy.[6]

To put the process plainly, then, both China and India have registered significant gains in their global economic weight between 1989 and 2001. This has made the two states, all other things being equal, considerably more powerful in terms of the global governance of economic accumulation, something that is also true for many other areas of geopolitics. This is a significant development, bound to exert profound pressures for change—first and foremost within these societies themselves.

As for the other pattern—the path of "enrichment without decipherable weight gain"—we see Luxembourg and Ireland, the two tiniest members of the European Union during the period: each has augmented its GDP per capita by a strikingly large amount—more than 150 percent of the world average GDP per capita between 1989 and 2001. The concrete mechanisms that have produced those results are radically different: off-shore "investment" paradise in Luxembourg, mid-to-high-tech, assembly-oriented boom, based on "green field" foreign direct investment and unprecedented levels of infrastructural EU subsidies in Ireland. In addition to these two, we do find a few additional West European states among those most successful in enriching themselves without gaining global economic weight, but the majority are outside of Europe. Here is the list of the world's societies that have been most enriched without much weight gain after Luxembourg and Ireland: Singapore (marked in figure 5.2 as Sin), South Korea (SK), Taiwan (TW), Trinidad and Tobago (T&T), Mauritius (Maur), Norway (N), Chile (Chi), the United Arab Emirates (UAE), the Netherlands (NL), Malaysia (Mal), Spain (E), Australia (Aus), Denmark (DK), Thailand (Thai), and so on. In other words, a handful of the twelve to fifteen member states of the European Union at the time—mainly the smaller ones—have been able to get in the group of greatest per capita achievers, but they certainly do not dominate this group. Even more striking is that the EU's larger, that is, globally more powerful, geopolitically most influential member states—incidentally, those that had obviously been most involved in the management of the European "theater" of the global strategic standoff—have had a strikingly unimpressive record during the first twelve years after the collapse of the bipolar setup in Europe. Although Britain was able to augment its status in terms of wealth by roughly 13 percent of the average world GDP per capita, its global weight has shrunk by a considerable amount (Britain lost approximately 0.3 percent of the gross world product). The stories of France and Italy are similar (only showing less enrichment), while the Federal Republic of Germany—which has, in the meantime, swallowed the German Democratic Republic—sustained losses in global position both in per capita terms and in its global weight. Having lost 1.25 percent of its global shares and the equivalent of more than 7 percent of the world average GDP per capita, Japan registers an even more dismal record in this period.

Most states of the world are tightly attached to the vertical axis of our figure — that is, their global weight has not changed much, while most of them show changes within the ±20 percent range with respect to the world mean GDP per capita. There is only one very distinct group of states that constitutes an exception from this rule, and I examine this group more closely next.

DIVERGING PATHS OF FORMERLY SOCIALIST STATES

Those states of the world that were members of the state-socialist "bloc" in 1989 have followed very peculiar mobility paths since the dismantling of the state socialist regimes in Europe. Figure 5.3 focuses on the trajectories of this group, including those that have reintroduced capitalism and those that have not undergone such a geopolitical treatment. Two of them (the People's Republic of China and the Socialist Republic of Vietnam) have already been mentioned: These states experienced no regime change. What they had instead was a steep economic upswing. They are examples of a peculiar kind of reform-state-socialist path — a direction that was experimented with in such states as Hungary, Poland, and Czechoslovakia during the late 1960s and 1970s but abandoned in favor of a full-swing return to capitalism later. The idea of this brand of late-state-socialism is that the state preserves single-party rule as its organizing principle and combines the basic institutional frameworks of state socialist socio-economic, socio-cultural, and socio-political systems with an economic management model that is very responsive to, indeed to a very large extent driven by, internal demand. The resulting increased turnover is widely expected by the reform-state-socialist political leaderships to augment their state's resource base, not only affording continued productive investment but also reinforcing collective consumption through the expansion of the socialist social-services sector, buffering social inequalities.

In its Chinese and Vietnamese variant, this model managed to do what critics of the economic hallmark of state socialism — the predominance of state ownership — have long thought, indeed argued very confidently, to be impossible: to create and maintain high rates of productivity in state-owned enterprises.[7] In addition, almost as an afterthought, China and Vietnam have recently begun experimenting, ever so gingerly, with a mixed-economy model: as table 5.1 shows for the ten Chinese enterprises with the greatest revenues in 2005, the Chinese state is encouraging the limited presence of foreign private capital — especially in the

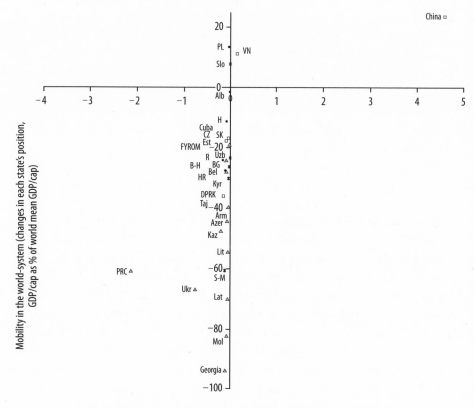

Figure 5.3. Global Trajectories of the States That Were State Socialist in 1989, 1989–2001

form of joint stock companies in which a commanding share of ownership is retained by the socialist state.

Some traces of domestic private capital are also allowed to coexist with state and cooperative ownership, but, at least so far, it is impossible to claim that private capital is the sole driving force in the spectacular growth of these predominantly state socialist mixed economies.[8] Whether continued implementation of this model will enhance the ability and willingness of Chinese and Vietnamese socialist states to deliver higher-quality collective consumption and decrease social inequality is too soon to tell.

Meanwhile, it would be a mistake to attribute geopolitical success in economic performance solely to the survival of state socialism per se: two additional state-socialist societies, the Democratic People's Republic of Korea—existing,

TABLE 5.1.
Largest Chinese Companies in Terms of Revenue

Rank	Company	Turnover (in million RMB)[a]	% owned by the state	% owned by domestic banks and asset management companies	% owned by foreign private capital	% owned by domestic capital
1	China Petroleum & Chemical (Sinopec)	590,632	67.92[b]	9.5	19.35	3.23
2	PetroChina	388,633	"commanding share"[c]			
3	China Mobile	192,381	100[d]			
4	China Telecom	161,212	72.09[e]	10.68	17.15	
5	China United Telecommunications	79,332	—			
6	China Netcom Group	64,922	100[f]			
7	Minmetals Development	64,593	100[g]			
8	Baoshan Iron & Steel	58,638	85[h]			
9	CNOOC	55,222	100[i]			
10	China Resources Enterprises	50,105	54.91[j]			
	GDP 2004 quarters 1–4	13,651,500[k]				

Source: The People's Daily Online, July 30, 2005
Additional sources (accessed August 3, 2005):

[a] http://english.people.com.cn/200507/30/eng20050730_199342
.html
[b] http://english.sinopec.com/en-company/938.shtml
[c] www.petrochina.com.cn/english/tzzgx/gszljg_6.htm
[d] www.chinamobile.com/english/Profile.html
[e] www.chinatelecom-h.com/company_e/company_e1_1.htm
[f] http://biz.yahoo.com/ic/106/106010.html and www.chinanetcom
.com.cn/en/zj/about/index.asp

[g] www.minmetals.com/English/intro/intro/intro/2003618001.htm
[h] www.baosteel.com/plc/english/index.htm
[i] http://210.77.145.59/tea/node/Ni6500L0P null.html
[j] www.cre.com.hk/aboutus.asp?lang=e
[k] www.stats.gov.cn/was40/detail?record=3&channelid=2118&
presearchword=gdp

pretty much throughout its entire history, in a model that can be described as war communism—and the Socialist Republic of Cuba—squeezed under an economic embargo by its erstwhile regional hegemon and main trading partner for more than four decades now—are showing steep declines in economic performance. North Korea and Cuba are reminders that pronouncements of the end of the Cold War are perhaps somewhat premature. If anything, it could be argued that the collapse of the Soviet pole of the global strategic standoff—and with it, the disappearance of subsidies and general geopolitical and economic support the Soviet Union provided—had made the predicament of those two, largely isolated, state-socialist regimes even more difficult, making the economic effects of their local Cold Wars ever more devastating for their societies.

Now let us look at that group of states that did undergo a post-state-socialist geopolitical transformation and became fully capitalist once again. There is no former-state-socialist state that would have been able to increase or even preserve its global weight since 1989: they are all on the left-hand side of the vertical axis of figure 5.3. As for their performance in terms of GDP per capita, we see two states that have improved their standing during the period under study: Poland (marked as PL)—which, as will be remembered, received a significant economic boost in the form of an act of debt forgiveness from the Paris Club in 1991, amounting to approximately 50 percent of its foreign debt (in terms of volume, the largest foreign debt in Eastern Europe at the time)—and Slovenia (Slo), formerly the wealthiest federal state of Yugoslavia, tightly reintegrated into the Austrian and Italian economies well before the demise of Yugoslavia, with improvements equivalent to 13 percent and 7.7 percent of the world average GDP per capita, respectively. Other than those two examples of success, *all post-state-socialist states of Eastern Europe and northern Eurasia have experienced a collapse in terms of the geopolitics of their economic standing after 1989.* The record of these post-state-socialist states is so dismal that except for Iraq—a state exposed to the ravages of several international and civil wars, dictatorship, and a long economic embargo during this period—all locations at the bottom part of the lower left quadrant of figure 5.3, reserved for those states that have undergone the most devastating geopolitical and economic collapse, are occupied by the former state-socialist states of Eastern Europe and northern Eurasia.

In figure 5.3, the states of Eastern Europe appear as small black circles. Relatively fortunate Poland and Slovenia are followed by Albania (which, being the smallest and poorest of the socialist "bloc," basically had almost nothing to lose). Hungary (H) is next in line (with a drop equivalent to 11.4 percent of the world average GDP per capita), followed by Slovakia (SK, a loss of 16.9 percent) and the Czech Republic (CZ, 17.9 percent). The extent of the economic devastation of Romania (R, 24.3 percent) and Bulgaria (BG, 27.6 percent) corresponds roughly to that of the post-Soviet republics—here, Estonia (EE) and Uzbekistan (Uzb)—with the least dismal economic record and the Former Yugoslav Republic of Macedonia (FYROM).

Two further observations ought to be made concerning the patterns presented in figure 5.3. First, overall, the former Soviet bloc's greatest losses have occurred in Russia (RU) and Ukraine (Ukr), both of which have undergone not only staggering impoverishment (losses equivalent to 60.9 percent and 67.1 percent of the world mean GDP per capita, respectively) during the first decade after state socialism, but also extremely significant losses of global economic weight (amounting to 2.1 percent and 0.8 percent of the gross world product) as well. Russia's global weight declined from 4.2 percent to 2.1 percent, and Ukraine's weight dropped from 1.15 percent to 0.35 percent during the period immediately after the collapse of state socialism in the U.S.S.R. Maddison's data suggest that, today, northern Eurasia's current position in the world (if taken to be the equivalent of the geographical area of the erstwhile U.S.S.R.) is worse than it has ever been since *before* 1700![9]

What is truly shocking, however, is the fate of those former Soviet republics that have had the most difficult time adjusting to the new, post-Soviet, capitalist conditions. Georgia (Geo) and Moldova (Mol) have become impoverished at rates unprecedented in peacetime, short of a major disaster like an earthquake or tsunami: They have lost the equivalent of 93.8 percent and 82.8 percent of the world average GDP per capita in the period after the dissolution of the U.S.S.R. Closely following them is Serbia-Montenegro (S-M), the only participant in all five of the post-Yugoslav wars, with a peripheralization of approximately 60 percent of the world mean GDP per capita.

Given these numbers, it is hardly surprising that the essentially urban, middle-class uprisings collectively labeled the "color revolutions" have thrived most in this exact segment of the post-state-socialist world: Serbia-Montenegro, followed by Georgia and Ukraine (and similar, foiled attempts by the political elites of Uzbekistan and Moldova). It appears plausible to assume that at least some of the middle-class unrest that took place recently in those societies may have had less to do with the inherent desirability of one political order over another than with the utter economic collapse of these societies, affecting most brutally the educated, urban middle classes of those post-state-socialist societies.

THE GEOPOLITICAL CONSEQUENCES OF
SHIFTING GLOBAL ECONOMIC WEIGHTS

In sum, the global system is in a great flux. That China's and India's "rises" manifest themselves primarily in weight gains has enormous geopolitical consequences—not only internally but externally as well. All of those changes apply in-
stantaneously, lending great volatility to the contemporary system. In addition to
these states' duly increased roles in the United Nations and other multilateral
intergovernmental fora, China's and India's pairwise geopolitical, economic, political, social, and cultural ties to each other and to other powerful actors—for instance, China-U.S., India-U.S., China-EU, India-EU, China-Russia, India-Russia,
China-Japan, and India-Japan relations—will acquire new global significance. Of
the many issues that this development raises, I confine myself to two remarks here.

First, it would be a complete falsification of history to narrate the rise of China
and India as something entirely new, a story without a precedent. We would be
well advised, instead, to remember that China and India were the world's two
most significant economic actors, at least from the fifteenth to the mid-nineteenth
century.

As the data in table 5.2, computed from Maddison (2003), suggest, it was not
until well into the second half of the nineteenth century that the combination
of various forms of imperialist geopolitics and colonialism brought China and
India down to levels that some of the most "successful" imperialist states of Western Europe have managed to attain—barely, and with enormous concerted effort.
(The West European record, Britain's top achievement, reached in the late nineteenth century, was 9.5 percent of the gross world product.) The history of global
capitalism—if it could ever be written without the pervasive Western Europe–
centric ballast that most of its forms carry—would have to be written mainly as
the history of China's and India's global economic weight. The recent, approximately 150-year history of the global "splendor" of the "West" would appear as a
brief and relatively insignificant interlude.[10] Whether the most powerful actors in
the "West," as well as the numerous organizational locations where the collective
interests and actions of the "West" are coordinated, have the moral, cultural, and
political tools necessary to acknowledge the fact of this brevity and insignificance,
and in what creative and peaceful institutional forms the "West" will be able to
exploit in order to adjust to the imminent end of its "splendor" is, no doubt, one
of the most fundamental questions of the survival of humankind.

Mere reference to China and India's global weight throughout of much of the
history of capitalism, however, does not solve the contemporary problems that

TABLE 5.2.
China's and India's Shares in the World Economy, 1500–1900 (in percentages)

	1500	1600	1700	1820	1870	1900
China	24.9	29.0	22.3	32.9	17.1	11.0
India	24.4	22.4	24.4	16.0	12.1	8.6

Source: Computed from Maddison 2003

this transformation produces for the stability of the world. For the capitalist world system has a few rather distinct features in its current form, features that make the contemporary situation particularly treacherous. I have already listed these new features in ten points above, so here I repeat only those two that I see as most dangerous in this regard: (1) the global military predominance of the declining economic hegemon of the twentieth century and (2) the pervasively Eurocentric and racist character of the political, moral, and ideological field of the contemporary system. Because of those two elements, a conscious effort is required on the part of global social organizations, politicians, states, intellectuals, and movements to focus on the creation of constructive institutional ways in which a devastating, Third (and this time, truly global) World War can be avoided. This is hardly an exercise in futuristic fantasy or science fiction: Significant outside efforts are already afoot pitting, for instance, the two engines of global growth, China and India, against each other.[11]

The other geopolitical issue has to do with the fact that none of the most successful states, those most able to increase their global weight (China, India, Indonesia, and Vietnam), is "Western."[12] Nor have the most affluent states of the world done particularly well. Taken as a single group, the wealthiest states of the world—the United States, the fifteen members of the EU as of 2001, and Japan—have sustained a 1.66 percent loss of economic weight during this period, a striking contrast to the collective achievement of 6.52 percent increase on the part of the four above Asian economies alone.

Instead of a reproduction of the often matter-of-factly assumed superior performance of the "West"—something that many observers of world politics as well as scholars of the political economy and geopolitics of the world system are used to and expect—what we see is quite a radical geographical shift. North America and Western Europe seem to have by and large been able to hold on to their wealth in per capita terms, but they also have been doing so with stagnating or outright declining economies, so that their ability to sustain their per capita wealth today is partly a product of a historical process that could be described as path dependence (that is, that ability is the result of these economies' previously advantageous positions in the world), partly an artifact of their declining shares in world population. Most important for their geopolitical position, their global economic weight is eroding. Maddison's data suggest that this has been the case for quite a while. Reported in the language of continents, the "engine" of the world economy is neither in Western Europe nor in North America. Instead, it has moved (back) to Asia.

Since, in a tightly integrated world system, the issue of global economic power is a near-zero-sum process, these results reveal the true global importance of the former state-socialist states of Eastern Europe and northern Eurasia. Plainly put, the collapse of Eastern Europe served as a global geopolitical buffer, delaying the point at which the societies of the "West," especially those of Western Europe, will gain a firsthand experience with the geopolitical effects of the drastic shrinkage of their economies in global terms. The last decade or so has seen the military pen-etration of western and central Asia by the United States and some of its Western allies through NATO as well as the creeping encirclement of both China and India, but Asia's rise has not created a more irritated, more openly belligerent re-sponse from the West, at least to some extent because most of the attendant losses of global position struck Eastern Europe and northern Eurasia.[13] The former So-viet bloc's losses of global weight (the equivalent of approximately 4.65 percent of the world economy) helped absorb the global effects of Asia's rise (without Japan, Asia as a whole shows an astonishing gain of 8 percent of the gross world product) so that the United States, the European Union, and Japan had to sustain, so far, only moderate losses of 1.66 percent. Part of the irony of the post–Cold War years is, of course, that the weight loss experienced by the regime-changing former state-socialist societies (altogether 4.65 percent of the gross world product) is al-most exactly equal to the gains made by the two successful, still state-socialist economies of the world, China and Vietnam (4.75 percent).

That the least impoverished ten member states on the western perimeter of the former Soviet bloc — including all of the social, cultural, political, and economic resources they have built up during the rapid, often forced social change that characterized their state-socialist histories — have recently been added to the Eu-ropean Union (this happened in May 2004 and January 2008, that is, after the point where Maddison's data stop) contributes further to subsidizing the West in terms of geopolitical resources. It is important to see, however, that both of those mitigating factors are distinctly short-term. The European Union is already run-ning out of semiperipheral, former state-socialist states that it could incorporate in its continued size-making effort, and there is no state-socialist bloc whose col-lapse could buffer the changes that Asia's continued rise is bound to set off in the global system of geopolitics of the near future. Short of another former Moscow bloc whose global weight could be sacrificed to weather the relative losses of economic weight required by Asia's continued rise, the losses will have to hit elsewhere, and the European Union and North America—which continue to be the two largest single markets in the world—inevitably will be affected by those transformations more adversely than they have been so far. To a large extent, attempts at placing such burdens on actors outside North America and Western Europe are likely to be the essence of the geopolitics of the states—the wealthiest and currently the geopolitically most powerful areas of the world. One plausible, related development would be a move toward matching the military-strategic structure of NATO with a "North Atlantic" single market—a project that already has powerful corporate lobbying support both in the United States and the EU—and, at least in the EU, legislative commitment as well.

It could be argued that the current situation is not entirely without precedent. After all, the societies of Japan and South Korea, non-Western as they are, both underwent spectacular economic upswings, resulting in steeply increased economic weights, in the decades following the Second World War. The current geopolitical situation, however, differs from those upswings in two crucial respects. First, those upswings took place on the pro-Western side of the global strategic standoff, that is, under geopolitical conditions in which a certain amount of Western goodwill and geo-economic patience was automatically granted to these societies, since their weight gains lent more economic power to the anticommunist bloc.

Second, both Japan and South Korea were under foreign military occupation during the period of their economic upswing, reducing their sovereignty—and, as a result, decreasing their states' capacity to act autonomously—with respect to the United States. The opportunities of direct Western political control that were in place in the myriad specific institutional forms both in Japan and in South Korea are, of course, not there in the current weight gainers of Asia, and the vanishing of the global logic of the strategic standoff took away much of those occasions for goodwill as well. Much of the global geopolitics of the next decade or two will be about how to manage the resultant tensions, conflicts, and face-offs.

Three basic, creative scenarios can be imagined. Given the exclusive nature of the "NATO matched by a North Atlantic single market" project, it is reasonable to expect that those scenarios will involve new and unprecedented forms of "lateral" regional cooperation among key actors outside of Western Europe and North America. They differ from each other only in terms of their scale and scope.

First, the two largest and currently most dynamic Asian states, China and India, could devise ways in which to implement an ambitious, stable, long-term development partnership—an idea that is clearly part of the two states' bilateral relations.[14] Since their economic organization is quite compatible and their strengths have sufficient complementarity, it might not be an impossible task for Asia's two successful developmental states to mobilize their impressive resources in key areas that contribute not only to solidifying the two economies' sustained growth but also to creating *a joint economic infrastructure* that would lead to a long-term commonality in economic-geopolitical interests between the two societies. Large-scale educational, cultural, research, and person-to-person exchanges would be logical components of such a project. This cooperation could invite Russia, whose fate is undeniably as much tied to Asia as to Europe. Its technologies, experience, and, perhaps even more significant, natural-resource base are, to some extent, located in Asia, and its geopolitical identity has always had a Asian component. The three large societies could form a truly powerful, single engine of Asian economic growth that is, frankly, unmatched in the modern history of the world.

Second, on a somewhat even greater scale, it is perhaps time to begin serious thinking about the viability of an Asian Union. Clearly, the political, social, and economic obstacles that such a project would have to overcome are enormous, but they are dwarfed by the difficulties, problems, and pains associated with economic growth that Asia would have to face in the absence of such an overarching organization. The great lesson from the emergence of the European Union is that there are truly significant advantages to be derived from a supra-state process that not only dismantles tariff barriers but also explicitly prescribes standards and the construction of overarching economic, legal, political, and social institutions that aim to ease and encourage flows of all kinds.

Finally, third, Asia's rise brings to the fore the question of alternative, "lateral" structures on the scale of the globe. It is clear that Asia's rise will affect the division of voice, tasks, and power within the United Nations, but, perhaps even more important, it also thematizes the issue of *alternative global organizations*. As the success of the ad hoc coalition of noncore, non-former-colonizer states at the last ministerial conference of the World Trade Organization (held in Cancún, Mexico, in September 2003) demonstrates, there are real opportunities for alternative global structures to form and exert serious influence on global affairs. One novel aspect of the G-20 summits, created in the wake of the global financial crisis of the autumn of 2008, was the prominent presence and important role played by China and India. The currently ongoing negotiations regarding the reform of the quota and voting systems of the International Monetary Fund also reflect the transformations in the global geopolitical-economic significance of the rising, large states of Asia.[15]

Asia's continued rise could provide not only a serious resource base but the powerful moral and political impetus for such a transformation as well. If such processes of integration are to take place in Asia, there is no better time to initiate them than at the point at which the region's two largest and most powerful economies are both on the upswing: It is much easier to create institutions under conditions of economic growth — indeed, some argue that it is only possible during such times. Many states in Asia have a relatively sizeable budgetary surplus nowadays. The historic question posed by Asia's ongoing rise is how wisely, with what kind of collective, global foresight, those resources will be expended. They could, of course, all be wasted on newer and newer weapons systems, aimed at each other or smaller neighbors. They could, on the other hand, be spent in a sensible, collectively rational, prudent, clever, and peaceful way. Those are the most important decisions that are being made at this very moment.

One thing is for sure: if any one, or any combination, of the above developments takes place, the character of the world will change — forever.

ACKNOWLEDGMENT

Parts of earlier versions of this chapter have been presented at the Challenging Entangled Hegemonies conference, organized by the Hungarian journal *Eszmélet* in Budapest, Hungary, October 14–16, 2005 and the author's keynote address as the recipient of the Immanuel Wallerstein Chair in Global Ethics at the University of Ghent, Belgium, in 2006. It elaborates a theme from the author's book *The European Union and Global Social Change: A Critical Geopolitical Economic Analysis*. The author is grateful to Mahua Sarkar for her advice, critique, and encouragement. He also thanks the Collegium Budapest Institute for Advanced Study for the residential fellowship that made completion of this project easier.

NOTES

1. Computed from the online data supplement published in conjunction with Maddison (2003).

2. Since this area of scholarship is widely known, I will just mention the most significant classics of this area that are available in English. In addition to work in-

cluded in this volume, see work by Fernand Braudel (especially 1981, 1982, 1986), Immanuel Wallerstein (e.g., 1974), Giovanni Arrighi (1996), Arrighi and Beverly Silver (1999), Samir Amin (1976), Janet Abu-Lughod (1989), André Gunder Frank (1998), Christopher Chase-Dunn (1998), Chase-Dunn and Thomas Hall (1997), and John M. Hobson (2004).

3. For more on the EU as a creative, new, nonstate form of public authority, see Böröcz and Sarkar (2005), and Böröcz (2009).

4. Here and throughout this chapter, I use the term geopolitics (as defined in the opening paragraph) as a shorthand reference to the ways in which organizations (states as well as other, non-state organizations) project their power into the world outside their boundaries.

5. Those states that had been dissolved since 1989—such as the formerly federal socialist states of Eastern Europe and Eurasia: the USSR, Yugoslavia, and Czechoslovakia—appear as their successor states. In such cases, the starting point of the comparison is the establishment of the new states.

6. On "peaceful rise," see, for instance, an editorial issued on May 2, 2004, in conjunction with the one-week holiday and related important celebrations commemorating International Labor Day: http://english.peopledaily.com.cn/200405/02/eng20040502_142255.html on the English-language website of the CCP's official newspaper, the People's Daily. Note also George W. Bush's reply seven weeks later, echoing the Chinese phrasing by pronouncing that "China's peaceful rise is very important" http://english.peopledaily.com.cn/200404/24/eng20040424_141421.shtml. Both websites accessed July 15, 2005.

7. This assumption was a defining feature of the economic literature during the last phase of state socialism in Eastern Europe. For an illustration, consider this exceptionally clear formulation by Harvard-based institutional economist János Kornai's monograph devoted to an analysis of the shortcomings of state-socialist economies: "Since the connection between the 'personal pocket' and the residual income of the state-owned firm is entirely absent, those who otherwise have deciding voice in how the residual income is used are not real owners at all from this point of view. The automatic, spontaneous incentive noted with private property does not apply" (Kornai 1992: 74).

8. Among the top ten, two enterprises mention this kind of ownership component, and only one has published specific data pertaining to this segment. There—in the case of Sinopec, the largest Chinese company to date—the proportion of private domestic capital ownership is 3.23 percent.

9. To be noted, again, is the fact that the recent "hydrocarbon bump" has, clearly, improved Russia's global position somewhat. The overall, long-term effects of this transformation are, however, beyond the scope of this chapter.

10. For more on this idea, see especially Frank (1998), Hobson (2004), and Böröcz (2009).

11. See, for example, "Washington Draws India in against China." People's Daily, English edition, available at http://english1.people.com.cn/200507/07/eng20050707_194676.html accessed July 26, 2005, cited in Friedman (2005).

12. Israel, whose record also shows a respectable increase in both per capita and global-weight terms, represents a case that stifles comparative analysis because it is impossible to decompose the statistical effects of foreign aid, especially military aid (a very significant component of the Israeli state budget), from intrinsic economic growth.

13. Meanwhile, it is possible to read the escalating Indo-Pakistani conflict against the backdrop of the structural transformation expressed in India's noticeable gain in global economic weight, a transformation not matched by Pakistan.

14. See, e.g., www.hindu.com/2005/04/10/stories/2005041003551000.htm and http://english.peopledaily.com.cn/200611/21/eng20061121_323795.html accessed December 11, 2008.

15. See, e.g., www.isn.ethz.ch/isn/Current-Affairs/Security-Watch/Detail/?ots591=4888CAA0-B3DB-1461–98B9-E20E7B9C13D4&lng=en&id=51755 or www.imf.org/external/pubs/ft/survey/so/2007/NEW057B.htm accessed December 11, 2008.

REFERENCES

Abu-Lughod, Janet. 1989. *Before European Hegemony: The World-System A.D. 1250–1350.* New York: Oxford University Press.

Amin, Samir. 1976. *Unequal Development: An Essay on the Social Formations of Peripheral Capitalism.* New York: Monthly Review Press.

Arrighi, Giovanni. 1994. *The Long Twentieth Century: Money, Power, and the Origins of Our Times.* London: Verso.

Arrighi, Giovanni, and Beverly J. Silver. 1999. *Chaos and Governance in the Modern World System.* Minneapolis: University of Minnesota Press.

Böröcz, József. 2005. "Redistributing Global Inequality: A Thought Experiment." *Economic and Political Weekly,* February 26.

Böröcz, József. 2009. The European Union and Global Social Change: A Critical Geopolitical Economic Analysis. London: Routledge.

Böröcz, József, and Mahua Sarkar. 2005. "What Is the EU?" *International Sociology* 20 no. 2:153–73.

Braudel, Fernand. 1981. *The Structure of Everyday Life, Civilization and Capitalism, 15th–18th Century.* Volume 1. Translated by Siân Reynolds. New York: Perennial Library, Harper and Row.

———. 1982. *The Perspective of the World: Civilization and Capitalism, 15th–18th Century.* Volume 3. Translated by Siân Reynolds. New York: Perennial Library, Harper and Row.

———. 1986. *The Wheels of Commerce: Civilization and Capitalism, 15th–18th Century.* Volume 2. Translated by Siân Reynolds. New York: Perennial Library, Harper and Row.

Chase-Dunn, Christopher. 1998. *Global Formation: Structures of the World-Economy.* Lanham, MD: Rowman and Littlefield.

Chase-Dunn, Christopher, and Thomas D. Hall. 1997. *Rise and Demise: Comparing World-Systems.* Boulder, CO: Westview Press.

Frank, André Gunder. 1998. ReORIENT: Global Economy in the Asian Age. Berkeley: University of California Press.

Friedman, George. 2005. "U.S.-Indian Relations and the Geopolitical System." Stratfor Analysis, July 20. Available at www.stratfor.com/products/enhanced/read_article .php?id=252087, accessed July 21, 2005.

Hobson, John M. 2004. The Eastern Origins of Western Civilisation. Cambridge, UK: Cambridge University Press.

Kornai, János. 1992. The Socialist System: The Political Economy of Communism. Princeton: Princeton University Press.

Maddison, Angus. 2001. The World Economy: A Millennial Perspective. Paris: Development Centre of the Organisation for Economic Cooperation and Development.

———. 2003. The World Economy: Historical Statistics. Paris: Development Centre of the Organisation for Economic Cooperation and Development. Data supplement available at www.theworldeconomy.org, accessed November 15, 2008.

Wallerstein, Immanuel. 1974. The Modern World-System: Capitalist Agriculture and the Origins of the European World-Economy in the Sixteenth Century. New York: Academic Press.

CHAPTER SIX

China's Economic Ascent and Japan's Raw-Materials Peripheries

PAUL S. CICCANTELL

China's rapid economic ascent during the past three decades offers an important opportunity to study national economic ascent and its potential to transform the world economy as it happens. World-systems analysis can study short-term fluctuations, medium-term trends, and potential long-term structural changes as China and other competitors challenge U.S. hegemony. This "real-time" opportunity avoids the analytic traps of post-hoc examinations of long-term structural change that may neglect agency, understate the role of competition between states and firms, and imply that the outcome was historically inevitable. The current severe challenges to U.S. hegemony economically and politically provide an analytical window for studying hegemonic competition and long-term change.

This chapter analyzes China's efforts to resolve the most fundamental obstacle to sustained, rapid economic ascent: how to achieve low-cost, secure access to a rapidly growing and increasingly diverse volume of raw materials that can provide a competitive advantage over other ascendant nations and the existing hegemon. China's raw-materials access strategies combine reliance on existing systems built by earlier ascendant economies with efforts to steal these earlier ascendants' raw-materials peripheries by offering what appear to be better deals to raw-materials–exporting states and firms. These strategies are quite similar to those the United States used against Great Britain during the nineteenth and twentieth centuries and those Japan used against the United States in the second half of the twentieth century. The success of these Chinese strategies is far from guaranteed, and this chapter analyzes these strategies and their successes and challenges in the early twenty-first century.

NEW HISTORICAL MATERIALISM

In any rising economy, strategies for economic ascent must respond to and take advantage of contemporary technological, geopolitical, environmental, and market conditions in the rest of the world and of the nation's position and location within that particular global economy. They must also coordinate the physical characteristics and location in space and in topography of the various raw-material resources actually or potentially available with the physical characteristics and location in space and topography of the national territory. The beginnings of economic ascent require successful coordination of domestic technological advances, particularly in heavy industry and transport, with the external solution of access to cheap and steady sources of the raw materials used for heavy industry. The raw materials used in greatest volume present the greatest challenge and best opportunity for economies of scale. These economies of scale, however, drive a contradictory increase in transport cost, as the closest reserves of raw materials are depleted more rapidly as the scale of their industrial transformation increases; for an extended presentation of this theoretical model, see Bunker and Ciccantell (2005).

The tension of this contradiction between the economies of scale and the cost of space foments technological innovation in raw-materials processing and transport. These innovations tend to generate further increases of scale, thus exacerbating over the long term the very contradiction between scale and space that they are designed to solve (Bunker and Ciccantell 2005).

The national economies that most successfully initiated technological and organizational solutions of this contradiction simultaneously generated their own rise to economic dominance, restructured the mechanisms and dynamics of systemic and hierarchic accumulation, and expanded and intensified the commercial arena of raw-materials trade and transport. Solutions to the raw-materials problem addressing the tension between increasing economies of scale in raw-materials extraction and transport and the accompanying diseconomies of the increasing cost of space require the coordination of multiple physical and social processes across geopolitical and physical space with domestic relations among firms, sectors, the state, labor, and new technologies. Rising economies resolve these problems at the same time as, or even before, they increase industrial competitiveness. These solutions stimulate complex processes of learning and institutional change that fundamentally mold the organization of the national economy at the same time that they change international markets and the rules binding participants in them (Bunker and Ciccantell 2005).

The challenges and the opportunities presented by the basic raw-materials industries and by the transport systems on which they depend foster generative sectors: sectors that create backward and forward links, stimulate a broad range of technical skills and learning along with formal institutions designed and funded to promote them, create vast and diversified instrumental knowledge held by interdependent specialists about the rest of the world, stimulate the development of financial institutions adapted to the requirements of large sunk costs in a variety of social and political contexts, and foment specific formal and informal relations among firms, sectors, and states, and the form of legal distinctions between public and private and between different levels of public jurisdiction (Bunker and Ciccantell 2005).

Generative sectors will be more numerous, more easily observed, and more efficacious in those national economies that are growing so rapidly that they must achieve massive increases in throughput and transformation of raw materials. The concept is relational, however, within a world-systems perspective, which implies that generative sectors in a rising economy will have significant consequences for economies that export raw materials or trade in other kinds of goods. This chapter is part of a series of comparative historical cases that analyze how generative sectors form around raw materials and transport (Bunker and Ciccantell 1995, 2003a, b). The lessons from these comparative historical analyses are used to diagnose a case of still uncertain outcomes, China's rapid economic ascent; for extended discussions of China's economic ascent, see Ciccantell and Bunker (2004) and Bunker and Ciccantell (2007).

Generative sectors are not necessarily the sectors in which profits are highest, even though high-profit sectors (whether gold and silver in the seventeenth century or computer technology in the twentieth century) typically attract the most analytical attention (see, for example, Arrighi 1994; O'Hearn 2001). However, as has been shown elsewhere (Bunker and Ciccantell 2003a, b), the sectors with the highest profits are not necessarily generative sectors. Instead, generative sectors provide the material building blocks, cost reductions across many sectors to increase competitiveness, and patterns of state-sector-firm relations and other institutions that combine to drive economic ascent.

How can rapidly growing economies acquire the raw materials essential to sustain these generative sectors, particularly in the face of domestic raw-materials depletion and the resulting diseconomies of space as these raw materials must be brought from more distant areas outside the political control of the ascendant state? One critical strategy to accomplish this task has been to steal raw-materials peripheries from earlier ascendant economies that have already undertaken the difficult and expensive tasks of building the necessary infrastructure; creating political, organizational, and legal forms that promote international trade and investment relations between a particular raw-materials–producing state and the world economy; and incorporating these peripheries economically and politically into the world economy. Earlier processes of economic ascent had progressively globalized the world economy and brought new raw-materials peripheries into the global trading system. Therefore, new ascendant economies and states have the opportunity initially to purchase raw materials from this established supply system.

The newer ascendants' rapid growth, however, means that their demand is increasing dramatically, necessitating a similar increase in supply if these growth rates are to be sustained. The combination of the existing social and material infrastructures in the raw-materials peripheries established by earlier ascendants, rapid demand growth in the ascendant economy, and the willingness of the newer ascendant economy to pay higher prices for raw materials in order to sustain their domestic growth creates an opportunity that states and firms in the raw-materials periphery find very attractive. Higher prices for rapidly increasing volumes of exports (in contrast to slower demand growth in the mature economies of the earlier ascendant) motivate firms and domestic elites in the periphery and even in the existing core powers with fewer opportunities for profitable investments to invest in production for export to the new ascendant. States in raw-materials–exporting regions typically support this investment with subsidies for transport and extraction, both in an effort to promote economic development and in the hopes of gaining better returns and more political freedom from the power of the existing hegemon. This is particularly apparent in postcolonial situations in which newly independent states seek to break free from neocolonial ties and in situations of resource nationalism in which states seek greater control over and benefits from raw-materials exports. Firms, elites, and states in raw-materials peripheries come to see the new ascendant as a potential ally in their attempts to promote political independence and economic development.

From the perspective of the new ascendant, building these relationships with existing raw-materials peripheries is much less expensive and difficult than creating their own new peripheries. One of the most important benefits is that most of the cost and risk of expanding extraction and transport is borne by firms and states in the extractive periphery and often by firms from the earlier ascendant. At the same time, these investments in mines and transport systems also often create opportunities for exports of industrial products from the ascendant economy to the periphery to support the development of these extractive industries and for consumption by the owners of and workers in these industries. "Stealing" these peripheries from earlier ascendants thus further enhances the rapid growth of the new ascendant; it reduces costs and risks while simultaneously creating significant new opportunities for profit from trade and investment.

During the last five hundred years, this process of stealing peripheries has been a key element in each case of rapid, transformative ascent (Bunker and Ciccantell 2005, 2007). For example, Holland progressively captured more and more of the Brazil trade from the waning Portuguese empire in the 1600s, taking control of much of the sugar, precious metals, and other raw-materials trade and capturing the benefits of this trade for its own domestic development in shipbuilding, shipping, finance, and other industries. Great Britain rapidly displaced the Dutch from North America, the Caribbean, India, and Southeast Asia in the late 1600s and 1700s and took control of trade in timber, sugar, and a host of other raw materials. During the nineteenth-century postcolonial era in Latin America, Great Britain similarly displaced the Spanish empire as the region's main trade and investment partner, inducing states to subsidize the construction of British-owned and manufactured railways to ensure high rates of profit and steady supplies of grain, silver, tin, and other products to British consumers and industries. The rapidly growing United States did the same to support its ascent in the nineteenth and twentieth centuries, displacing Great Britain first in much of North America and later in Canada, Latin America, and the Caribbean to acquire the raw materials for U.S. industrialization. The United States often used the opportunity to escape British hegemony as a key enticement for firms and states to redirect their exports of copper, bauxite, and other raw materials to the U.S. market with its rapidly growing demand.

Moreover, this process has continued in the late twentieth and early twenty-first centuries. After World War II, the United States effectively took control of Australia's resources in order to establish a supply relationship with Japan, over Australia's objections, in order to support U.S. Cold War efforts in Asia by rebuilding Japan. This U.S.-led reorganization of Australia's raw-materials trade relations created the pattern for Japan's progressive globalization of the iron and coal industries via long-term contracts and joint ventures. This raw-materials access strategy came to rely on its seeming support for resource nationalism (often to escape the control of the U.S. hegemon and its firms), but it greatly benefited Japanese firms and the Japanese state by transferring much of the costs and risks of supplying Japan's industries to states and firms in Australia, Brazil, Canada, and other nations. The raw-materials peripheries that Japanese strategies stole from the United States and Great Britain provided billions of dollars in subsidies to Japanese industrial development and global competitiveness in the form of lower raw-materials costs. They formed a key pillar of Japan's rapid economic ascent and ensured that the raw-materials–intensive industries that states and firms in these raw-materials–exporting regions wanted to develop using revenues from raw-materials exports to Japan were instead built in Japan itself (Bunker and Ciccantell 2007).

But why should raw materials continue to be a concern in the current era of high-technology industries and supposed dematerialization (see, for example, Herman et al. 1989)? Claims about dematerialization became possible as heavy industry in the United States and Western Europe became increasingly uncompetitive from the 1970s onward and much of it closed. However, these industries were simply relocating to less expensive nations in the semiperiphery and periphery such as South Korea, Brazil, and especially China. The world economy uses more material every year; it is just increasingly produced outside the core nations. World steel production in 2007, for example, was 1.34 billion metric tons, an increase of 7.5 percent in comparison with 2006, the fifth year in a row of growth of more than 7 percent. This is the largest volume of steel production in history, and more than 36 percent of this steel was made in China (*Skillings Mining Review* 2008a). Steel today, for example, is seen as an anachronistic relic in the United States because of the industry's collapse since the early 1970s in the face of first Japanese and later other global competition. However, under conditions of rapid economic growth in China in recent years, huge and rapidly growing quantities of steel are needed to build office buildings, factories, roads, and other infrastructure, in addition to the products being exported. The Chinese steel industry simultaneously generates huge profits for steel-producing firms, many of them operating in partnership with Japanese, South Korean, and European steel firms. Steel may be past its prime in the product life cycle of U.S. industry, but it remains a key ingredient in the rapid economic ascent in China.

CHINA'S RAPID ECONOMIC ASCENT

By any measure, the economic ascent of China in the past three decades is the most dramatic change in the capitalist world economy of the late twentieth and early twenty-first centuries. In the steel industry, Chinese steel production increased from 158,000 tons in 1949 to forty million tons in 1980 and to 489 million tons in 2007, 36 percent of total world steel production (Hogan 1999a and 1999b; Brizendine and Oliver 2001; Serchuk 2001; *Skillings Mining Review* 2008a). The Chinese government is closing small, globally uncompetitive steel mills and building new coastal steel mills using the latest technology and the least costly globally available coal and iron ore, rather than relying on lower-quality, higher-cost domestic resources, as was formerly done under state policies of domestic economic self-sufficiency (Hogan 1999a). China is now the world's leading producer of steel, surpassing Japan, the United States, and Europe (Serchuk 2001: 32). China also became one of the world's largest importers of iron ore, using a global system of raw-materials supply created by Japan during its economic ascent via a variety of innovations in technology and social organization of steel production, ocean shipping, and raw-materials supply agreements (Bunker and Ciccantell 2007).

The steel, transport, and other linked industries in the generative sectors of China began to develop during the first half of the twentieth century under the aegis of invading imperial powers, most importantly the Japanese, who built China's first steel mill at Anshan. The Communist Party emphasized the continued development of the industry from the 1950s through the 1980s (Hogan 1999a; Serchuk 2001). These steel mills were relatively small in scale and, for security purposes, often located far inland. Rural areas of China supplied coal and iron ore, and the coal industry became one of the most important employers in rural China, producing 871 million tons of coal in 1985 and employing millions of people. The mines and steel mills were linked by a limited and antiquated railroad transport system that severely limited interregional trade and raised the costs of production. This transport system also made imports and exports of resources extremely difficult. The problems of this rail system were highlighted by weather problems in early 2008 that caused huge backlogs for New Year's vacation travelers, while rail closures threatened coal-fired power production.

Chinese government policies for steel, coal, and linked industries began to change in 1978, with minerals and metals industries planned to be key components of efforts to expand China's role in the global economy (Dorian 1999; Schneider et al. 2000). The pace of change accelerated in the 1980s as part of the broader process of economic reform instituted by the Communist Party (Dorian 1999). To supply these mills, imports of far higher-quality Australian, Brazilian, and other imported iron ore increased rapidly, and several ports serving coastal steel mills were expanded to accommodate very large bulk carriers (Hogan 1999a, b; *International Bulk Journal* 2002: 27–28).

By 1995, China was the world's largest steel producer. This dramatic increase in capacity and production, however, encountered three major problems: (1) limitations on the quality and product lines of the Chinese steel mills required significant volumes of imports of products such as steel sheet (Hogan 1999a, b;

Serchuk 2001: 32); (2) aging and often antiquated technologies created quality problems, management difficulties, and environmental problems (Hogan 1999a, b; Brizendine and Oliver 2001; Serchuk 2001); and (3) extremely low levels of productivity per worker made Chinese steel uncompetitive globally without extremely low-cost labor (Brizendine and Oliver 2001: 22).

The Chinese government instituted a series of new policies during the next decade in order to address these problems in the steel and coal industries in particular and more generally to prepare the broader economy for joining the World Trade Organization and to increase global competitiveness. These policies include restructuring steel mills and firms to improve productivity and reduce employment, closing many small steel mills and coal mines and encouraging concentration into a smaller number of more competitive and potentially more profitable firms (Mehta 1998; Hogan 1999a, b; Brizendine and Oliver 2001), refocusing investment in steel to improve quality and broadening production into high-end product lines to replace imported steel (Hogan 1999a, b; Brizendine and Oliver 2001; Serchuk 2001), and attracting foreign firms as joint-venture partners and technology suppliers (Dorian 1999; Hogan 1999a, b; Brizendine and Oliver 2001; Huskonen 2001). Chinese steel firms have also begun cooperating with foreign firms to create joint ventures in iron ore, copper, and other types of mines and steel mills in Australia, Papua New Guinea, Chile, Peru, the Philippines, and New Zealand (Dorian 1999; Tse 2000). These overseas investments by Chinese firms as minority joint-venture partners and buyers of output under long-term contracts are explicitly modeled on the raw-materials access strategies of Japanese steel firms. They reduce the costs and risks to the Chinese importing firms while transferring the vast majority of the costs and risks of large investments in mines and infrastructure to firms and states in the exporting region.

Based on earlier research on the process of hegemonic succession (Bunker and Ciccantell 2005, 2007) and the work of Arrighi (1994), one of the most interesting questions about the long-term sustainability of China's economic ascent is the role played by Japan in that ascent. In each earlier case of rapid ascent, the existing hegemon played a key role as the supplier of capital and technology to the rising economy, as part of what Arrighi (1994) analyzed as the period of financialization and decline in the existing hegemon and the efforts of financial capital in the hegemon to find new opportunities for investment in rapidly growing economies. At least to some extent, Japanese firms play this role in the ascent of China in raw materials, transport, and many other industries. The largest and most modern steel mill in China, Baoshan, on the southeastern coast near Shanghai, was built with technical assistance from Nippon Steel and other Japanese companies

(Hogan 1999a), an explicit replication of the Japanese steel-based Maritime Industrial Development Areas (MIDAs) program. Japanese steel firms are joint-venture partners in several steel mills and steel-processing plants, supplying capital and technology to their Chinese partners (Tse 2000). In other raw-materials industries, a wide variety of Japanese raw-materials–processing firms, trading companies, and banks are playing similar roles (Tse 2000).

China is following the Japanese model of coastal greenfield heavy industrialization to supply other industries at low cost as state policies focus on deepening industrialization in steel, shipbuilding, and other heavy industries (Todd 1996; Hogan 1999a). However, following the models of earlier ascendant economies, even in terms of fomenting what have historically been key generative sectors in the most successful cases of ascent, does not guarantee success. This is in part because older models may prove to be surpassed by new technological and organizational innovations by other competitors and in part because successful sustained ascent is a relational process of competition with the existing hegemon and other ascendant economies. China's efforts to follow Japan's model of ascent confront challenges from the existing hegemon, the United States, and other competitors, including the European Union, Japan, and Russia. The economic and social consequences of closing or ending state support for inland industry, especially in the Northeast, are also a potential internal limitation of China's ascent (Ciccantell and Bunker 2004).

These explicit efforts to follow the Japanese post–World War II model of development illustrate both the potential benefits and risks of following this model and creating an integrated set of generative sectors in steel and transport. Steel and other heavy industry–based growth poles following this model can be found on the coasts of a number of nations in Europe, Asia, Latin America, and Africa. However, most remain at best poorly integrated enclaves that have failed to generate sustained economic growth. State policies and the availability of funding are only parts of the broader process of international competition that shapes the developmental trajectories of particular growth poles, regions, and states within the world economy. The strategies, successes, and failures of other ascendant economies and the existing hegemon shape the technological, organizational, socioeconomic, and political parameters that determine global competitiveness, and more successful rivals can effectively circumscribe the best policy choices and largest investments of other competitors. The outcomes of these developmental efforts are highly contingent on the strategies of other competing economies, and the long-term sustainability of China's efforts to continue its economic ascent by following the Japanese model is far from assured.

CHINA'S STRATEGIES TO BUILD ITS
RAW-MATERIALS PERIPHERIES

From the 1950s through the 1980s, Japan's steel industry led the world in growth rates, exports, and technological innovations. The Japanese steel firms and trading companies, initially supported by the U.S. government and the World Bank, fomented the creation of a global coal industry in socially remote areas of Australia, Canada, South Africa, and several other nations that transformed coal from a local and regional industry into a truly global industry. The Japanese steel firms drove a similar dramatic change in the iron-ore industry during this period, creating a global industry oriented toward supplying the rapidly growing Japanese steel industry.

Japanese strategies to gain access to coal from these new raw-materials peripheries fomented a huge excess capacity in the metallurgical coal industry by the mid-1980s, as new firms and mines entered production based on expectations of continually rising Japanese demand and steadily increasing prices. Intense global competition and excess capacity fomented by Japanese long-term contracts lowered raw-materials prices and reduced or eliminated rents (as demonstrated by the halving of real costs of importing coal into Japan between 1959 and 1998 from $86.65 in 1992 dollars to $43.63; Ciccantell and Bunker 2005: 188–89), putting intense pressure on exporting firms to reduce costs or face bankruptcy. The resulting restructuring from the late 1980s through the early 2000s bankrupted firms, closed mines, and devastated communities (Bunker and Ciccantell 2007).

The growth of Chinese steel production and consumption transformed the gloomy situation of coal-producing firms and regions. Rapidly growing metallurgical coal consumption by China's steel industry transformed China from a metallurgical coal exporter to an importer in the early 2000s. Chinese coal imports soaked up existing excess coal capacity and stimulated a huge investment rush in Canada, Australia, and other coal-mining regions (Morrison 2004), resulting in metallurgical coal contract prices exceeding $100 per ton and spot prices exceeding $150 per ton in 2004, the highest level in more than twenty years (Wailes 2004). Further increases in the past four years are even more dramatic, with Canadian coal firms signing contracts for $275–300 per ton for 2008–09 (*Canadian Mining Journal*, May 18, 2008). Coal firms are reopening mines closed because of uncompetitively high costs and are investing in previously economically unattractive mining projects around the world (Hayes 2004; Wailes 2004; Morrison 2004; Bunker and Ciccantell 2007).

As was the case in the coal industry, the rapid growth of the Japanese steel industry from the 1950s through the 1980s allowed Japanese steel firms to foment the development of a global iron-ore industry structured to supply iron ore at low cost to Japan. The Japanese steel firms formed joint ventures, signed long-term contracts, created transport systems, and organized a global market in which the firms, as a cartel of tightly coordinated buyers, cut their real iron-ore import costs in half in the late twentieth century (Bunker and Ciccantell 2005, 2007). For iron-ore–exporting states and firms, these Japanese strategies created a situation of excess capacity and low prices by the late 1980s and early 1990s (Bunker and Ciccantell 2007). China's rapid economic ascent has transformed the global iron-ore industry in recent years, just as was the case in the coal industry.

The major iron-ore firms are expanding production around the world, often in partnership with large iron-ore consumers in Japan, South Korea, and China. The vast bulk of this expansion relies on plans to export not to the relatively stagnant Japanese steel industry but instead to the rapidly growing Chinese steel industry (Hextall 2002: 67; *Mining Journal* 2002). A Salomon Smith Barney report issued in 2003 argued that "in a relative sense, China is now more important to the metals and mining sector than, say, Japan in the 1960s and 1970s, since at that time Japan was growing against a backdrop of reasonable global growth whereas Chinese growth has occurred in relative isolation" (cited in Hextall 2003: 63). The two major iron-ore mining firms in Australia, RTZ and BHP, have signed a number of long-term contracts with Chinese steel firms, some of which include joint-venture investment from the Chinese steel firms and from Japanese trading companies that will facilitate coordination and shipping (Kirk 2004: 5; Callick 2004; AFX.COM, March 1, 2004; *Kyodo News*, March 1, 2004; Sinocast, March 3, 2004; *Global Newswire*, April 20, 2004). One Chinese steel firm, Sinosteel, sought to take over a midsize Australian iron-ore mining firm, Midwest Corp., but another Australian firm outbid it (*Skillings Mining Review* 2008e).

In recent years, Chinese steel firms have typically paid $3.50 to $4.00 more per ton for iron ore than do Japanese steel firms, even though China is the world's largest iron-ore importer, because the Chinese steel firms have not coordinated their purchases. However, the recent long-term contracts and joint-venture investments represent a situation in which, as one industry analyst describes it, "in some ways the Chinese are beginning to do what the Japanese steel industry has already done to get pricing power" (AFX-Asia, March 1, 2004). The Chinese steel firms are trying to learn from the Japanese model of forming joint ventures among themselves in order to increase bargaining power with the iron-ore oligopoly and are seeking to take a leading role in the annual negotiations over iron-ore prices. The Chinese steel mills and the Chinese state fought hard against price increases in 2006, arguing that iron-ore and steel prices in China were too low to support more increases and that because of the huge size of the Chinese market, Chinese steel firms should be the lead negotiators for setting prices. The Chinese state sought to intervene directly in price negotiations in 2006 (*Xinhua*, February 17, 2006; *Lloyd's List*, March 10, 2006). These efforts by the Chinese government to obtain lower prices drew strong negative reactions from Australia and Brazil, including efforts by Brazil's mining industry association to get the Brazilian government to appeal to the World Trade Organization for violations of free-trade rules because of Chinese government intervention in the negotiations (Wilson 2006; *Skillings*, April 21, 2006). The Chinese government even sought to work cooperatively with Nippon Steel to block efforts to increase iron-ore prices, but all of these efforts failed (McGregor 2006: 2; *Skillings*, April 2006: 4; *Skillings*, April 21, 2006; Sinocast, May 26, 2006; *Skillings*, June 2006: 28). Chinese firms were forced to accept the prices negotiated by Japanese and European steel firms (Bunker and Ciccantell 2007).

The first price negotiations for 2008, which were concluded in February 2008, continued this pattern of Japanese and Korean steel firms setting prices that the Chinese firms are likely to be forced to accept. CVRD of Brazil negotiated an increase of another 65 percent in iron prices for 2008 with the Japanese steel mills and POSCO of South Korea (*Skillings Mining Review* 2008b). Despite coordinating their contract negotiations with CVRD under the leadership of Baosteel, China's largest steel firm, the Chinese steel firms accepted the same 65 percent price increase four days later (*Skillings Mining Review* 2008d). However, the Australian iron-ore mining firms are not satisfied with this increase, arguing that the much shorter sea voyage from Australia makes their ore more valuable to the Chinese steel mills than Brazilian ore. BHP and RTZ's hard-line negotiating strategy aimed to achieve a price increase of greater than 100 percent, and the smaller Chinese steel firms have already agreed to a 95 percent price increase (*Skillings Mining Review* 2008g), and the large Chinese steel firms eventually accepted a 95 percent increase as well (*Skillings Mining Review* 2008f), for the first time establishing a freight differential for Australian iron ore. BHP is seeking to gain even greater market power by attempting to take over RTZ, although these efforts have so far been successfully rebuffed, and by cornering the market for chartered large bulk carriers, driving up costs for competing firms and the Chinese steel firms, and pushing ocean shipping rates to their highest levels ever (*Skillings Mining Review* 2008h). The daily cost to charter a very large bulk carrier in 2002 was $17,000 per day; the mid-2008 rate is $303,000 per day because of BHP's efforts and the broader demand for raw-materials shipping to serve the rapidly growing Chinese market (*Skillings Mining Review* 2008h, 2008i). Chinese steel firms and the Chinese state have sought to use the strategies developed by Japanese steel firms and the Japanese state to control their iron-ore costs. However, China's own dramatic economic ascent, based on heavy industrialization, has so far undercut these strategies and left the Chinese steel firms paying ever-increasing iron-ore prices (Bunker and Ciccantell 2007).

Given these difficulties in gaining more control over price negotiations, Chinese firms have begun to try to acquire larger ownership stakes in iron-ore–exporting firms. The extremely high profits to be made from selling iron ore and steel today have spawned a wave of merger activity in these industries globally. BHP, the world's second largest iron-ore producer and exporter and itself a product of a recent merger, has proposed a hostile takeover of RTZ, the third largest iron-ore miner and a firm that has recently purchased Alcan, one of the world's largest aluminum firms, and a number of other raw-materials firms. This attempted takeover and the high degree of concentration that would result in the global iron-ore industry has prompted major iron-ore consumers, including Chinese steel firms and the Chinese state, to look for ways to prevent this takeover using China's huge volume of foreign-currency reserves. The Chinese government has hired investment-banking firms and authorized state-owned firms to bid for a stake in RTZ large enough to block BHP's takeover effort. Chinalco, a Chinese state-owned aluminum firm, formed a joint venture with Alcoa, the U.S.-based world's largest aluminum firm, to buy a 12 percent stake in RTZ for $14 billion in January 2008. This share may be large enough to block BHP or to force RTZ to sell key parts of its business to Chinalco and Alcoa (Hoffman 2008; Werdigier and Lague 2008; *Skillings Mining Review* 2008c).

This strategic effort is remarkable in a number of ways. The partnership with Alcoa in a potential hostile takeover bid would be a first for a Chinese state-owned firm, and this effort to intervene directly in restructuring the global iron-ore industry is a dramatic expansion of Chinese strategies to gain control over this industry. Raw-materials costs-driven inflation is a severe economic problem in China, and the Chinese state is seeking to use its massive trade surplus to find a global solution to this increasingly pressing domestic problem. This investment is the largest international foreign investment made by a Chinese state-owned firm. In this era of globalization and neoliberal reductions in the role of the state in the economy, this strategic action by a state-owned firm to take a leading role in a global industry is a glaring exception to the neoliberal model.

The emergence of the Chinese steel industry with the support of Japanese steel mills may transform the global steel and iron-ore industries, just as the development of the Japanese steel industry did after World War II. Japan's creation of a global iron-ore industry opened the door for China's raw-materials–based industrial deepening and potentially its sustained ascent by bringing into production new mines and firms in previously socially remote regions. These mining firms needed new markets after the long stagnation of Japanese steel production in the 1990s. Chinese steel firms are using this opportunity and importing capital and technology from Japan to become the world's largest iron-ore importer and steel producer. Chinese strategies to improve their negotiating position and control over the global iron-ore industry, however, confront major challenges.

Chinese raw-materials access strategies in the oil industry are following a similar pattern. The Chinese government and Chinese oil firms are creating joint-venture and long-term contract relationships to acquire oil and gas to fuel China's economic growth in many other nations. Russia, Iran, Sudan, and Venezuela are becoming major oil and gas exporters to China, based on the potential for long-term, rapid economic growth in China and these states' desires to reduce dependence on U.S. firms and vulnerability to U.S. government geopolitical control. The Chinese government has also arranged oil and natural-gas supply deals in Cameroon, Nigeria, Gabon, Angola, Brazil, Peru, Kazakhstan, Azerbaijan, Saudi Arabia, and even in Canada's oil sands region of Alberta, creating a great deal of concern for the U.S. and Japanese governments about future access to oil supplies for their own nations (York 2004; EIA 2004; Ebner 2004; Alberta Oil 2005; Luciw 2005; *Reuters*, June 18, 2005; Fattah 2006; Engdahl 2006; Cheng 2006). The U.S. State Department recently appointed a special envoy for energy issues, with the explicit goal of supporting access by U.S. oil firms to resources around the world (McCarthy 2008).

Perhaps most important, the Chinese and Russian governments are developing close economic and political relationships, motivated both by goals of creating a counterweight to U.S. hegemony and by efforts to promote domestic economic development. Russian raw materials feed a growing share of Chinese industry. Petroleum exports to China receive the greatest attention, most notably Chinese government support for Russian government renationalization of Yukos via a long-term contract and $6 billion credit arrangement between the state-owned China National Petroleum Corporation and Russian state-owned Rosneft (Arvedlund and Romero 2004; Watson 2005; Buckley 2005; *Reuters* 2005; Arvedlund 2005).

China's rapidly growing petroleum imports motivate an intense search for supplies of oil from many parts of the world. The failed effort to acquire Unocal of the United States by the China National Offshore Oil Corporation (CNOOC) because of Unocal's extensive Asian oil reserves marked a new escalation of this rivalry between major oil importers. Members of the U.S. Congress called for hearings on the proposed takeover as a potential national security threat, highlighting the intense economic and political rivalry over raw-materials supplies between China and the existing hegemon (Lohr 2005; King, Hitt, and Ball 2005; Wayne and Barboza 2005). China's leading global role as an oil importer discouraged other global oil firms from bidding against CNOOC for Unocal because these oil firms feared damaging their potential future sales to China (FT.com, March 3, 2005). Unocal accepted a bid from Chevron after CNOOC withdrew its bid because of political opposition in the United States, but this will not end China's efforts to acquire oil around the world (Sorkin and Mouawad 2005).

This takeover battle signified a major change in China's role in the global economy, even though it ultimately failed, because it laid the groundwork for efforts like Chinalco's recent investment in RTZ. As one international banker noted, "It is a wake up call for the global financial community. China is no longer a hunting ground for foreign investors. It has become a source of takeover activity" (FT.com, June 22, 2005). The Chinese government's development strategy now emphasizes both acquiring raw materials around the world and creating globally competitive enterprises. One advisor to the Chinese government reported that the effort to buy Unocal was not just about oil fields but also about promoting foreign investment by Chinese firms, with the National Development and Reform Commission, the leading economic planning agency, guiding CNOOC's bid for Unocal (FT.com, June 23, 2005). Rapid economic growth depends on rapidly growing supplies of raw materials, and the Chinese state now focuses a great deal of effort on establishing raw-materials supply relationships around the world. These efforts often come into conflict with efforts by the United States, Japan, and the European Union to gain access to these same resources, especially energy resources. These economic conflicts, particularly in conjunction with what some analysts argue is the impending peak in global oil production (see, for example, Simmons 2005), threaten to create political and even military conflicts over scarce resources in the coming years (Zweig and Jianhai 2005).

Just as in the case of China's relationship with the United States, significant conflicts and rivalries also mark the relationship between China and Japan. Energy supplies are one major arena of conflict, most notably over supplies of oil and gas from Russia (Kenny 2004). Japan's government won one recent battle by promising billions of dollars to build a $15.5 billion oil pipeline to move Russian oil to a port for export to Japan, but the Chinese and Japanese governments both seek to buy natural gas from a major development at Sakhalin Island (Brooke 2004, 2005a). The Chinese government is exploring a potential natural-gas field in an area of the East China Sea that both China and Japan claim, and the Chinese government refuses to halt exploration despite repeated Japanese requests (*Reuters*, May 31, 2005). Rivalries over oil, iron ore, coal, and other raw materials are critical components of China's relationship with Japan (Bunker and Ciccantell 2007).

However, China and the existing hegemon, the United States, are not simply rivals over raw-materials imports; the relationship between the United States and rapidly ascending China is far more complex. The Chinese government buys tens of billions of dollars per year of U.S. government Treasury bonds and holds immense foreign-currency reserves (mainly of U.S. dollars), all of which support U.S. government operations and the value of the U.S. dollar. Chinese firms supply huge and growing volumes of manufactured goods to the United States, and Chinese firms buy billions of dollars of imports from the United States. As one recent analysis argues, "The result is a historically unusual relationship in which the rising power, developing China, provides both exports (second-leading supplier) and loans (second-leading holder of government debt) to the superpower, the industrialized United States" (Deng and Moore 2004: 132). This parallels Japan's relationship with the United States since the 1970s after more than two decades of rapid industrial development in Japan; China is playing this same role for the United States after two decades of rapid economic ascent in China. However, no similar relationship developed during earlier processes of economic ascent (Bunker and Ciccantell 2005, 2007).

The emphasis on current and potential rivalry obscures the close cooperative relationship between the United States and China, which is largely responsible for China's economic ascent during the past three decades. Shared opposition to the Soviet Union led the United States and China to form what Henry Kissinger referred to as a "tacit alliance" by 1973, during which "Washington proceeded to support, arm, share intelligence with and nurture the economy of a Chinese government it had previously attempted to overthrow" (Mann 1999: 8, cited in Nayar 2004: 31). The U.S. government supported China's military modernization and, by granting Most Favored Nation trading status to China, supported the origin and development of China's export-led development strategy (Nayar 2004; Mahbubani 2005; Bunker and Ciccantell 2007). Further, another analyst argued that "the training of People's Republic of China (PRC) students and scholars in the West, most importantly in the United States, by itself constitutes the most significant transfer of technology to one country in a short period of time ever.

Without doubt, over the past twenty years, China has obtained what it needed for its economic modernization from abroad (capital, technology and access to markets) in greater amounts and at less cost than any country previously" (Van Ness 2002: 133). This tacit alliance played a critical role in helping the United States in its geopolitical rivalry with its most formidable political rival of the mid–twentieth century, the Soviet Union, but, just as with Japan-U.S. relations after World War II, it led to the dramatic rise of a new economic and political ally and rival that transformed the world economy. As in the earlier cases of rapid and systemically transformative economic ascent, the existing hegemon unintentionally created a major new rival (Bunker and Ciccantell 2005, 2007).

CONCLUSION: HISTORICAL COMPARISONS

Overall, in the context of competition in the global economy, replicating a highly successful model created during the 1950s and 1960s by Japanese firms and the Japanese state may not be sufficient to overcome existing and potential future challengers for economic ascent and hegemony. The next decade may bring a fundamental restructuring of the capitalist world economy in support of sustained Chinese economic ascent, but that ascent also could prove to be sharply constrained by economic and political competition, including the emergence of new organizational, technological, socioeconomic, or political innovations that increase scale and competitiveness in a rival economy and render China's immense investments in steel mills, coal mines, shipyards, and other industries as relics of an earlier era of the capitalist world economy.

From a long-term historical and theoretical perspective, China's increasing efforts to gain access to raw materials around the world may mark the latest example of what can be termed an ascendant economy stealing raw-materials peripheries from an earlier ascendant. Stealing these peripheries fuels economic ascent in the rapidly rising economy and simultaneously restructures the world economy in support of its ascent. Historically, the United States stole Canada, Mexico, and Brazil from Great Britain in the late 1800s and early 1900s, refocusing raw-materials exports from these areas to supply U.S. factories. After World War II, the United States did the same with several remaining British colonies, including Jamaica's bauxite reserves and, in the case of coal, Australia in order to give Japan the coal resources it needed to rebuild its economy. Japan later took Brazil, Indonesia, and much of western Canada from the United States. China is now seeking to take the oil sands and other western Canadian resources from the United States and the resources of Brazil, Australia, Russia, and other regions away from

Japan. When such strategies to take raw-materials peripheries away from earlier ascendant economies succeed, they provide raw materials at a lower cost to the rapidly growing economy than would be possible via imperial conquest or starting from scratch in new raw-materials–producing areas, thus increasing the rapidly growing economy's global competitiveness. China's success or failure in these efforts to take existing raw-materials peripheries away from the United States and Japan will prove critical to the sustained ascent of China's economy in the twenty-first century.

REFERENCES

AFX News. 2004. "BHP Wins 9 Bln. USD, 25-Year Iron Ore Supply Deal with 4 China Steel Cos." March 1.

Alberta Oil. 2005. "Fueling the Dragon." *Alberta Oil* 1, no. 2: 28–29.

Arrighi, Giovanni. 1994. *The Long Twentieth Century: Money, Power, and the Origins of Our Times.* London: Verso.

Arvedlund, Erin. 2005. "China Denies It Had a Role in Sale of Yukos Gas Unit." *New York Times*, February 4.

Arvedlund, Erin, and Simon Romero. 2004. "Kremlin Reasserts Hold on Russia's Oil and Gas." *New York Times*, December 17.

Brizendine, Thomas, and Charles Oliver. 2001. "China's Steel Sector in Transition." *China Business Review*, January-February: 22–26.

Buckley, Chris. 2005. "Calling In Envoy, Beijing Assails Pentagon Report." *New York Times*, July 21.

Bunker, Stephen G., and Paul S. Ciccantell. 2003a. "Transporting Raw Materials and Shaping the World-System: Creating Hegemony via Raw Materials Access Strategies in Holland and Japan." *Review of the Fernand Braudel Center* 26, no. 4: 339–80.

———. 2003b. "Generative Sectors and the New Historical Materialism: Economic Ascent and the Cumulatively Sequential Restructuring of the World Economy." *Studies in Comparative International Development* 37, no. 4: 3–30.

———. 2005. *Globalization and the Race for Resources.* Baltimore: Johns Hopkins University Press.

———. 2007. *An East Asian World Economy: Japan's Ascent, with Implications for China.* Baltimore: Johns Hopkins University Press.

Callick, Rowan. 2004. "Beijing's First-Stop Shop for Resources." *Australian Financial Review*, March 2: 16.

Canadian Mining Journal. 2008. "Coal Price: Fording, Western Canadian Set 2008 Prices." May 18, 2008.

Cheng Wing-Gar. 2006. "CNOOC to Buy Nigerian Oil Field State for $2.27 Bln." Bloomberg.com, January 9.

Ciccantell, Paul S., and Stephen G. Bunker. 2004. "The Economic Ascent of China and the Potential for Restructuring the Capitalist World-Economy." *Journal of World-Systems Research* 10, no. 3: 565–89.

Deng Yong and Thomas Moore. 2004. "China Views Globalization: Toward a New Great-Power Politics?" *Washington Quarterly* 27, no. 3: 117–36.

Dorian, James. 1999. "Mining in China: An Update." *Mining Engineering* 51, no. 2: 35–34.

Ebner, Dave. 2004. "China's Oil Sands Role Tests U.S." *Globe and Mail*, December 30.

Energy Information Agency (EIA). 2004. "Country Analysis Briefs: China." July.

Engdahl, F. William. 2005. "China Lays Down Gauntlet in Energy War: The Geopolitics of Oil, Central Asia, and the United States." JapanFocus.org, December 22.

Fattah, Hassan. 2006. "Chinese Leader Increases Trade Ties with Saudi Arabia." *New York Times*, April 23.

Financial Times. 2005a. "Oil Groups Fear Upsetting China." *New York Times*, March 3.

———. 2005b. "CNOOC Offer May Be a First Salvo." *New York Times*, June 22.

———. 2005c. "Beijing Policy Steers CNOOC Ambitions." *New York Times*, June 23.

Global News Wire. 2004. "Steel Companies Seek Steady Ore Supply From Australia." April 20.

Hayes, Jason. 2004. "Canadian Metallurgical Coal Market Expanding." *CIM Bulletin* 97, no. 1082: 15–16.

Herman, R. et al. 1989. "Dematerialization." In *Technology and Environment*, ed. J. Ausubel and H. Sladovich, 50–69. Washington, D.C.: National Academy Press.

Hextall, Bruce. 2002. "Miners in Ore Over Pilbara's Key to China." *Australian Financial Review*, May 24: 67.

Hoffman, Andy. 2008. "New Rio Tinto Investors Eye Alcan Assets." *Globe and Mail*, February 1.

Hogan, William. 1999a. *The Steel Industry of China: Its Present Status and Future Potential*. Lanham, MD: Lexington Books.

———. 1999b. "The Changing Shape of the Chinese Industry." *New Steel* 15, no. 11: 28–29.

Huskonen, Wallace. 2001. "China Adds Three New Steel Mills." 33 *Metalproducing*, April: 26–27.

International Bulk Journal. 2002. "China Has Its Irons in the Fire." May: 28.

Kenny, Henry. 2004. "China and the Competition for Oil and Gas in Asia." *Asia-Pacific Review* 11, no. 2: 36–47.

King, Neil Jr., Gregg Hitt, and Jeffrey Ball. 2005. "Oil Battles Sets Showdown over China." *Wall Street Journal*, June 24, A1, A10.

Kirk, William. 2004. "BHP Billiton Iron Ore Supply Contracts and Expansions." *Skillings Mining Review* 93, no. 11: 5.

Kyodo News International. 2004. "Japan Traders Itochu, Mitsui to Invest in Iron-Ore Joint Venture in Australia." *Kyodo News International*, March 1.

Lloyd's List. 2006. "China Backs Steel Mills' Price Battle." March 10: 4.

Lohr, Steve. 2005. "Unocal Bid Opens Up New Issues of Security." *New York Times*, July 13.

Luciw, Roma. 2005. "China Tries Oil Sands." *Globe and Mail*, April 12.

Mahbubani, Kishore. 2005. "Understanding China." *Foreign Affairs* 84, no. 5: 49–60.

McCarthy, Shawn. 2008. "U.S. on Offensive to Secure Energy Supplies." *Globe and Mail*, February 13.

McGregor, Richard. 2006. "China Excluded from Iron Ore Pricing." *Financial Times*, February 20: 2.

Mehta, Manik. 1998. "Winds of Change in China and India." *Steel Times International*, May.

Mining Journal. 2002. "WA Iron Ore: China's Impact." November 29: 377.

Morrison, Kevin. 2004. "Voracious Demand Fuels Miners' Challenge." *Financial Times*, April 23: 24.

Nayar, Baldev Raj. 2004. "The Geopolitics of China's Economic Miracle." *China Report* 40, no. 1: 19–47.

O'Hearn, Denis. 2001. *The Atlantic Economy: Britain, the U.S., and Ireland.* Manchester: Manchester University Press.

Reuters. 2005a. "China Refuses Japan Request over Gas Project." *New York Times*, May 31.

———. 2005b. "Venezuela to Sell Fuel Oil to China." *New York Times*, June 18.

Schneider, Karen, Wu Zhonghu, Dai Lin, and Vivek Tulpule. 2000. *Supplying Coal to South East China: Impacts of China's Market Liberalisation.* Canberra: ABARE.

Serchuk, Alan. 2001. "Chinese Steel: Rousing the Phoenix." *Modern Metals* 57, no. 1: 32–43.

Simmons, Matthew. 2005. *Twilight in the Desert: The Coming Saudi Oil Shock and the World Economy.* Hoboken, NJ: John Wiley and Sons.

Sinocast. 2004. "Four Chinese Steel Makers Acquired Overseas Iron Mine Equity." March 3.

———. 2006. "CVRD Said to Be Suspect of Violating Negotiation Rules." May 26.

Skillings. 2008a. "Total 2007 World Steel Production." *Skillings Mining Review*, January 28.

———. 2008b. "Vale Settles Iron Ore Price." *Skillings Mining Review*, February 18.

———. 2008c. "China Studies Actions to Thwart BHP/Rio Combo." *Skillings Mining Review*, January 28.

———. 2008d. "Vale Settles Benchmark with Chinese Steelmaker." *Skillings Mining Review*, February 22.

———. 2008e. "Murchison, Midwest Agree to Merge; Sinosteel Still on Sidelines." *Skillings Mining Review*, May 27.

———. 2008f. "Iron Ore Talks Expected to Conclude Soon." *Skillings Mining Review*, June 3.

———. 2008g. "Rio, Small Chinese Mills Agree to 95% Iron Ore Price Hike. *Skillings Mining Review*, June 10.

———. 2008h. "BHP Billiton Monopolizes Bulk Carriers." *Skillings Mining Review*, June 3.

———. 2008i. "BHP Pushes Ship Charter Rates to Record." *Skillings Mining Review*, May 20.

Skillings Mining Review. 2006. "Brazilian Iron Miners Ask Government to Confront China." April 21.

Sorkin, Andrew Ross, and Jad Mouawad. 2005. "Bid by Chevron in Big Oil Deal Thwarts China." *New York Times*, July 20.

Todd, Daniel. 1996. "Coal Shipment from Northern China and its Implications for the Ports." *Dock and Harbour Authority* 76, no. 868: 49–58.

Tse Pui-Kwan. 2000. *The Mineral Industry of China*. Washington, D.C.: U.S. Geological Survey.

Van Ness, Peter. 2002. "Hegemony, Not Anarchy: Why China and Japan Are not Balancing U.S. Unipolar Power." *International Relations of the Asia-Pacific* 2, no. 1: 131–50.

Wailes, Graham. 2004. "Export Metallurgical Coal Mine Costs." *AusIMM Bulletin* 2: 44–45.

Watson, Nick. 2005. "China Helps Rosneft Pay for Yukos." *Thedeal.com*, January 24.

Wayne, Leslie, and David Barboza. 2005. "Unocal Deal: A Lot More Than Money Is at Issue." *New York Times*, June 24.

Werdigier, Julia, and David Lague. 2008. "Rio Tinto Rejects Latest Offer." *New York Times*, February 7.

Wilson, Alex. 2006. "Rio Tinto Doubles Annual Profit to US$5.2 Billion." *AAP Newsfeed*, February 2.

Xinhua. 2006. "China to Resist Iron Ore Price Increase at Global Negotiations." *Global News Wire*, February 17.

York, Geoffrey. 2004. "China Frantic for Energy Supplies." *Globe and Mail*, November 29.

Zweig, David, and Bi Jianhai. 2005. "China's Global Hunt for Energy." *Foreign Affairs* 84, no. 5: 25–38.

CHAPTER SEVEN

Sino-Russian Geoeconomic Integration

An Alternative to Chinese Hegemony on a Shrinking Planet

JOHN GULICK

For many years running, U.S. scholars of various stripes have contended that the ultimate challenge to U.S. primacy in the global system rests in the startling economic and military rise of China (Righter 2008). Proponents of this position come from myriad coordinates on the political grid. On the hawkish right, academics embedded in think tanks such as the International Institute for Strategic Studies depict China as an increasingly potent threat to U.S. military dominance over the maritime space of the western Pacific and geostrategic sea lanes elsewhere (Glaser and Skanderup 2005). In the establishment center, figures affiliated with august bodies such as the Council on Foreign Relations fret that China's already mighty economic clout and successful South-South diplomatic outreach is putting downward pressure on the global human-rights standards professed by the United States (Economy 2007b). On the liberal left, advocates of East Asian regionalism herald China's emergence as an economic pole of attraction and multilateral power broker, arguing that over the medium run it will probably yield a Sinocentric East Asian order (Feffer 2006). Finally, academics more openly disdainful of U.S. imperialism hold out hope that China is accruing the power needed to capsize U.S. primacy. In his latest magnum opus, Giovanni Arrighi spells out how the costly U.S. immobilization in Iraq and Afghanistan is both rendering it ever more reliant on Chinese subsidy of its current account deficit and freeing China to undertake ambitious trade, investment, and raw-materials–sourcing diplomacy in sub-Saharan Africa, Latin America, and Central and Southeast Asia (Arrighi 2007). China's unbroken twenty-five-year run of vigorous growth, its climbing of the research and development and production technology ladders, and its successful prosecution of commercial diplomacy (Kurlantzick 2007) have all compelled Arrighi to aver that China could very well be the seat of a coming East Asia–centered hegemonic regime (Arrighi 2007).

In so arguing, Arrighi sidelines a set of analytical observations he made more than ten years earlier in *The Long Twentieth Century*. This is unfortunate because these observations illuminate the serious barriers to China's ostensible hegemonic ascent and hence have special relevance today. In *The Long Twentieth Century*, Arrighi contends that as the global capitalist order matures through consecutive systemic cycles of accumulation (or hegemonies), contradictory structural trends mount. Foremost among these tensions is the increasing deficit of territorial scale and organizational resources that any hegemonic leader or aspirant enjoys relative to a world system that accretes new layers of complexity and interdependence with each successive cycle. The upshot is that with each new epoch, it becomes more difficult for a hegemonic power to orchestrate the institutional underpinnings of an expanded world system (Arrighi 1994: 32–33). Arrighi concludes not only that another round of world-system expansion will require leadership by actors harboring endowments exponentially greater than those harbored by their predecessors during the U.S.-anchored "long twentieth century" but also that the fabric of the world system has simply become too densely interwoven to accommodate hegemonic leadership by an entity that has not burst the fetters of the orthodox state form (Arrighi 1994: 32–33). In other words, in the years to come, political dominance in the world system will no longer be centered in the vehicle of a singular, territorially bounded state deploying superior financial, productive, military, or international rule- and norm-making capabilities.

Per Arrighi's acute insights of more than a decade ago, no candidate for hegemonic leadership today possesses the scale and capability endowments sufficient to engineer new conditions of global rule and accumulation in a more thickly layered world system—not even China. China boasts quasi-continental reach and an impressive portfolio of strengths. Among these strengths are a precipitously growing base of manufacturing capacity and, concomitantly, a precipitously growing share of global economic output (Glyn 2005), in the neighborhood of two trillion dollars of currency reserves (Li 2008: 22), and an increasingly potent arsenal of conventional and nuclear military forces (Righter 2008). But many of the traits that make China appear to be a viable hegemonic successor merit qualification. China's reputation as the world economy's workshop may be well deserved, but the World Bank's long overdue recalibration of comparative GDP measures shows that China is not the economic colossus that many have perceived and al-

ternately feared or celebrated (Mead 2007). Most of China's exports to core capitalist markets are "manufactured as foreign brands by foreign-owned companies . . . as part of cross-national production chains. . . . China pockets only a
small part of the gain" (Shirk 2007: 26; see also Hart-Landsberg and Burkett 2004:
13 and Harvey 2005: 124). Along the same lines, China's strides in breakthrough
technological innovations have been overblown (Engardio et al. 2007; Hart-
Landsberg 2008). The historic deflation of the U.S. housing bubble and the con-
comitant turmoil in U.S. financial markets and reversal of U.S. economic growth
have exposed the ultimate dependence of China's development model on the unsustainable debt-leveraged consumption of the United States (Hung 2008; Li
2008: 28–29); the gloomy economic forecast now haunting the PRC proves the
lie of the "decoupling" thesis, which lamely suggested that Chinese accumulation would churn along at its customary pace even if the economies of the Euro-
American capitalist core contracted (Hart-Landsberg 2008; Jacobs and Barboza
2008). China's hoard of foreign exchange may seem huge, but until Wall Street's
recent nosedive the sum of its value did not top the net assets of the largest mutual fund in the United States (Righter 2008). And despite the overheated rhetoric of Pentagon intelligence sources about China developing offensive naval and
airborne capabilities contesting U.S. military supremacy in the western Pacific,
China's military modernization campaign has focused on the simple development (and purchase) of assets enabling it to neutralize a U.S. intervention on behalf of Taiwan (Klare 2005; Negroponte 2007).

Moreover, nearly all scholarship favorably weighing the prospects of Chinese
hegemonic succession is essentially blind to the ways in which accumulation and
territorial pursuits in the world system are always already embedded in entropic
transformations of the natural environment by human society (Hornborg 2001;
Biel 2006; Clark and York 2008: 13). Past campaigns of capitalist power ascent
occurred during a geohistorically specific epoch when centuries of the world
system's material expansion had yet to strain unduly the biospheric conditions in-
visibly framing that very expansion; optimistic assessments of China's hegemonic
destiny typically overlook this. More to the point, these assessments all too often
neglect the ominous fact that perhaps the most fundamental of these biospheric
conditions, a heretofore oblique configuration of the carbon cycle, is eroding before our very eyes.[1] Ever since the widespread adoption of the coal-powered steam
engine in capitalist raw-material extraction, transport, and industry, it is the continuous increase in labor productivity that has propelled world-systemic expansion (Christie 1980: 16; Altvater 1998: 23–25). But this secular trend has itself been
rooted in a peculiar structuring of the carbon cycle, one allowing for a long se-

quence of sociotechnical revolutions in value production: a distinctive geophysical ensemble of ample supplies of commercially recoverable fossil energy resources (Alvater 2006: 42) combined with climates (in the meteorological sense) sufficiently stable and benign to encourage and reward the mobilization of wage labor-saving investment (Clark and York 2005: 403–409; Simms 2005). In an age of incipient "peak oil" and with runaway global warming now far from inconceivable, a growing cast of historical social scientists recognizes that this ensemble is vanishing (Grimes 1999; Foster 2005: 1–2; Li 2007: 2–3).

CHINA'S HEGEMONIC AMBITION?

The acknowledgment of this emergent reality is built on the latest and best findings of energy economists and climatologists. The customarily cautious International Energy Agency (IEA) has joined the chorus of sober energy economists (Cavallo 2005) who argue that within the next decade or so—and very possibly sooner—the total global output of conventional crude oil will plateau and then irreversibly decline (Foster 2008: 24–28; Klare 2008: 35–43). China's thirst for petroleum has played a significant role in this dawning era of socially induced oil scarcity. Since the turn of the century, it has accounted for between 30 and 40 percent of the total world increase in petroleum demand (Hatemi and Wedeman 2007: 104; Rachman 2008). Extrapolating from the recent past, the U.S. Energy Information Agency (EIA) envisions that by 2025, China's per capita oil consumption will triple (Hatemi and Wedeman 2007: 104). But in the wake of unanticipated global production shortfalls reported by the IEA and others, to be perfectly blunt, this scenario is a mirage.

A believable analysis of whether China's climb will proceed must entertain how plausible it will be for China to steer away from its previously projected levels of petroleum consumption growth, and in particular to source viable transportation fuel alternatives, one of oil's more stubbornly nonsubstitutable use values (Li 2007). Already the rapid conversion of world cropland and the diversion of water supplies from food to biofuel production have negatively impacted the diets and caloric intake of the Global South's landless and poor (Magdoff 2008: 3); China's winter 2008 of discontent, with popular protest related to hydrocarbon energy bottlenecks and food price hikes, may provide a glimpse of its very own bad future (Ford 2008). As for seeking nonpetroleum-based inputs for electricity generation, China will continue relying heavily on aggressive exploitation and oxidation of its domestic (and dirty brown) coal reserves (Wen and Li 2006: 141–42; Li 2008: 30). By augmenting China's substantial and rapidly escalating contribution to net global greenhouse emissions, this adjustment to looming "peak oil" will of course only further disrupt the carbon configuration that secretly underpinned centuries of world capitalist expansion (Economy 2007a). Considering that nearly every credible scientific study conducted since the Intergovernmental Panel on Climate Change's Fourth Assessment Report of 2007 suggests that anthropogenic climate forcing is unfolding more quickly and with graver consequences than previously understood (Hansen et al. 2008; Tin 2008), China's hewing to a largely coal-dependent energy regime should be cause for great alarm. This is all the more true from the perspective of China's own social stability. For example, the effects of climate change are already stirring up unrest by environmental refugees suffering from longer and more intense droughts and by antipollution protestors victimized by insufficiently flushed toxic waterways (Gulick 2007). In short, through the pathway of socioecological disorder engendered by industrial growth, China's ascent undercuts itself.

What is more, the preceding commentary tenuously assumes that the Chinese Communist Party (CCP) seeks to thrust China into the role of hegemonic power, with the attendant burden of managing the myriad contradictions of capital accumulation on a world scale. Will not China's ruling circles be more preoccupied for quite some time with the onerous task of resolving its own unresolved "agrarian question"—that is, how to balance the competing imperatives of adjusting China's economy to the global law of value and finding gainful employment for its swelling reserve army of rural surplus labor (Negroponte 2007)? The Hu-Wen leadership has launched several initiatives under the banner of the "new socialist countryside" to elevate lagging peasant incomes, thereby gearing China's development drive toward broadened internal demand (Aiyar 2007). But the jury is out as to whether this approach is working. The much-ballyhooed abolition of the agriculture tax in 2006 does little to ease the economic burdens on China's rural poor (French 2008). Although the state took 60 billion yuan in revenues from the tax in 2003, by 2005 many provinces had already phased it out. Even if the tax amounted to about 10 percent of the average farmer's income before it was eliminated, to this day farmers are still burdened with many illicit local taxes and levies (French 2008). This raises a fundamental question: will local party-state notables who have gotten rich through abusing their rural subjects—and whose disobedience of central-government directives aimed at alleviating social inequities has become legendary—tolerate, at their own expense, policies that try to improve the living standards of farmers (Engardio et al. 2007; French 2008; Righter 2008)?

Two other late-breaking factors promise to undermine party-state attempts to boost mass consumption in the countryside. One, the prospective de facto privatization of agricultural land use rights might make a significant number of enterprising peasants considerably wealthier, but the resulting consolidation of leased plots might also make an even larger share of peasants essentially landless and destitute (Andreas 2008: 133–34). Two, as thousands of urban coastal plants shutter their gates in the face of a global economic recession unseen since at least the 1980s and quite possibly since the 1930s (Landler 2008), millions of migrant workers are being laid off, depriving their rural families of much-needed remittance income (Wong 2008). Expending voluminous currency reserves on a $586 billion crash program of accelerated infrastructure building—effectively employing displaced smallholders and idled factory hands as hardhats—appears to be the party-state's preferred antidote (Barboza 2008). However, expert judgments differ on how willing and able PRC officialdom is to reorient economic output away from global supply chains, even in the midst of collapsing world demand for China's exports (Harvey 2005: 130–32; Walker and Buck 2007; Hart-Landsberg 2008).

If the Arrighi of *The Long Twentieth Century* is indeed correct in claiming that a reconstitution of the world system on new foundations will require its authors to wield exponentially greater economic resources and international authority, then this admittedly incomplete yet telling inventory of China's internal endowments relative to the global arena—including its geophysical attributes relative to world-historical time—suggests that it alone cannot spearhead such a reconstitution. Given China's limitations, its ongoing ascent is feasible if, and only if, it continues to draw upon complementary factors furnished by political and economic agencies who perceive that relieving China of its many burdens and assisting its upward trajectory yields net gains for all concerned. Who or what might these agencies be?

Even though it is quite commonplace to assert that the United States (especially the United States under George W. Bush's executive hand) has expedited China's rise (Wallerstein 2004; Palat 2005; Arrighi 2007), most scholars who examine this dynamic regard its outcome as unintended by the United States. Accordingly, they buy into the trope of a Sino-American geopolitics in which Chinese and U.S. interests are diametrically opposed. Given how intimately intertwined capital valorization processes in both the United States and China have become in the last decade (encased in the maxim "China earns and lends and the U.S. borrows and spends"), a case can be made that this picture is quite mistaken (Jones 2005: 108; Petras 2007).[2] Rather than signaling a deeply held hostility toward China's ascent per se, soundings of the "China threat" enunciated in Washington, D.C. may have the effect of ensuring that the two political economies interlock in a manner that prolongs rather than erodes U.S. centrality in the world system (Barma, Ratner, and Weber 2007; Paulson 2008). That is, although a menacing "China threat" discourse may issue from the Pentagon and kindred think tanks from time to time, its latent function may be the wresting of concessions from the CCP—regarding enforcement of copyrights and patents, for example—such that ongoing market reforms disproportionately advantage the U.S. Chamber of Commerce and U.S. financial institutions (McGregor 2005; Weisman 2006).

However, the extension of U.S. preeminence by structurally tying China's development model to Wall Street and the imperial dollar works only insofar as the populist-protectionist bloc in the United States plays the subordinate role of useful pawn on behalf of U.S. transnational capital, especially its financial wing (Petras 2005). Even though for many years the preponderant U.S. strategic stance toward China has accented the tactics of economic entanglement rather than those of military encirclement (Higgins 2004; Barma, Ratner, and Weber 2007; Bhadrakumar 2007), the PRC leadership now has solid grounds for worrying that the surprisingly commodious relationship it enjoyed with the United States during Bush's reign may be in jeopardy. Gathering evidence shows that a cross-class coalition of populists and protectionists has acquired enough independent momentum such that the "business internationalist" delegation in Washington can no longer manipulate the populist-protectionist bloc in support of its agenda (Hutzler 2006; Arrighi 2007: 295). The 2006 congressional races saw the election of a crop of "Lou Dobbs Democrats" sour on globalism, seeing globalism less as a benign vehicle of liberal market virtue than a malevolent force that strengthens China (or, at best, unpatriotic corporate betrayers of the national interest such as Wal-Mart) and enfeebles the United States (Weisberg 2006). Not coincidentally, the congressional session of 2007 featured the revival of pressure on China to cease its alleged "currency manipulation" or suffer trade sanctions; at the behest of Congress, the United States Trade Representative appealed to the World Trade Organization to get China to desist from its "illegal subsidies" to exporters (The Economist 2007a; Mekay 2007). The peculiar conjuncture of the worldwide financial panic and economic meltdown offers yet more fertile conditions for the augmentation of nationalist-populist and anti-PRC social forces in U.S. political culture. To be more specific, while the United States is rapidly hemorrhaging jobs, the international flight of capital to the ostensible safety of the U.S. Treasury is propping up the dollar and hence the value of the dollar vis à vis the yuan (Jacobs and Barboza 2008); the corresponding dissonance between massive U.S. employment losses and the persisting huge Chinese trade surplus with the United States is likely to amplify nationalist-protectionist voices all over the U.S. political

spectrum (Faiola and Cha 2008). Finally, the foremost domestic imperative con-
fronting the PRC—the stimulation of internal growth through public spending
on infrastructure—necessitates that the Bank of China reorder the PRC's economic model away from the underwriting of U.S. purchasing power by cautiously
but decisively reducing its investments in U.S. government securities (Norris 2007;
Bezlova 2008).

If recently revealed frailties in Sino-American economic interdependence further manifest themselves, toward which foreign sources of aggrandizement might
the Chinese valorization process increasingly orient itself in order to avert a severe and dangerous accumulation slowdown? Prior to their being stricken by
the financial contagion that originated in lower Manhattan and then engulfed
the global economy with lightning velocity (Davis 2008; Faiola and Cha 2008),
both Japan and the European Union seemed to be plausible candidates. In 2004,
for the first time since the United States initially draped East Asia in its Cold War
shadow, China and Japan became one another's top trading partners (Keliher
2004). Many observers foresee closer economic links leading to a lessening of
bilateral tensions, which will in turn expedite greater commercial ties. Some go
so far as to predict that successively broader and deeper economic links will spur
Chinese and Japanese ruling elites to collaborate in building pan–East Asian institutions for dealing with monetary cooperation and regional security issues independent of U.S. mediation (Palat 2005).[3] On the face of it, this is not a fanciful
proposition; after all, in the wake of the exchange rate volatility that has jolted
Northeast Asia, China and Japan (and South Korea) have expanded on the currency swap format put into place after financial and monetary instability last
swept over the region in 1997 and 1998 (Al Jazeera 2008). But nonetheless, to forecast that intensified commercial ties will eventuate in a grand geopolitical payoff
that marginalizes the United States is to be too formulaic. As R. Taggart Murphy
succinctly explains, evolving Sino-Japanese economic integration may do more
to accentuate than reduce Japan's geostrategic subordination to the U.S. im-
perium: "Japan's long postwar acquiescence to the status of an American protec-
torate is in part . . . due to the belief, held by much of Tokyo's political elite, that
the alternative to American protection is incorporation into a new Chinese Empire as a tributary state. As Japan's economic dependence on China deepens, the
rationale for an American counterweight becomes all the more obvious" (Murphy 2005: 58). For Japan to play a commensurate role in a truly independent
framework for coordinating East Asian affairs, it would have to assert its autonomy
from U.S. superintendence in a decisive way. Sixty years of being a pliant vassal
of U.S. imperialism has thoroughly encoded the genetic structure of Japanese

politics and society, and the constellation of political forces that could press for a radical break with the United States is almost entirely absent (MacCormack 2007).

China's central bank may be furtively and gradually shifting currency reserves into euro-denominated instruments, but in many fields Sino-European tensions resemble and even exceed Sino-American tensions. If anything, European small manufacturers and what is left of the European workers' movement are more fiercely opposed to Europe being turned into a sales floor for consumer goods made in China than their U.S. counterparts are opposed to the "Wal-Marting" of the United States (*The Economist* 2007b). In an episode resembling the U.S. furor over the Chinese National Overseas Oil Company's proposed takeover of the Unocal Corporation, China Development Bank's bid to participate in the buyout of the British bank Barclays PLC spurred the European Union to contemplate measures prohibiting takeovers by "politically motivated buyers" from the developing world (Singer et al. 2007). Furthermore, the tide of electoral politics in most EU countries is not in China's favor. For example, like most putative neoliberals the world over, President Nicolas Sarkozy of France is not a consistent and principled defender of the free market. Sarkozy may rail against France's antiquated welfare state, but he also steadfastly holds to an industrial policy that will protect the markets and assets of French and EU "champions" against Chinese penetration (Pfaff 2007). And to the sensibilities of many Chinese, the European Union is an even more obnoxious purveyor of hypocritical human rights imperialism than the United States, epitomized by the pro-Tibetan protests that interrupted the Beijing Olympics torch procession in Sarkozy's France (Anderson 2002; Bennhold 2008).

EMERGING SINO-RUSSIAN PARTNERSHIP IN THE 1990S

Rather than pursue the elusive grail of global hegemony in the face of the aforementioned impasses, China might instead transform its strengthened "strategic partnership" with Russia into genuine geoeconomic integration. More than most critical scholars have acknowledged, from the latter half of the 1990s forward, U.S. geostrategy has largely been geared toward boxing in the ostensible regional ambitions of bureaucratic capitalist China and seizing on postcommunist Russia's disarray to prevent it from regaining sway over its "near abroad" (Johnson 1999: 44–51; Achcar 2000: 109–11; Klare 2006). The perennial challenge facing foreign policy makers in Washington has been executing this two-pronged strategy in a manner that does not drive the Asian giants into a permanent embrace (Achcar 2000: 111); the difficulty of pulling off this high-wire act was proven during the eight years that the administration of George W. Bush held power. The aggressive antics of U.S. imperialism in Central and Western Asia have made it plain to both China and Russia that the pillars of U.S. geostrategy include controlling China's access to sources of imported oil and controlling Russia's access to markets for exported hydrocarbons. But the blatant geopolitical maneuvering of the United States in and around the Persian Gulf and the Caspian Basin may eventuate precisely what U.S. post–Cold War geostrategy avows to prevent—a potential alliance between two powers with combined resources and credibility sufficient to challenge U.S. global primacy (Gowan 2006).

Entering the 1990s, China and Russia alike were preoccupied with adjusting their geopolitical orientations and political economies to the dawning of the post–Cold War era, its trademark feature being the victory of capitalist globalization under revived U.S. leadership. Its once-despised Soviet rival radically weakened by permanent stagnation and political turmoil in the Baltic republics, China looked to counterbalance magnified U.S. global hegemony by building on the normalization of Sino-Soviet diplomatic relations put in motion by Gorbachev (Ferdinand 2007b: 842). In 1994, the bilateral relationship was officially dubbed a "constructive partnership" (Garnett 2001: 46). Barred from the Western market in arms, China quickly established itself as the top customer of Russian military hardware (Achcar 2000: 130; Deng 2002: 130). As control over U.S. East Asian policy passed from a Commerce Department bent on mercantilist brinkmanship with Japan to rabidly anti-PRC Republicans in Congress, the incentive for China to solidify its partnership with Russia grew (Castro 2000: 210). No longer predicated on the rudimentary norms of mere peaceful coexistence—vowing to settle differences amicably, respecting one another's internal affairs, and so on (Wishnick 2001: 104–5)—the Sino-Russian relationship increasingly became informed by a joint wariness of U.S. "hegemonism" (Gittings 2000: 399).

Russia and especially China were now irrevocably entangled in a world capitalist order in which access to some combination of U.S. finance, investment, and markets was important to their flourishing or at least survival. At the same time, neither stood to benefit from participating in an order in which U.S.-dictated rules and actions determined the terms of engagement. In other words, Beijing and Moscow both wanted a fluid global system enhancing the welfare of all imperial and subimperial stakeholders rather than one consisting of a dominant United States and subordinate deputies doing its bidding (Achcar 2000: 132–33). Consequently, in 1996, Beijing and Moscow upgraded their constructive partnership to a "strategic partnership . . . of mutual coordination directed towards the 21st Century." By letting Washington know that their global capitalist incorporation neither precluded horizontal relationship building nor equaled acceptance of a world system privileging the United States, China and Russia's declaration of the strategic partnership tried to establish more equilibrating balance in the U.S.-China-Russia "triangle" (Wishnick 2001: 126; Deng 2002: 119; Cheng 2004: 484). This strategic move also attempted to promote a system of global governance grounded in principles that, if observed, would inhibit U.S. geopolitical freedom of maneuver. More precisely, it emphasized the sovereign equality of the big powers, their right to territorial integrity, and international conflict resolution that paid deference to the consensual decision making of the UN Security Council (Lo 2004: 296; Wang 2006: 25; Ferdinand 2007b: 860). In line with this, China vowed to remain silent about Russia's ruthless war against Chechen separatists. Russia in turn pledged its opposition to Taiwan publicly pronouncing its independence (Wishnick 2001: 126–27; Lo 2004: 296) and sold China destroyers, antiship missiles, and air defense systems for the explicit purpose of blunting U.S. intervention on behalf of a breakaway Taiwan (Achcar 2000: 131–32; Garnett 2001: 45). Later in the decade, both countries upbraided the United States for bypassing UN Security Council authorization and goading NATO into the bombing of Serbia (Achcar 2000: 131–32; Wang 2006: 25). The devastating effect to which U.S. smart bombs were used in Serbia also further convinced Chinese military officials of the necessity to upgrade their arsenal (Gittings 2000: 398), and Russian arms producers and sellers were more than eager to oblige (Deng 2002: 130). However, despite the ratcheting up of Sino-Russian coordination in the geopolitical sphere, bilateral trade figures fell far short of the U.S. $20 billion mark optimistically envisaged early in the 1990s (Wishnick 2001: 131–33). Grand issues of international power politics defined the scope of the strategic partnership; neither Beijing nor Moscow was willing to make pecuniary sacrifices that would give the partnership complementary economic substance (Wishnick 2001: 153; Kerr 2005: 417).

ACCELERATING SINO-RUSSIAN INTEGRATION IN THE POST-9/11 WORLD

When George W. Bush assumed office, an administration populated with neo-conservatives and hawks accentuated China's emergence as a surefire threat to the politico-military position of the United States in East Asia, rather than the virtues of commercial entanglement. Accordingly, the 2001 Quadrennial Defense Review reclassified China as a "strategic competitor" (Wang 2006: 9). Prior to September 11, this more aggressive U.S. posture toward China induced deeper

Sino-Russian cooperation. In June 2001, China, Russia, and four Central Asian states officially formed the Shanghai Cooperation Organization (SCO), a forum to address common dangers to regional stability (especially Islamist irredentist movements), which served as an illustrious example of the multilateral problem management void of U.S. participation (Kerr 2005: 415; Wang 2006: 24). This was followed in July 2001 by Beijing and Moscow inking the "Treaty of Good Neighborliness and Friendly Cooperation," a pact reaffirming their commitment to a multipolar international order (Garnett 2001: 41). To defense intellectuals in Washington, these developments constituted proof positive that the Sino-Russian partnership was acquiring a distinctly anti-U.S. hue (Garnett 2001: 41).

Initially, the opportunistic response of the United States to the attacks of September 11 impacted the Sino-Russian strategic partnership by weakening it. By lending their support to the idea of a long-term, U.S.-led international operation against fundamentalist Muslim terrorism, both Beijing and Moscow put themselves in a reactive mode in which narrow individual calculations trumped their joint interests (Ferdinand 2007b: 854). In some respects, both Russia and China were trying to make the best of a new situation, turning the "global war on terror" declared by the United States into a chance to gain some ground against ethnoreligious separatist insurgencies that had long troubled their southern and western perimeters, respectively (Anderson 2002: 14). But both were significantly more inclined than they had been just a few months earlier to cut separate deals with the United States, each scrambling to take advantage of bold new security gambits rolling out of Washington. The opening act of the U.S. "long war" in the world of radical Islamic strongholds, the attempted dislodging of the Taliban from Afghanistan, involved the United States getting the Kremlin's express permission to lease military bases in Uzbekistan and Kyrgyzstan and to secure flyover rights from other former Soviet republics (Lanteigne 2004). During the waning months of 2001, op-ed pages in the trans-Atlantic realm resounded with visions of Russia maturing into the advanced capitalist West's most reliable supplier of suitably priced oil, soon to displace the Wah'habist-ridden emirates of the Persian Gulf (Trilling 2002). British Prime Minister Tony Blair even entertained the fanciful notion of allowing Russia to play a "consult and advise" role within NATO (Trilling 2002; Lanteigne 2004: 6). Moreover, even though hostility to a missile defense scheme was a point of unity between Beijing and Moscow at their summit of a mere half-year earlier (Cheng 2004: 487; Lanteigne 2004: 7), Putin did not raise much of a fuss when the United States "rewarded" Russia for its obeisance in Central Asia by unilaterally withdrawing from the ABM Treaty, which forbade signatories from implementing antiballistic missile weaponry (Lo 2004:

305; Ferdinand 2007b: 844). Russia's serial gifts to the United States portended a nascent quid pro quo between Moscow and Washington, suggesting that in the unfolding post–September 11 era, the United States could successfully cultivate ties with Russia, which it could then use to pressure China on a variety of fronts (Cheng 2004: 488; Lo 2004: 299).

China's top decision makers may have been dismayed by the degree to which Russia had acquiesced on a host of issues to the advanced capitalist West in general and the United States in particular. However, most intuitively understood this as a tactical retreat rather than a strategic capitulation on the part of Russia, an adjustment that did not represent a sundering of the Russo-Chinese partnership (Rozman 2004: 336; Kerr 2005: 419). After all, Beijing itself had hopped aboard the "global war on terror" express, not least because for all the success of its "self-strengthening" program—the core element of which was economic modernization through sequenced world market integration—the CCP could not brook overt confrontation with its largest export market and a leading source of its foreign capital, the United States (Kerr 2005: 414; Wang 2006: 9, 15). In any event, the short-lived U.S. courtship of Russia did nothing to depress Chinese and Russian aspirations that bilateral trade would constitute a more prominent part of their strategic partnership. With the deliberate aim of expanding Sino-Russian trade relations, on several occasions in 2001 and 2002 China and Russia hosted high-level trade delegations (Rozman 2004: 334–36). Crucially for the cause of Sino-Russian economic integration, by the early 2000s the value of Chinese joint ventures with Russian firms in the Russian Far East had surpassed that of Japan, South Korea, and the United States combined (Brooke 2004). And as 2002 unfolded, the faction in the Kremlin that had counseled the Putin administration to offer concessions to the advanced capitalist West lost its stature, embarrassed by the high-handedness of a United States that added to the insult of ripping up the ABM Treaty the injury of negotiating an arms "reduction" agreement with Russia in which it was allowed to mothball, rather than destroy, its nuclear warheads (Trilling 2002; Kerr 2005: 419).

However much the strategic partnership wavered in the immediate post–September 11 environment, it got back on track (and then some) as a result of the Bush administration's determination to invade and occupy Iraq despite the strenuous objections of the vast majority of international civil society, which included the rather more tepid objections of Russia and China themselves (Wang 2006: 25). The U.S.-led campaign flouted all of the principles underlying the partnership. The United States flagrantly disrespected the consultative mechanisms of the UN Security Council, rushed to war to advantage its own narrow imperial interests, and cynically deployed "democracy promotion" and "human rights" rhetoric strongly distasteful to both Beijing and Moscow (Deng 2002: 120–21). Russian officials may have been mildly disappointed by China's reluctance to take a vocal stand against the blatant U.S. violation of international law, but Russia's decision to side with France and Germany in opposing unabashed U.S. unilateralism was sufficient evidence to convince Chinese officials that Russia had abandoned hopes of courting U.S. favor (Ferdinand 2007b: 849). Once the deepening of the Sino-Russian strategic partnership was back on the agenda, the growing U.S. immobilization in the quagmire of post-Saddam Iraq allowed China and Russia the leeway to do so without inviting the heavy sanction of the United States (Yang 2003). The United States could scarcely afford to confront China outright over its resuming deeper cooperation with Russia; after all, China was effectively paying the freight for the increasingly costly U.S. imperial adventures by means of its increasingly voluminous purchase of U.S. Treasury securities (Arrighi 2005: 76). By 2005, through their SCO mouthpiece, China and Russia were demanding that the United States draft a plan to end its airbase leases in Kyrgyzstan and Uzbekistan (Wang 2006: 25). Even more provocatively, their militaries conducted joint war-gaming exercises ("Friendship 2005") for the first time since the Sino-Soviet split of the late 1950s, with a repeat performance in 2007 (Wang 2006: 26; Ferdinand 2007b: 854). Meanwhile, in 2004, Sino-Russian trade surpassed the long-sought mark of $20 billion (a fourfold increase over 1999; Lo 2004: 297) and is expected to approach $60 billion by the end of the decade (Lomanov 2005). Economic transactions once limited mostly to Chinese consumer goods and foodstuffs in exchange for Russian armaments and natural resources increasingly diversified (Lo 2004: 297). Take, for example, Akademgorodok, a Soviet-era suburb of Novosibirsk, home to fifty-two scientific institutes and some eighteen thousand scientists, including half a dozen Nobel Prize winners. Eighty percent of Akademgorodok's income derives from filling Chinese orders for everything from wind tunnels and soil analyzers to lasers, DNA labs, and electron accelerators (Matthews and Nemtsova 2006).

It would still be fair to say that Russia and China each values the strategic partnership partly because tighter bilateral links bolster their leverage in their respective individual dealings with the "indispensable" United States (Lo 2004: 299; Rozman 2004: 332–38; Ferdinand 2007b: 866). For example, as the Pentagon and the U.S. Congress in 2005 ratcheted up demagogic rhetoric about China's supposed expansionist ambitions in the western Pacific (Klare 2006; Wang 2006: 10), its central bank's so-called manipulation of the value of the yuan, and other alleged misbehaviors, China's diplomatic corps gamely played the Russo-Chinese strategic partnership card to prompt the militarist and protectionist wing of the U.S. ruling class to dial down its complaints (Petras 2005). Yet as it were inadvertently, a threshold of mutual trust between Russia and China appears to have been crossed, and changing world-systemic realities have increasingly placed the strategic partnership on a footing independent of the imperative for each big Asian power to triangulate against the United States (Lo 2004: 306–7). Perhaps top among these realities is the nakedness with which the bipartisan U.S. security establishment now displays its resolve to prolong U.S. global primacy in the face of China's rise and Russia's resurgence (Cheng 2004: 485–86). The more nakedly these tactics reveal U.S. imperial resolve, the more compelling becomes the Russian and Chinese attraction to one another, notwithstanding China's and Russia's distinctly modest and nonrevolutionary goals of being accorded roles in the transnational capitalist order commensurate with their civilizational weight (Achcar 2005; Trenin 2007). U.S. foreign policy opinion across the spectrum currently insists that the "authoritarian capitalisms" of China and Russia represent a serious threat to the international community of "free and democratic countries" because of their mutual disrespect for economic liberalism and accountable government at home and their blasé attitude toward nuclear proliferation abroad (Kagan 2006; Gat 2007). This resolve prevails even though China's and Russia's ruling cliques embrace the distinctly nonrevolutionary goals of forging deeper global economic integration and incubating yet more dollar billionaires who faithfully attend the annual World Economic Forum, while simultaneously aiming to contain the socioeconomic contradictions of this project by keeping the nouveau riche bourgeoisie politically dependent and the popular masses quiescent through nationalist posturing and moderate doses of welfare spending (Kagarlitsky 2004; Ferdinand 2007a: 671–76).

Once world energy prices began to climb out of their fifteen-year trough in 2000, Russia's plan for bouncing back from the catastrophe of the 1990s hinged on the state reclaiming command over hydrocarbon export policy in a time of tight world energy markets (Lavelle 2004). However, as Russo-American relations began to deteriorate after the short-lived honeymoon of late 2001, the United States began to ratchet up geopolitical pressure on Russia's western flank (Cohen 2006). U.S. aid to "color revolutions" in Georgia and Ukraine, the proposed extension of NATO to Russia's front porch, and the agenda to shield the Czech Republic and Poland with antiballistic missiles all clearly signaled to the Kremlin U.S. intent to create a belt of satellites poised between Russia and its prosperous energy customers in Central and Western Europe (Trenin 2007). The U.S. gambit to surround Russia may have suffered a temporary setback when Georgia,

Washington's wildcat client in the Caucasus, picked a fight with Russia in South Ossetia it was doomed to lose; the refusal of the European Union to one-sidedly condemn Russia's short-lived march into Georgia added to the apparent failure of U.S. geostrategy (Wallerstein 2008). Bear in mind, however, that prior to this incident both the U.S.-abetted "color revolutions" and a further round of NATO expansion received EU backing (Trenin 2007). Bear in mind also that one of the top foreign policy priorities of the new team in the White House is rehabilitating the frayed Euro-American alliance so that the containing of Russia can proceed with renewed multilateral legitimacy (Consortiumnews.com 2008). The sum of these events should reaffirm Russia's understanding that it must seek ever more avidly to cultivate primary-energy-starved China as the client that will salvage its hydrocarbon-exporting development model (Saunders 2006).

On the flip side of the equation in China, political stability depended on the continuation of high-speed GDP growth, as had long been the case in the era of economic reform. More than ever before, however, this high-speed growth in turn depended on China's importing progressively greater volumes of natural gas and oil. The U.S. grand scheme to impose neoliberal democracies by force in West Asia, be its result imperial victory or regional chaos, signaled to China the necessity of reducing its reliance on Persian Gulf sources of oil and gas, thrusting energy-resource cooperation with Russia to the forefront (Kerr 2005: 417). By 2005 and 2006, China had increasing reason to suspect that the United States had undertaken the (by now disastrous) Iraq incursion precisely to gain leverage over China's meteoric rise. The rhetoric emanating from Washington became more bellicose, and at the same time the Pentagon concluded a burden-sharing agreement with the Japanese military allowing the United States to forward position more troops, nuclear-powered submarines, and long-range bombers at the edge of China's Pacific perimeter (Klare 2006; Wang 2006: 10–12). It is hardly a mystery why such provocations would drive China to value its strategic partnership with Russia all the more forcefully, especially when the relationship is predicated on solidarity against the United States because it is likely to push the envelope in exactly this manner. Not least among the concrete elements of the partnership is a putative commitment by Russia to assist China in its quest to meet its exploding demand for primary energy imports (Kerr 2005).

Fast-forward to today. As the bad mortgage-debt crisis winds out from Wall Street to envelop the entire world-system, tapping larger proportions of its hydrocarbon imports from Asian Russia acquires even greater urgency for China. While one paradoxical effect of the global metastasizing of the crisis has been the rallying of the dollar, the medium-range prognosis for the dollar's strength is not good. Presupposing the likelihood that the dollar is forced to adjust downwards in line with the diminishing financial preeminence of the United States, China will be moved to avoid a repeat performance of 2007 and early 2008, when the plummeting dollar raised the bill for its dollar-invoiced oil and gas imports and provoked consumer panic and social instability (Bezlova 2007). To ensure that the construction of the East Siberian Pacific Ocean (ESPO) pipeline from the trans-Baikal to the Far East will allow China to receive fifty million tons of petroleum (fully one-third of its import needs) by 2010—more than ever before—it is imperative for China to cozy up to Russia (Ferdinand 2007b: 851–52). By guaranteeing credit to a Russian hydrocarbon sector suddenly starved for capital by global debt deflation, China has virtually guaranteed that the second leg of the ESPO pipeline will terminate on northeastern Chinese soil (Helmer 2008). While the orchestrated cooperation of China and Russia originated largely as a defensive buffer against the reckless "hegemonism" of the United States, the mere fact of their strategic collaboration validates the growing perception of some in the U.S. power elite that the two Asian giants proactively constitute the greatest danger to a liberal international order (Lobe 2006). U.S. aggressions and provocations on the extremities of the contiguous Sino-Russian landmass convince China and Russia, in turn, that bolstering their strategic partnership with economic cooperation, especially in the critical sphere of developing and delivering hydrocarbon energy resources, is the prudent choice.

NOTES

1. There are salutary exceptions, such as Li (2008).

2. Jones colorfully likens the mutual dependence of China and the United States to a "tight embrace, performing a minuet which is part dance of death."

3. Palat limns a more sophisticated version of this argument, maintaining that China's rise as an East Asian economic power attenuates regional fears of recrudescent Japanese imperialism; thus, overlapping and complementary Japanese and Chinese trade and investment networks in East Asia as a whole boost the possibilities of autochthonous regional monetary and even security cooperation.

REFERENCES

Achcar, Gilbert. 2000. "The Strategic Triad: USA, China, Russia." In *Masters of the Universe*, ed. Tariq Ali, 99–144. London: Verso.

——. 2005. "China: Capitalist Superpower?" *IV Online Magazine*, June. Available at www.internationalviewpoint.org/spip.php?article827, accessed November 15, 2008.

Aiyar, Pallavi. 2007. "China: More Rights for Millionaires." *Asia Times Online*, March 22. Available at www.atimes.com/atimes/China/IC22Ad01.html, accessed November 15, 2008.

Al Jazeera. 2008. "Economic Crisis Unites Asian Giants." December 13. Available at http://english.aljazeera.net/news/asia-pacific/2008/12/200812138361719177.html, accessed December 13, 2008.

Altvater, Elmar. 1998. "Global Order and Nature." In *Political Ecology: Global and Local*, ed. David Bell, Leesa Fawcett, Roger Keil, and Peter Penz, 19–45. London: Routledge.

——. 2006. "The Social and Natural Environment of Fossil Capitalism." In *Socialist Register 2007: Coming to Terms with Nature*, ed. Leo Panitch and Colin Leys, 37–59. London: Merlin.

Anderson, Perry. 2002. "Force and Consent." *New Left Review* 17: 5–30.

Andreas, Joel. 2008. "Changing Colours in China." *New Left Review* 54: 123–42.

Arrighi, Giovanni. 1994. *The Long Twentieth Century: Money, Power, and the Origins of Our Times*. London: Verso.

——. 2005. "Hegemony Unravelling." Part 1. *New Left Review* 32: 23–80.

——. 2007. *Adam Smith in Beijing: Lineages of the Twenty-First Century*. London: Verso.

Barboza, David. 2008. "China Unveils Sweeping Plan for Economy." *New York Times*, November 10.

Barma, Naazneen, Ely Ratner, and Steven Weber. 2007. "A World without the West." *National Interest online*, July 1. Available at www.nationalinterest.org/General .aspx?id=92&id2=14798, accessed November 15, 2008.

Bennhold, Katrin. 2008. "Paris Mounts Diplomatic Charm Offensive to Mollify China." *International Herald Tribune*, April 21. Available at www.iht.com/bin/ printfriendly.php?id=12200062, accessed April 21, 2008.

Bezlova, Antoaneta. 2007. "Economy—China: Jittery as Fuel Prices Rise." *InterPress Service*, November 14. Available at http://ipsnews.net/print.asp?idnews=40046, accessed November 15, 2008.

——. 2008. "Balking at Changing Dollar-Centric Economic Order." *InterPress Service*, November 14. Available at www.ipsnews.net/print.asp?idnews=44800, accessed November 22, 2008.

Bhadrakumar, M. K. 2007. "China Begins to Define the Rules." *Asia Times Online*, January 20. Available at www.atimes.com/atimes/China/IA20Ad03.html, accessed April 9, 2008.

Biel, Robert. 2006. "The Interplay between Social and Ecological Degradation in the Development of the International Political Economy." *Journal of World-Systems Research* 12, no. 1: 109–47.

Brooke, James. 2004. "Russia Catches China Fever." *New York Times*, March 30, W1.

Cavallo, Alfred. 2005. "Oil: Caveat Empty." *Bulletin of Atomic Scientists* 61, no. 3: 16–18.

Cheng, Joseph Y. S. 2004. "Challenges to China's Russia Policy in Early 21st Century." *Journal of Contemporary Asia* 34, no. 4: 480–502.

Christie, Renfrew. 1980. "Why Does Capital Need Energy?" In *Oil and Class Struggle*, ed. Petter Nore and Terisa Turner. London: Zed.

Clark, Brett, and Richard York. 2005. "Carbon Metabolism: Global Capitalism, Climate Change, and the Biospheric Rift." *Theory and Society* 34: 391–438.

———. 2008. "Rifts and Shifts: Getting to the Root of Environmental Crises." *Monthly Review* 60, no. 6: 13–24.

Cohen, Stephen. 2006. "The New American Cold War." *The Nation*, June 21, 9.

Consortiumnews.com. 2008. "Obama and U.S.-Russia Tensions." December 14. Available at www.consortiumnews.com/Print/2008/121408a.html, accessed December 15, 2008.

Davis, Mike. 2008. "Can Obama See the Grand Canyon?" TomDispatch.com, October 15. Available at www.tomdispatch.com/post/174989, accessed December 16, 2008.

De la Castro, Renato Cruz. 2000. "Whither Geoeconomics?" *Asian Affairs, An American Review* 24, no. 4: 201–21.

Deng Peng. 2002. "Embracing the Polar Bear? Sino-Russian Relations in the 1990s." *Journal of Third World Studies* 19, no. 2: 113–39.

The Economist. 2007a. "Lost in Translation: China and U.S. Trade." May 17.

———. 2007b. "The World Does Not Shake China," December 1–7, 34–36.

Economy, Elizabeth. 2007a. "China Vs. Earth." *The Nation*, May 7. Available at www.thenation.com/doc/20070507/economy, accessed November 15, 2008.

———. 2007b. "China's Missile Message." *Washington Post*, January 25, A25. Available at www.washingtonpost.com/wp-dyn/content/article/2007/01/24/AR2007012401646 .html, accessed November 15, 2008.

Engardio, Pete, Dexter Roberts, Frederik Balfour, and Bruce Einhorn. 2007. "Broken China." *Business Week*, July 23. Available at www.businessweek.com/magazine/ content/07_30/b4043001.htm, accessed November 15, 2008.

Faiola, Anthony, and Ariana Eunjung Cha. 2008. "Downturn Choking Global Commerce." *Washington Post*, December 11, A01.

Feffer, John. 2006. "China and the Uses of Uncertainty." *Foreign Policy in Focus*, December 12. Available at www.fpif.org/fpiftxt/3781, accessed November 15, 2008.

Ferdinand, Peter. 2007a. "Russia and China: Converging Responses to Globalization." *International Affairs* 83, no. 4: 655–80.

———. 2007b. "Sunset, Sunrise: China and Russia Construct a New Relationship." *International Affairs* 83, no. 5: 841–67.

Ford, Peter. 2008. "China Battles Rising Prices, Snowstorms." *Christian Science Monitor*, February 1. Available at www.csmonitor.com/2008/0201/p01s01-woap.html, accessed November 15, 2008.

Foster, John Bellamy. 2005. "Organizing Ecological Revolution." *Monthly Review* 57, no. 5: 1–10.

———. 2008. "Peak Oil and Energy Imperialism." *Monthly Review* 60, no. 3: 12–33.

French, Howard. 2008. "Lives of Poverty, Untouched by China's Boom." *New York Times*, January 13.

Garnett, Sherman. 2001. "Challenges of the Sino-Russian Strategic Partnership." *Washington Quarterly* 24, no. 4: 41–54.

Gat, Azar. 2007. "The Return of Authoritarian Great Powers." *Foreign Affairs* 86, no. 4. Available at www.foreignaffairs.org/20070701faessay86405/azar-gat/the-return-of-authoritarian-great-powers.html, accessed November 15, 2008.

Gittings, John. 2000. "The China Card." In *Masters of the Universe,* ed. Tariq Ali, 397–402. London: Verso.

Glaser, Bonnie S., and Jane Skanderup. 2005. "U.S.-China Relations: Disharmony Signals End to Post–Sept. 11 Honeymoon." *Comparative Connections* 7, no. 2: 27–42.

Glyn, Andrew. 2005. "Imbalances of the Global Economy." *New Left Review* 34: 5–37.

Gowan, Peter. 2006. "A Radical Realist." *New Left Review* 41: 127–37.

Grimes, Peter. 1999. "The Horsemen and the Killing Fields: The Final Contradiction of Capitalism." In *Ecology and the World-System,* ed. Walter Goldfrank, David Goodman, and Andrew Szasz, 13–42. Westport, CT: Greenwood Press.

Gulick, John. 2007. "Socio-Ecological Instability in China." *Peace Review* 19: 315–22.

Hansen, James, Makiko Sato, Pushker Kharecha, David Beerling, Robert Berner, Valerie Masson-Delmotte, Mark Pagani, Maureen Raymo, Dana L. Royer, and James C. Zachos. 2008. "Target Atmospheric CO_2: Where Should Humanity Aim?" *Open Atmospheric Science Journal* 2: 217–31.

Hart-Landsberg, Martin. 2008. "The Realities of China Today." *Against the Current,* November/December. Available at www.solidarity-us.org/node/1940, accessed November 15, 2008.

Hart-Landsberg, Martin, and Paul Burkett. 2004. "China and Socialism: Market Reforms and Class Struggle." *Monthly Review* 56, no. 3: 7–123.

Harvey, David. 2005. *A Brief History of Neoliberalism.* Oxford, UK: Oxford University Press.

Hatemi, Peter, and Andrew Wedeman. "Oil and Conflict in Sino-American Relations." *China Security* 3, no. 3: 95–118.

Helmer, John. 2008. "China Ties Up Russia's Crude—Again." *Asia Times Online,* November 1. Available at www.atimes.com/atimes/China_Business/JK01Cb01.html, accessed December 10, 2008.

Higgins, Andrew. 2004. "As China Surges, It Also Proves a Buttress to American Strength." *Wall Street Journal,* January 2004.

Hornborg, Alf. 2001. *The Power of the Machine.* Walnut Creek, CA: Altamira.

Hung Ho-fung. 2008. "Rise of China and the Global Overaccumulation Crisis." *Review of International Political Economy* 15, no. 2: 149–79.

Hutzler, Charles. 2006. "China Anticipates Bumpy Road with U.S." *Associated Press Wire Service,* November 9. Available at http://news.yahoo.com/s/ap/20061109/ap_on_re_as/china_us_elections, accessed November 11, 2006.

Jacobs, Andrew, and David Barboza. "Unexpected Drop in China's Imports and Exports." *New York Times,* December 11.

Johnson, Chalmers. 1999. "In Search of a New Cold War." *Bulletin of the Atomic Scientists* 55, no. 5: 44–51.

Jones, Mark. 2005. "Battle of the Titans." In *The Final Energy Crisis*, ed. Andrew McKillop and Sheila Newman, 105–15. Pluto Press: London.

Kagan, Robert. 2006. "League of Dictators?" *Washington Post*, April 30, B7.

Kagarlitsky, Boris. 2004. "The Russian State in the Age of American Empire." In *Socialist Register 2005: The Empire Reloaded*, ed. Leo Panitch and Colin Leys, 271–83. London: Merlin Press.

Keliher, Macabe. 2004. "Replacing U.S. in Asian Export Market." *Asia Times Online*, February 11. Available at www.atimes.com/atimes/China/FB11Ad01.html, accessed November 15, 2008.

Kerr, David. 2005. "The Sino-Russian Partnership and U.S. Policy toward North Korea: From Hegemony to Concert in East Asia." *International Studies Quarterly* 49: 411–37.

Klare, Michael. 2005. "Revving Up the China Threat." *The Nation*, October 24. Available at www.thenation.com/doc/20051024/klare, accessed November 15, 2008.

——. 2006. "Containing China." *TomDispatch*, April 18. Available at www.tom dispatch.com/index.mhtml?pid=78021, accessed November 15, 2008.

——. 2008. *Rising Powers, Shrinking Planet*. New York: Metropolitan Books.

Kurlantzick, Joshua. 2007. *Charm Offensive: How China's Soft Power Is Transforming the World*. New Haven: Yale University Press.

Landler, Mark. 2008. "Dire Forecast for Global Economy and Trade." *New York Times*, December 10.

Lanteigne, Marc. 2004. "Uncertain Ground: Sino-Russian Strategic Relations and Shifts in Great Power Politics." Paper presented at the 45th Annual International Studies Association (ISA) Conference in Montreal, Canada.

Lavelle, Peter. 2004. "What Does Putin Want?" *Current History* 103: 314–18.

Li Minqi. 2007. "Capitalism with Zero Profit Rate? Limits to Growth and the Law of the Tendency of the Rate of Profit to Fall." University of Utah Department of Economics Working Paper Series, no. 2007–05. Available at www.econ.utah.edu/ activities/papers/2007_05.pdf, accessed November 15, 2008.

——. 2008. "An Age of Transition: The United States, China, Peak Oil, and the Demise of Neoliberalism." *Monthly Review* 59, no. 11: 20–34.

Lo Bobo. 2004. "The Long Sunset of Strategic Partnership: Russia's Evolving China Policy." *International Affairs* 80, no. 2: 295–309.

Lobe, Jim. 2006. "Hawks Looking for New and Bigger Enemies?" *InterPress Service*, May 5. Available at http://ipsnews.net/news.asp?idnews=33143, accessed November 15, 2008.

Lomanov, Aleksandr. 2005. "China's Hu in Russia for Summit." *Vremya novostei*, July 1.

MacCormack, Gavan. 2007. *Client State: Japan in the American Embrace*. London and New York: Verso Press.

Magdoff, Fred. 2008. "The World Food Crisis: Sources and Solutions." *Monthly Review* 60, no. 1: 1–15.

Matthews, Owen, and Anna Nemtsova. 2006. "Russia: Putin's China Problem." *Newsweek International*, March 27.

McGregor, James. 2005. "Advantage, China." *Washington Post*, July 31.

Mead, Walter Russell. 2007. "The Great Fall of China." *Los Angeles Times*, December 30.

Mekay, Emad. 2007. "Play by the Rules, Washington Tells China." *InterPress Service*, February 2. Available at www.ipsnews.net/news.asp?idnews=36427, accessed February 3, 2007.

Murphy, R. Taggart. 2006. "East Asia's Dollars." *New Left Review* 40: 39–64.

Negroponte, John. 2007. *Annual Threat Assessment of the Director of National Intelligence.* Washington, D.C.: Office of the Director of National Intelligence.

Norris, Floyd. 2007. "China Less Willing to Be America's Piggy Bank." *New York Times*, December 22.

Palat, Ravi. 2005. "On New Rules for Destroying Old Countries." *Critical Asian Studies* 37, no. 1: 75–94.

Paulson, Henry A. Jr. 2008. "A Strategic Economic Engagement: Strengthening U.S.-Chinese Ties." *Foreign Affairs* 87, no. 5. Available at www.foreignaffairs.org/2008 0901faessay87504/henry-m-paulson-jr/a-strategic-economic-engagement.html, accessed December 14, 2008.

Petras, James. 2005. "Statism or Free Markets? China Bashing and the Loss of U.S. Competitiveness." *Counterpunch Online*, October 22–23. Available at www.counter punch.org/petras10222005.html, accessed November 15, 2008.

———. 2007. "China: Is High Growth–High Risk Liberalization the Only Alternative?" *The James Petras Website*, September 10. Available at http://petras.lahaine .org/articulo.php?p=1710, accessed November 15, 2008.

Pfaff, William. 2007. "In Sarkoland." *New York Review of Books*, June 14. Available at www.nybooks.com/articles/20254, accessed November 15, 2008.

Rachman, Gideon. 2008. "The Battle for Food, Oil, and Water." *Financial Times*, January 29. Available at www.ft.com/cms/s/0/c6f6f012-ceob-11dc-9e4e-000077b07658 .html, accessed November 15, 2008.

Righter, Rosemary. 2008. "Black Smoke over China." *Times Literary Supplement*, January 30. Available at http://entertainment.timesonline.co.uk/tol/arts_and_entertain ment/the_tls/article3276851.ece, accessed November 15, 2008.

Rozman, Gilbert. 2004. *Northeast Asia's Stunted Regionalism.* Cambridge, UK: Cambridge University Press.

Saunders, Paul. 2006. "Putin Advances his World View." *Asia Times Online*, September 29. Available at www.atimes.com/atimes/Central_Asia/HI29Ago2.html, accessed November 15, 2008.

Shirk, Susan. 2007. *China: Fragile Superpower.* Oxford, UK: Oxford University Press.

Simms, Andrew. 2005. *Ecological Debt.* London: Pluto.

Singer, Jason, Henry Sender, Jason Dean, and Marcus Walker. 2007. "Governments Get Bolder in Buying Equity Stakes." *Wall Street Journal*, July 24.

Tin, Tina. 2008. *Climate Change: Faster, Stronger, Sooner.* Brussels: World Wildlife Foundation European Office.

Trenin, Dmitri. 2006. "Russia Leaves the West." *Foreign Affairs* 85, no. 4: 87–96.

Trilling, Roger. 2002. "Bushido—The Way of Oil." *Village Voice*, January 16–22. Available at www.villagevoice.com/news/0203,trilling,31517,1.html, accessed November 15, 2008.

Walker, Richard, and Daniel Buck. 2007. "The Chinese Road." *New Left Review* 46: 39–66.

Wallerstein, Immanuel. 2004. "China and the U.S.: Competing Geopolitical Strategies." *Commentary*, December 15. Available at www.binghamton.edu/fbc/151en .htm, accessed November 15, 2008.

———. 2008. "Geopolitical Chess: Background to a Mini-war in the Caucasus." *Commentary*, August 15. Available at http://fbc.binghamton.edu/239en.htm, accessed August 19, 2008.

Wang Yuan-Kang. 2006. *China's Grand Strategy and U.S. Primacy: Is China Balancing American Power?* Washington, D.C.: Brookings Institution.

Weisberg, Jacob. 2006. "The Lou Dobbs Democrats." *Slate.com*, November 8. Available at www.slate.com/id/2153271, accessed December 10, 2008.

Weisman, Steven. 2006. "China Trip by Paulson Lifts Stakes." *New York Times*, December 8.

Wen Dale and Minqi Li. 2006. "China: Hyper-Development and Environmental Crisis." In *Coming to Terms with Nature*, ed. Leo Panitch and Colin Leys. Monmouth, UK: Merlin Press.

Wishnick, Elizabeth. 2001. *Mending Fences*. Seattle: University of Washington Press.

Wong, Edward. 2008. "As Factories Close, Chinese Workers Suffer." *International Herald Tribune*, November 14.

Yang Jieman. 2003. "Zhongyao Zhanlue Jiyu Qi Yu Zhongguo Waijiao De Lishi Renwu (Important period of strategic opportunity and the historical mission of Chinese diplomacy)." *Mao Zedong Deng Xiaoping lilun yanjiu* (Study of Mao Zedong and Deng Xiaoping theories) 4: 60–67.

CHAPTER EIGHT

China and the U.S. Labor Movement

STEPHANIE LUCE AND EDNA BONACICH

China frequently has been used as a code word in American discourse.[1] As Thomas Friedman points out, forty years ago, China was seen as a country of starving children who would take our food if they could (Friedman 2005). Today, China is the country "stealing our jobs." While not everyone buys into the hysteria about the "China threat," it is clear that much of the U.S. labor movement feels that the country poses a challenge to the strength and viability of union power. The United States has lost more than three million manufacturing jobs since 2000, while imports from China have increased more than 200 percent, creating fear among U.S. workers.[2] James P. Hoffa, president of the International Brotherhood of Teamsters, wrote a few years ago that China is "stealing the good middle-class, industrial jobs that keep America running."[3]

Just how big a threat is China for the U.S. labor movement? In this chapter, we examine the evidence on the impact of China's growth on workers in the United States and offer a list of approaches that address the fundamental challenges facing the working class.

CHINA IN THE GLOBAL ECONOMY

The first problem with current rhetoric about China "stealing jobs" is that it exaggerates the role of China in the world economy. China is not the only country to which the United States and other countries of the Global North are losing jobs. India is a growing player in global production, as is Vietnam. Canada and

Mexico are still major trading partners. The demonization of China implies that it is the primary source of U.S. job loss, which is false.

That said, we should recognize that China is a major exporter of manufactured goods that is growing at a rapid rate, and the United States is a major importer of Chinese-made goods. Other chapters in this volume provide detail on the enormous growth of the Chinese economy during the last several decades. We do not repeat that discussion here but instead examine the impact of this growth on U.S. jobs.

China had already become the world's fastest growing economy by the early 1990s, when President Bill Clinton decided to reverse his campaign promises and extend Most Favored Nation (MFN) status to China.[4] Despite opposition in both parties, Clinton stated that trade with China was clearly in the interest of the United States and that exports to China would support American jobs (Devroy 1994). President Clinton was only extending the trade status the United States had granted to China every year since 1980; however, he took relations with China to a new level a few years later when he pushed for China's acceptance into the World Trade Organization (WTO).

Clinton and other policy makers, along with neoliberal economists, argued that free trade benefits all involved. It allows countries to pursue their comparative advantage, producing what they can produce at the lowest cost, and to trade with other countries to get a full range of goods and services produced in the most efficient way. In this case, China's entry into the global economy would open up a vast new market of consumers ready to buy U.S.-made products, thereby creating new jobs. U.S. businesses also would be able to buy cheaper inputs from China, allowing them to sell goods more cheaply and become more competitive.

Despite the rhetoric, there is scant evidence that trade with China has created or supported U.S. jobs. Rather, as exports from China to the United States far exceed U.S. exports to China, and as U.S.-based transnational corporations increasingly move jobs to China or expand operations there, it is more likely that China's economic growth and its trade with the United States has cost U.S. jobs. But just how many jobs?

Critics assert that job threats come from three main sources. First, Chinese manufacturers can produce goods and services much more cheaply in China because of much lower wages, harsh working conditions, and poor health, safety, and environmental standards. This means that U.S. consumers can purchase goods and services at a much lower price and will stop buying from U.S.-based companies, thereby causing those companies to lay off workers. Second, China does not allow its currency to float and pegs it at a rate that many economists claim is artificially low. This makes Chinese goods even cheaper and enhances the incentive for U.S. consumers to purchase Chinese products. Third, U.S.-based multinationals, in search of lower wages and less regulation, are directly moving production and jobs from the United States to China (offshoring) or choosing to locate new production or expansions in China rather than in the United States.

IMPORTS AND CURRENCY VALUATION

Unfortunately, there is little hard data available that measure the impact of these three trends. Rather, most studies are either theoretical or estimates extrapolated from trade data. The most consistent source of estimates on U.S. jobs lost due to increased trade with China comes from the Economic Policy Institute (EPI). EPI economist Robert Scott measured total exports and imports between the United States and China for the past ten years, and he found that imports from China displaced more than 2.1 million job opportunities—jobs that could have been supported through domestic production—between 1996 and 2007, after accounting for jobs supported through exports. Furthermore, while imports were displacing an average of 101,000 job opportunities per year before 2001, that number rose to 353,000 per year after China entered the WTO that year.

Scott notes that the trade imbalance between the two countries is exacerbated by China's fixed currency. China had set the value of the yuan pegged to a fixed rate of 8.28 yuan to the U.S. dollar. After mounting pressure, China changed its practice in 2005, pegging the yuan to a market basket of currencies. But the yuan is still fixed within a certain range. Financial analysts say that the real value of the yuan, if allowed to float freely on the open market, would be as much as 40 percent higher because of China's massive growth. A higher value would make Chinese goods and services more expensive to buy. A range of actors, including the National Association of Manufacturers, the EPI, and the AFL-CIO, have called on China to float its currency, allowing its value to rise. In turn, they argue, this would make Chinese goods less competitive—thereby helping domestic production and jobs. Richard Trumka, AFL-CIO secretary-treasurer, co-chaired the China Currency Coalition, which called on Congress to take a number of measures to deal with "the tragic impact of China's unfair trade practices." It demanded that Congress pass a bipartisan bill that would create more WTO mechanisms for U.S. manufacturers to address China's currency manipulation (Trumka 2005).

While the majority of economists agree that China should stop fixing its currency value, not all agree that a higher value would necessarily lead to more U.S. production and jobs. For example, Alan Greenspan remarked in 2005 that a higher valuation would likely decrease Chinese imports but increase imports from other Asian countries. Greenspan added that the growing U.S. trade deficit with China actually in part reflects a shift of trade from a range of Asian countries to more trade with China (Hagenbaugh 2005). Reducing total imports could also possibly reduce jobs in the logistics and retail sector.

In addition, labor-market analyst Kim Moody believes that the EPI studies overestimate actual jobs lost. For example, EPI finds that there were 677,000 job opportunities lost because of the trade imbalance from 1997 through 2003, which, Moody says, "would account for 23 percent of all jobs that actually disappeared during those years." However, in that time period, Chinese imports comprised only between 6.5 and 12 percent of all imports into the United States (Moody 2007). As of 2006, Canada was still the country that sent the most goods to the United States, in total dollar value, accounting for 17.4 percent of imports in the year ending in May 2006.[5] Mexico, Japan, and Germany together still account for more than 20 percent of imports into the United States.

OFFSHORING

In addition to job opportunities lost because of imports, U.S.-based companies are also directly moving some jobs to China, in search of lower production costs (including much lower wages). In a recent study that charted the actual closing of plants and their reopening offshore, Kate Bronfenbrenner and Stephanie Luce found that only about 24 percent of the jobs shifted from the United States to other countries in 2004 went to China. Mexico remained the top destination for jobs, accounting for about 34 percent (Bronfenbrenner and Luce 2004). Still, the total jobs lost by being shifted overseas was small in comparison to the total jobs lost for all reasons within the United States. For example, in the first quarter of 2004, about twenty-five thousand jobs were moved from the United States to China, and another thirty-five thousand to Mexico, out of 7.3 million private-sector jobs that were lost because of closing and contracting (downsizing) in the United States.[6] The bulk of this job loss, in absolute numbers, was in service-providing industries, with far more jobs lost in professional and business services, leisure and hospitality, and retail trade than in manufacturing. Note that this study looks only at jobs that can be clearly documented as shifting. Unfortunately, we do not have a measure of all of the subcontracting and arm's-length agreements to produce goods to meet U.S. corporations' specifications that go on in other countries, including China, and that involve no direct transfer of jobs. For example, giant retailers such as Wal-Mart import tons of goods from offshore, including imports totaling $18 billion from China in 2005, yet they did not directly "shift" production, since they do not engage in it. Instead, they shifted their suppliers, leading indirectly to U.S. job loss.

A host of studies have employed other methodologies in an attempt to measure the impact of offshoring. In a 2006 paper, economist Alan Blinder estimated the potentially devastating impacts of massive job loss in the coming years. Blinder rated jobs on how easy it would be to offshore them, and he found that between 22 and 29 percent of jobs held by U.S. workers will potentially be offshored within the next twenty years. The paper caught the public's attention in part because Blinder considers himself a supporter of free trade, but he notes that the transition to a true global free market will be costly and painful, particularly for U.S. workers (Blinder 2006).

Economists from the right and left agree that a global economy means more competition among workers. According to Richard Freeman, the global workforce essentially doubled during the past two decades as China, India, and the former Soviet bloc countries entered global capitalism. Michael Yates adds that the continuous churning caused by free trade and structural adjustment policies pushes people out of agriculture and into wage-labor markets, further increasing the pool of potential labor (Yates 2003). The end result is that employers can engage in "global labor arbitrage" and pit workers against one another in an effort to drive down wages, speed up production, and avoid unions and regulations.

Labor arbitrage is not new. Moody provides a thorough case for how employers employed similar tactics in moving production from the U.S. north to the U.S. south for many decades. But as the global economy expands and as policy makers deregulate many sectors to allow more freedom of movement for capital, the possibilities increase, particularly as workers do not enjoy similar freedom of movement.

Hence, China's entry into the global market is an extension of trends that had already been occurring for U.S. workers, who have steadily been losing power with respect to capital since the 1950s. There is no doubt that U.S. employers have moved some jobs from the United States to China and that some job opportunities have been lost because of the large trade imbalance. This reduces workers' power. In addition, the emergence of China, with its massive size and growth, significantly increases employers' use of a credible threat of movement, further reducing workers' power.

IMPACT ON U.S. WORKERS AND LABOR

Some labor leaders single out China for its "unfair trade practices": fixed currency rates; failure to enforce labor and human rights; failure to enforce adequate safety, health, and environmental regulations; and provision of subsidies to business not allowed under WTO rules. Chinese workers are not entitled to real freedom of association, as their only choice for union representation is the government-controlled All-China Federation of Trade Unions (ACFTU). While China's situation is extreme in terms of the size of its economy and its repression of rights, other countries—including the United States—also engage in some of these unfair practices.

While China is not necessarily unique, its impact on the global labor market is large because of the size of its workforce and productive capacity. Average wages in China are much lower than those in the United States, but they also are lower than those in Mexico, the Caribbean, and a number of Asian countries, further contributing to the "race to the bottom" in wages and working conditions.

China's growth comes in a period of instability in the global labor market. According to the International Labour Organization (ILO), global unemployment in 2007 stood at 6 percent, and the number of people without work—almost two hundred million—is also at a record high (ILO 2008). This rate does not include workers in the informal economy, who, in many countries, comprise the largest share of the workforce. Global unemployment did not fall, despite record economic growth as measured by GDP. The world economy was strong and growing from 2002 to early 2008, based on GDP, but there was still a very large pool of workers looking to sell their labor power. The ILO predicts that absolute unemployment and the unemployment rate will increase significantly with global economic turbulence, increasing the pool of people looking for work.

This results in competition among workers and among countries. Some workers are able to get living-wage work, but most must take work at low wages or try to survive in the informal sector. Worldwide, a greater share of total output goes to capital. Stephen Roach, former chief economist at Morgan Stanley, wrote in 2007: "The pendulum of economic power is at unsustainable extremes in the developed world. For a broad collection of major industrial economies—the United States, the euro zone, Japan, Canada and the U.K.—the share of economic rewards going to labor stands at a historical low of less than 54% of national income—down from 56% in 2001. Meanwhile, the share going to corporate profits stands at a record high of nearly 16%—a striking increase from the 10% reading five years ago" (Roach 2007).

Of course, this is not just a "China effect"; labor has been losing power relative to capital for the past thirty or more years, long before China entered the picture in a serious way. As Moody and others argue, there are other forces at work that explain job loss, such as technological innovation and lean production (Moody 2007). But the trend intensified as China entered the world market, increasing employers' ability to use the threat of capital flight against workers trying to organize or push for higher wages. China also has concentrated more of the production in one country, making it a larger target for wrath—or a more powerful potential ally. Interestingly, this may end up changing the power dynamics within global supply chains. As Chinese manufacturers grow in size and capacity, relations between producers and the retailers or brands that purchase their products may shift in favor of China.

THE U.S. LABOR MOVEMENT'S RESPONSE

The U.S. labor movement has responded to the emergence of China primarily by trying to curtail imports of Chinese-made goods to the U.S. market. The AFL-CIO opposed granting China MFN trade status and establishing permanent normal trade relations (PNTR; Bello and Mittal 2000). It fought against the entry of China into the WTO, then called on the Bush administration to sanction China for unfair trade based on its labor policy. To this end, the AFL-CIO filed a petition with the U.S. Trade Representative (USTR) in 2004 and again in 2006, calling on Bush to use the sanctions allowed for under section 301 of the 1974 Trade Act. In particular, that section lays out trade practices that impose unreasonable burdens on U.S. commerce, which include the denial of workers' rights. The AFL-CIO filed its petition arguing that the Chinese government allows violations of child labor, minimum wage, and human-rights laws. Both times, the USTR decided against accepting the petition for a hearing.

The efforts to exclude Chinese-made goods are predicated, in part, on the idea that the Chinese working class is especially oppressed and that the Chinese labor movement is completely compromised as a puppet of the Chinese government. Apart from the issue of singling out China in a manner disproportionate to its significance in world trade, we have three other criticisms of the U.S. labor movement's approach for most of its history.

First, the AFL-CIO has a notorious record of undermining progressive labor struggles in the Global South during the Cold War (Frutiger 2002; Scipes 2006). Indeed, it was nicknamed by some as the AFL-CIA for its active participation in support of U.S. goals to crush communism and expand its own empire (Blain 2001). U.S. unions would attack left-leaning unions around the world in the name of "independent unionism" while trying to create and support business unions.

Fortunately, the AFL-CIO is no longer dominated by Cold Warriors. Still, anti-communism has not disappeared completely, and some of the anger toward China can be seen as expressing Cold War sentiments.

Second, the mainstream labor-movement stance toward China suffers from a long history of racism toward Chinese workers (see Wong and Bernard 2000). Most unions supported the 1882 Chinese Exclusion Act, and California unions were particularly extreme in keeping out Chinese and other Asian workers (Saxton 1975). The anti-Chinese position was built on a racist notion of Chinese workers as "the other": a faceless mass coming to steal jobs from native-born workers. While Andrew Gyory (1998) argues that there was not necessarily a unified anti-Chinese view among the U.S. working class, history is rife with anti-Chinese sentiment by labor leaders. Denis Kearney and H. L. Knight, of the Working-man's Party of California, waged a "Chinese Must Go" campaign in 1878, writing that "California must be all American or all Chinese. We are resolved that it shall be American, and are prepared to make it so" (Kearney and Knight 1878).

The anti-Chinese attacks from union leaders picked up steam and took a new direction after the Chinese Revolution of 1949, combining racism with Cold War themes. Although it was not always the majority view in the labor movement, it still worked to keep workers divided across national borders.

Finally, the U.S. labor movement has also turned to protectionism as a response to job loss. While the fear of job loss is sometimes exaggerated beyond the reality, employers do use threats of bringing in new groups of workers and, more recently, sending jobs overseas as a way to keep workers in line. According to Kate Bronfenbrenner (2000), employers have increased the use of the "threat effect" after the passage of the North American Free Trade Agreement (NAFTA). "Free trade" allowed employers to move jobs out of the United States more easily, thus enabling them to make a more credible threat of job shifts.

In response to threatened and actual job loss, unions have frequently relied on protectionist responses to keep jobs in the United States. Examples of recent protectionist policies include the efforts by unions and some politicians to ban state and local governments from contracting out public-sector work overseas (but not necessarily against contracting out in general), to pass "consumers' right to know" legislation that would allow customers to find out in which country their call-center service representative is located, and to require employers to give three months' notice to any employees whose jobs are being moved overseas.

Given that there are essentially no other policy alternatives available, protectionism seems a rational response for individual workers and union leaders. But its long-term effects are deadly, as we shall see.

The larger problem that unions face is the lack of a serious analysis of the dynamics of global capitalism and the relationship of forces it creates. The source of the problem lies in a variety of factors, including U.S. labor law, U.S. foreign policy, the lack of limits on transnational corporations, and the lack of any kind of industrial policy or ideological vision among U.S. unions (Bonacich, Fletcher, and Hermanson 2007). Without a larger analysis of how the global economy works and what alternative models the labor movement should strive for, unions tend to react to global developments on an ad hoc basis, responding to each crisis as it arises, without an overarching understanding of how these crises are linked together.

GLOBAL CAPITALISM AND THE RELATIONSHIP OF FORCES

The labor movement needs an analysis of China that is situated in an understanding of the complexities of global capitalism. The relationship between the United States and China is multifaceted. Many U.S. leaders are fearful that China will gain military might and threaten U.S. dominance. However, a large share of corporations have a strong interest in exploiting the economic opportunities presented by China, whether it's selling to the Chinese market or employing low-cost labor. At the same time, U.S. companies are not completely united on a China agenda. Smaller companies, which are far more numerous than the giant transnational corporations (TNCs), often do not have the capacity to move offshore and so have an interest in protecting domestic production. This split emerged at a meeting of the National Association of Manufacturers (NAM), during which a resolution was passed essentially condemning China for keeping the value of its currency artificially low. Some TNC members of NAM were strongly opposed and threatened to leave the organization.[7]

China itself is a complicated country. On the one hand, its very strong state refuses to allow foreign capital to enter the country without considerable oversight, and in this sense, it challenges the neoliberal model. On the other hand, its firm embrace of markets is encouraging the massive movement of capital to China, not only in direct investment but also in the form of contracting arrangements (Ross 2006). In terms of foreign investment, China has seen massive growth in recent years, surpassing $80 billion in utilized FDI in 2007.[8] Because China exercises considerable control over its labor force, especially in the export sector, it is able to woo foreign capital to come and "exploit" its workers. The combination of a strong state, a commitment to capitalist development, and a huge peasantry that is rapidly being proletarianized leads China to be an especially attractive manufacturing site.

Finally, workers and unions in the United States and China are not mono-lithic forces. In the United States, unions represent only about one in ten work-ers, so labor leaders cannot speak for all workers. Even within the labor move-ment, there is a range of opinion about how to address China, as mentioned above. In China, while the ACFTU is huge, it also doesn't represent all workers. In particular, it does not represent most of the workers employed by transnational corporations or in the special economic zones. The result is that the working class is divided, both within countries and between countries.

DILEMMAS OF A DIVIDED WORKING CLASS

The relationship between Western and Chinese labor is quite similar to the rela-tionship between white and black labor during much of U.S. history—including the "Chinese immigration" question of the nineteenth century and the treatment of Latinos, under conquest and as immigrants, and that goes equally for the pres-ent moment. One might argue that it resembles most relationships between the working classes of colonial powers and the working classes of the peoples they have colonized, whether these working classes occupy territories distant from each other or coexist within the same state. Coexistence can arise because of working-class settlement of colonized territories or the movement of peoples—as slaves, indentured servants, guest workers, or "free" immigrants—to areas where the colonizer working class is already settled.

All of these situations have in common the following structure:

First, the capitalist class employs both sets of workers but under very different circumstances. The "advantaged" workers are usually able to win citizenship rights for themselves, form unions, and struggle to improve their position in rela-tion to the employer (Glenn 2003). The colonized or racialized workers have no such political standing. Racial ideology is one mechanism used to justify the dif-ference in treatment, including beliefs in the biological or cultural inferiority of the workers and their greater expendability. Their lives are deemed less impor-tant than those of the colonizers, regardless of class differences among the latter, so that exposing them to hazardous work situations or to excessively long hours of work is acceptable.

One can argue that capitalists merely take advantage of preexisting differences between workers, rooted in levels of development, conquest, and so on. Or one may contend that capitalists play an active role in constructing this division by taking advantage of the political "weaknesses" of the colonized/racialized workers. Even if they do not initiate a division, they may elaborate on it and worsen conditions for the colonized/racialized.

Regardless of how the division got started, capital takes advantage of the split and pits one group against the other. One form that this takes is to shift production away from the more advantaged workers and move it to the colonized/racialized workers, paying them less and getting them to work harder under much worse conditions. The more advantaged workers are disciplined by having to face job loss or a reduction in standards in order to become "more competitive," a win-win situation for capital.

Second, the two working classes have different views of each other. The advantaged working class tends to see the colonized/racialized working class as a threat. Sometimes they buy into the images of racial inferiority promoted by the ruling class and feel no affinity with them as fellow workers. Moreover, they sometimes blame the colonized/racialized workers for their situation, claiming that they lack the courage to stand up for themselves and prevent being dominated.

The colonized/racialized workers may see the advantaged working class as partners in the structure that oppresses them. The class differences among the colonizers seem irrelevant; they all participate in the exploitation of the colonized, and all appear to benefit from it. Even if some more advantaged workers see themselves as exploited and are engaged in a struggle against capital, they all appear to have the opportunity for upward mobility.

Third, the more advantaged workers may try to protect their jobs and living standards by preventing capital's access to the racialized labor force. This approach can entail preventing racialized workers from entering the labor market (exclusion)—for example, the anti-Chinese movement on the West Coast of the United States and Canada in the late nineteenth century—or creating structures that keep them out of certain jobs (exclusiveness), as exemplified by the apartheid system in South Africa or the *hukou* household registration system in China (Alexander and Chan 2004). There is a long history of craft unions holding monopolies on training and job access and imposing racial (and gender) restrictions on membership.

An alternative approach is to pursue solidarity with the colonized/racialized working class by fighting for their rights and helping them gain access to full citizenship. The goal here is to recognize that the two working classes share a common enemy in the capitalist class and that they need to prevent themselves from being divided and pitted against each other by uniting and standing behind one another. Of course, this is the basic idea of unionism to begin with. Here it incorporates not only individuals but also groups. The principle of solidarity is extended to all workers.

All workers must have basic political rights so that they can protect themselves against excessive exploitation. One goal is to be able to set standards, or floors, that limit competition among workers so that they are not in a position of being forced to undercut each other. Workers may be compelled to compete on a variety of other issues, but not on matters of basic pay, benefits, and hours of work, thereby weakening the threat of job displacement through undercutting.

Ultimately, however, there are no real mechanisms for enforcing the rights of workers under the current system. Therefore, the long-term goal is to develop the power of the working class so that it can either modify the global capitalist system significantly and gain the right for labor and other interests (such as ethnic, racial, and gender groups) to be part of the decision-making process in terms of planning the rules of the global political economy or eliminate capitalism as an organizing principle entirely.

WHAT IS BEING TRIED? WHAT IS POSSIBLE?

Fortunately, there are a few places where workers and unions in the United States and China are attempting to build alliances and solidarity. Here we review a few of the efforts that labor leaders and activists are pursuing to build international solidarity.

Working with the ACFTU

Until 2008, the AFL-CIO leadership had refused to meet with or recognize the ACFTU, an organization with almost two hundred million members. However, the federation appears to be changing its stance, and recently sent their general counsel to visit the country. At the same time, the International Trade Union Confederation (ITUC), with 167 million members in 153 countries, announced that it would open dialogue with the ACFTU after a vote in Brussels in December 2007 (Vandaele 2008).

The other U.S. labor federation, Change to Win (CTW), has been meeting with the ACFTU for some time. Andy Stern, president of the largest CTW union, the Service Employees International Union (SEIU), made an official visit to China in 2002, while he was still part of the AFL-CIO—much to the dismay of the AFL-CIO leadership. Stern and other CTW leaders have traveled to China to meet with ACFTU officials on numerous occasions. Stern explains that SEIU has conducted a seminar on organizing for the ACFTU and that the organizations share information about their common employers.

Some U.S. activists acknowledge the limitations of the ACFTU but have decided to pursue relations with them. For example, Kent Wong, head of the UCLA Center for Labor Research and Education, argues that the labor movements of the West cannot ignore such a large organization that strives to represent the interests of Chinese workers. One might criticize it for lacking independence from the government, but that is true for trade-union federations in a number of countries.

Some observers argue that the ACFTU has always been an organization in flux and that that tendency to change continues today. According to researcher Jude Howell (2006), the ACFTU has begun the process of holding direct elections for local union officials. While experiences and attitudes toward direct elections are mixed, the ACFTU in Guangdong Province began experimenting with them in 1986, in part to try to build more working-class consciousness among migrant workers. Howell claims that by early 2004, "one-third of all unions in foreign-invested enterprises in the province had chairs and committees directly elected by workers." In most cases, the elections were a result of pressure from international NGOs and consumer groups. The actual details of the cases vary considerably, with some candidates being selected by management and some coming from the workers.

It is difficult to say how much impact these direct elections have had in building an independent trade-union movement in China. Critics claim that these elections have had little effect in changing conditions. However, the elections point to heterogeneity in experiences within the ACFTU, which creates openings for possible change. Howell concludes, "The international trade union movement's refusal to engage with China ironically contributes to the slow progress of reform within the ACFTU."

Whether because of internal changes or other reasons, in 2006 and 2007 the ACFTU launched major organizing campaigns at U.S. multinationals in China, resulting in union representation at seventy Wal-Mart stores and more than four hundred McDonalds and KFC restaurants. Anita Chan writes that the effort at Wal-Mart contained some elements of an authentic organizing drive, starting with some Wal-Mart employees who met clandestinely with coworkers to build support for the union and the establishment of a worker committee (Chan 2007). On the other hand, the drive turned into a top-down effort, with little real worker support or involvement at many of the branches. However, there has been some evidence of worker organizing in some Wal-Mart stores (Chinese Labor News Translations 2008).

Still, some U.S. labor activists remain optimistic. Kent Wong has made a number of efforts to get U.S. labor leaders to visit China and host Chinese labor leaders in the United States. After a visit to China in 2007, Los Angeles County Federation of Labor president Maria Elena Durazo established a formal sister-city relationship with the Shanghai Municipal Trade Union Council.

There are still some critics who argue strongly against engaging with the ACFTU, as it is a government-controlled body that does not allow authentic worker organization. When the ITUC voted to open dialogue with the ACFTU in December 2007, it faced dissent from Hong Kong trade unions, Solidarnosc (Poland), and the Dutch trade-union federation (Vandaele 2008). Dan Gallin, chair of the Geneva-based Global Labour Institute, argues that formal relations with ACFTU affiliates can actually hurt real organizing, as it legitimates the ACFTU and does not lead to real change. Gallin cites the Hong Kong Confederation of Trade Unions and *China Labour Bulletin*, which noted that the ACFTU had already entertained dozens of official visits of trade unionists from around the world by the 1990s, and despite establishing hundreds of formal relationships, there had been no change within the ACFTU (Gallin 2008).

Bottom-up Organizing

Despite potential openings in the ACFTU, other activists feel that other avenues of labor organizing are more likely to lead to change in China and perhaps in U.S.-China worker relations. This includes work with grassroots organizations that are trying to develop independent NGOs for Chinese workers. This is difficult in mainland China, as independent worker organizations are illegal. However, there is more political space for NGOs in Hong Kong, and organizations based there, such as the Chinese Working Women's Network (CWWN), work with workers on the mainland when possible. Some NGOs have received financial support from U.S. unions for their work. For a while, the CWWN sponsored a bus that would visit worksites in Guangdong Province to help workers learn their rights (Chan 2006). However, the boundaries of what is allowed by local police and Chinese authorities are constantly in flux.

In addition to organizational ties, Katie Quan, longtime trade-union activist and scholar, writes that it is also important to develop "people-to-people relations," building off the model of "ping-pong diplomacy of the 1970s." Through worker relations as well as increased "research, media coverage and other dissemination of public information," the foundations for greater collaboration will develop (Quan 2004). To this end, scholars and journalists are helping to get information out about the labor situation in China. Despite the view that some have of Chinese workers as passive victims of corporate abuse, there is wide-scale protest occurring on a regular basis in the country, and it appears to be on the rise (Lee 2005). In the mid-1990s, there was an average of ten thousand large-scale workplace protests a year in China; by 2005, this was up to almost ninety thousand a year (Costello, Smith, and Brecher 2006). Workers are also filing complaints against employers who violate labor law: individual and collective labor dispute cases number in the tens of thousands each year. U.S. unionists can do little to support this bottom-up worker organizing in China directly, but this information exchange helped build the foundation for collaboration on labor-law reform. China passed an initial law in 1994 but has revisited it on several occasions. In 2006, a new section of law was drafted that would provide significant improvements to the rights of migrant and short-term contract workers. TNCs, led by the American Chamber of Commerce, immediately attacked the law, telling the Chinese government that it must reject such changes or face capital flight.

Activists fought back. They worked to get the word out in the U.S. and European press and to highlight the hypocrisy of corporations claiming to be in China to serve the Chinese people yet fighting against worker rights (Costello, Smith, and Brecher 2006). Ellen David Friedman, a former union organizer in the United States, helped coordinate a speaking tour for Professor Liu Cheng, one of the leading labor legal scholars in China. Professor Cheng spoke with unions, academics, and lawyers across the country. U.S. activists mobilized to pressure Congress to call on the corporations to back off. Several unions representing workers at GE successfully pushed that company to withdraw its protests against the law. The final law, which went into effect in January 2008, was weaker than the draft, but it did include new rights for contract workers.

This example shows how the U.S. labor movement can work in solidarity with Chinese workers at home by getting their corporations and government to support, or at least not block, efforts to improve workers' rights in China.

The Antisweatshop Movement and Corporate Social Responsibility

Western activists have developed campaigns to pressure the TNCs to improve their labor relations around the world, using the threat of consumer boycotts and the loss of credibility for their brands. Independent NGOs, such as the Workers Rights Consortium, work to monitor suppliers. These efforts have received significant support from some U.S. unions, such as UNITE HERE and the United Steelworkers.

In addition, many corporations have set up their own monitoring programs to oversee their offshore suppliers. Corporate social responsibility (CSR) is a broad term that incorporates many variations of activity, but it includes efforts by corporations to engage in socially responsible activity in regard to labor relations and environmental practices. While some have argued that this is "the fox guarding the chicken coop" and numerous critiques have been written about the various programs that have been tried (for example, Esbenshade 2004), the corporations have not been able to disregard this pressure entirely and have, at times, made some significant changes, such as Reebok's attempts to support worker organizing within Chinese factories. Most large TNC brands now have a corporate code of conduct as well as staff assigned to address the concerns raised by antisweatshop activists. For some corporations, this is a significant operation involving dozens of staff and budgets of hundreds of thousands of dollars.

In many ways, the end results of the antisweatshop and CSR campaigns are similar: codes of conduct relating to corporate activity. However, we distinguish between those efforts initiated by corporations concerned about their brand image and those initiated by activists concerned about workers' rights. The motivations and goals of the two efforts differ, even if the on-the-ground activity often looks similar.

CSR has been a hotly contested issue among activists, economists, and corporate executives. While there is a range of opinions on the value of CSR in general, most commentators conclude that CSR has made a small dent, if any, in China. This failure is due in part to the massive size of the country and workforce. It is also due to complicated relations among brand names, retailers, factories, and subcontractors. Finally, there have been numerous challenges navigating relations with the ACFTU, local police, and other forces in China, which have at times impeded the opportunities to push for workers' rights.[9]

Possibility of Supply-Chain Campaigns

Another approach, one not yet tried, is to develop the concept of supply-chain campaigns—in particular, combining the interests of Chinese (and other Asian) production workers with U.S. (and other Western) distribution workers, especially those involved in the logistics sector, namely, transportation and warehousing, but not excluding sales workers. Both of these groups have been hurt by globalization, so they might find common cause in cooperating, without the condescending illusion that U.S. unions will "help the poor Chinese workers learn how to organize."

Production and distribution workers who work for the same TNC, such as a giant retailer like Wal-Mart, could take advantage of certain weaknesses and vulnerabilities in the global logistics system. Among them is the fact that goods are now supposed to move on a just-in-time basis, so that companies can save on carrying less inventory. In addition, a global supply chain means "long supply lines"—products shipped long distances, by ship, air, and train. As Bonacich and Wilson (2007) explain, "The longer the line the more the opportunities for discontented workers to rebel somewhere along it, slowing down the movement of freight." Moreover, goods must pass through certain choke points, such as the major container ports (for example, the ports of Los Angeles and Long Beach, which account for 40 percent of total containerized imports to the United States and an even higher percentage of the imports from China).

A more detailed proposal for supply-chain organizing is provided in Bonacich and Wilson (2007). We highlight here a few of the key steps needed to pursue this approach that are most relevant to what this discussion. First, a global workers' movement must continue to insist on the right of workers everywhere to form independent trade unions. Even when engaging with the ACFTU, workers and their advocates must hold this as a goal. Second, labor must take part in the development of a global development plan. This requires continued dialogue among workers' organizations as well as with the rest of civil society. Third, this global plan must include efforts to restructure the rules of global investment and to reform or abolish the International Monetary Fund, the World Bank, and other neoliberal institutions.

Bonacich and Wilson put forth ideas about how workers in the United States could begin the efforts for global supply-chain organizing right in Southern California. This would help build a solid foundation for collaboration with Chinese workers on the other side of the supply chain.

CONCLUSION

There is no question that China has emerged as a major player in the global economy. Many U.S. observers have noted, with awe and fear, its rapid growth, large population and workforce, and low wages. We argue that China's entry into the global economy is notable, although it more likely intensifies trends that were already occurring rather than representing something fundamentally new and unique. Still, China's size and political economy have created the conditions for it to be a major site of capital investment. In this sense, China does have an impact on the conditions of work for workers around the world. On the other hand, we believe that the framework of "U.S. versus China" is not helpful in understanding the dynamics or the possible strategies for organizing.

U.S. unions must find ways to build solidarity and connections with Chinese workers. The problems created by global capitalism cannot be resolved solely through collective bargaining agreements. They require major changes to the rules of the game. The only way to achieve this is by developing the social power to force them. Global labor can and must be a key partner in the exercise of such power.

The strategies that we list above represent small, initial steps. None of these efforts has yet gained significant traction. Some may fail completely. In the early stages of collaboration, it may be necessary to experiment widely. But in pursuing any of the strategies we list above, the goal should not be limited to improving the situation of the employees (whether direct or contracted) of the TNCs in question; rather, the focus should be on gaining power for the working class as a whole in relation to transnational capital. One very important demand is to require that the global economy no longer be run solely by corporate capital and its state supporters. The entire world political economy needs to be opened up to democratic participation by all significant social sectors, including, importantly, labor.

NOTES

1. We use China as shorthand for the People's Republic of China.

2. Employment data from the U.S. Bureau of Labor Statistics, Current Employment Statistics Survey, Table B-1 for 2000 and 2007. Imports data from U.S. Census Bureau, Foreign Trade Statistics, "Trade in Goods with China" for 2000 and 2007.

3. James P. Hoffa, "Bush to Hu: 'Huh?'" April 23, 2006, available at www.huffington post.com/james-p-hoffa/bush-to-hu-huh_b_19657.html, accessed November 12, 2008.

4. The United States had granted temporary MFN status to China every year since 1980. In 1998, the term was changed to Normal Trading Relations. China was granted Permanent Normal Trading Relations status by Congress in 2000.

5. U.S. Census, "Imports (Goods)," Foreign Trade Statistics, available at www .census.gov/foreign-trade/statistics/highlights/top/top0605.html#imports, accessed November 12, 2008.

6. Bureau of Labor Statistics. Business Employment Dynamics, First Quarter 2004.

7. "Domestic Manufacturers Force the National Association of Manufacturers' Big Members to Take a Stand on China," Manufacturing News, July 7, 2006, vol. 13, no. 13. It is interesting to note that U.S. labor-movement leaders and domestic capital are often on the same side of this issue.

8. The largest source of FDI into China comes from Hong Kong, followed by the British Virgin Islands, South Korea, Japan, Singapore, and the United States. See U.S.-China Business Council, "Foreign Investment in China: Forecast 2008," avail-

able at http://uschina.org/public/documents/2008/02/2008-foreign-investment.pdf, accessed December 10, 2008.

9. Others have noted the weakness position of CSR in other countries and contexts as well (for example, Ballinger 2008).

REFERENCES

Alexander, Peter, and Anita Chan. 2004. "Does China Have an Apartheid Pass System?" *Journal of Ethnic and Migration Studies* 30: 609–29.

Ballinger, Jeff. 2008. "No Sweat? Corporate Social Responsibility and the Dilemma of Anti-Sweatshop Activism." *New Labor Forum* 17, no. 2: 91–98.

Bello, Walden and Anuradha Mittal. 2000. "Backgrounder: Dangerous Liaisons: Progressives, the Right, and the Anti-China Trade Campaign." Available at www.food first.org/node/224, accessed November 15, 2008.

Blain, Mike. 2001. "Skeletons May Emerge from AFL-CIO Cupboard." *Seattle Independent Media Center*, March 9, Available at www.labournet.net/world/0109/aflcio1.html, accessed January 30, 2008.

Blinder, Alan S. 2006. "Offshoring: The Next Industrial Revolution?" *Foreign Affairs*, March/April.

Bonacich, Edna, Bill Fletcher Jr., and Jeff Hermanson. 2007. "Breaking with the System: A Reply to Stephen Lerner." *New Labor Forum* 16, no. 3–4: 116–27.

Bonacich, Edna, and Jake B. Wilson. 2007. *Getting the Goods: Ports, Labor, and the Logistics Revolution*. Ithaca: Cornell University Press.

Bronfenbrenner, Kate. 2000. "Uneasy Terrain: The Impact of Capital Mobility on Workers, Wages, and Union Organizing." Report submitted to the U.S. Trade Deficit Review Commission, September 6.

Bronfenbrenner, Kate, and Stephanie Luce. 2004. "The Changing Nature of Corporate Global Restructuring: The Impact of Production Shifts on Jobs in the U.S., China, and Around the Globe." Report submitted to the U.S.-China Economic and Security Review Commission. Available at www.news.cornell.edu/releases/Oct04/jobs.outsourcing.rpt.04.pdf, accessed November 12, 2008.

Center for Labor Research and Education. 2007. "L.A. Labor Builds Solidarity in Shanghai."
Available at www.labor.ucla.edu/updates/shanghai.html, accessed November 15, 2008.

Chan, Anita. 2007. "Organizing Wal-Mart in China: Two Steps Forward, One Step Back for China's Unions." *New Labor Forum* 16, no. 2: 87–96.

Chan, Jenny Wai-ling. Spring 2006. "Chinese Women Workers Organize in the Export Zone." *New Labor Forum* 15: 19–27.

Chinese Labor News Translations. 2008. "The Emergence of Real Trade Unionism in Wal-Mart Stores." May 4. Available at www.clntranslations.org/article/30/draft, accessed June 12, 2008.

Costello, Tim, Brendan Smith, and Jeremy Brecher. 2006. "Labor in China." *Foreign Policy in Focus*, December 29.

Devroy, Ann. 1994. "Clinton Grants China MFN, Reversing Campaign Pledge." *Washington Post*, May 27.

Esbenshade, Jill. 2004. *Monitoring Sweatshops: Workers, Consumers, and the Global Apparel Industry*. Philadelphia: Temple University Press.

Friedman, Thomas L. 2005. *The World Is Flat: A Brief History of the Twenty-First Century*. New York: Farrar, Straus, and Giroux.

Frutiger, Dean. 2002. "AFL-CIO China Policy: Labor's New Step Forward or the Cold War Revisited?" *Labor Studies* 27, no. 3: 67–80.

Gallin, Dan. 2008. "Looking for the Quick Fix: Reviewing Andy Stern." Union Ideas Network. Available at http://uin.org.uk/content/view/256/68/, accessed January 10, 2008.

Glenn, Evelyn Nakano. 2003. *Unequal Freedom: How Race and Gender Shaped American Citizenship and Labor*. Cambridge, MA: Harvard University Press.

Gyory, Andrew. 1998. *Closing the Gate: Race, Politics, and the Chinese Exclusion Act*. Chapel Hill: University of North Carolina Press.

Hagenbaugh, Barbara. 2005. "Greenspan: China Policy Change No Quick Job Fix." *USA Today*, June 24, 1b.

Hong Kong Confederation of Trade Unionists and China Labor Bulletin. 2001. "Rethinking the Rethink." January 18. Available at www.hrichina.org/public/contents/article?revision%5fid=4192&item%5fid=4191, accessed January 31, 2008.

Howell, Jude. 2006. "New Democratic Trends in China: Reforming the All-China Federation of Trade Unions." IDS Working Paper 263. Sussex, UK: Institute of Development Studies.

International Labour Organization. 2008. "Global Employment Trends January 2008." Geneva: International Labour Office.

Kearney, Dennis, and H. L. Knight. 1878. "Appeal from California. The Chinese Invasion. Workingmen's Address." *Indianapolis Times*, February 28. See http://history matters.gmu.edu/d/5046/, accessed November 15, 2008.

Lee Ching Kwan. 2005. "China's Contentious Transition: Labor Protest in China's Rustbelt and Sunbelt." Talk delivered at UCLA, October 27. Based on book of the same title to be published by University of California Press.

Moody, Kim. 2007. *U.S. Labor in Trouble and Transition*. New York: Verso.

Quan, Katie. 2004. "Workers Need Relations with Chinese Unions." International Centre for Trade Union Rights. November 19. Available at www.ictur.org/Quan .html, accessed January 10, 2008.

Roach, Stephen S. 2007. "The Davos Disconnect." Morgan Stanley Global Economic Forum, January 30. Available at www.morganstanley.com/views/gef/archive/2007/20070130-Tue.html, accessed January 10, 2008.

Ross, Andrew. 2006. *Fast Boast to China: Corporate Flight and the Consequences of Free Trade*. New York: Pantheon.

Saxton, Alexander. 1975. *The Indispensable Enemy: Labor and the Anti-Chinese Movement in California*. Berkeley: University of California Press.

Scipes, Kim. 2006. "When Will the AFL-CIO Leadership Quit Blaming the Chinese Government for Multinational Corporate Decisions, U.S. Government Policies, and U.S. Labor Leaders' Inept Responses?" *Monthly Review*, July 3. Available at http://mrzine.monthlyreview.org/scipes030706.html, accessed November 15, 2008.

Trumka, Richard. 2005. "Remarks by AFL-CIO Secretary-Treasurer Richard Trumka at China Currency Coalition Press Briefing at National Press Club." AFL-CIO Press Release, October 13.

Vandaele, John. 2008. "International Union Sets Up Chinese Links." Interpress Service, January 22. Available at www.ipsnews.net/news.asp?idnews=40871, accessed January 31, 2008.

Wong, Kent, and Elaine Bernard. 2000. "Labor's Mistaken Anti-China Campaign." *New Labor Forum* 9: 19–23.

Yates, Michael D. 2003. *Naming the System: Inequality and Work in the Global Economy*. New York: Monthly Review Press.

CHAPTER NINE

China as an Emerging Epicenter of World Labor Unrest

BEVERLY J. SILVER AND LU ZHANG

A common theme in the literature on globalization has been that the fast growth of manufacturing in China has sounded the death knell for workers' capacity for collective resistance in both the Global North and Global South. With the mobilization of China's vast reserves of cheap and disciplined labor, it is argued that a "race to the bottom" has been unleashed, producing an endless downward spiral in workers' power and welfare.

Notwithstanding its popularity in the literature, the thesis that capital mobility produces a straightforward race to the bottom is suspect on theoretical-empirical grounds. Rather, the historical pattern is one in which capital does indeed recurrently relocate geographically in search of cheaper or more docile labor but ends up creating new working classes and new rounds of labor-capital conflict in each favored site of production. Whether we look at the history of the diffusion of mass production in textiles globally in the late nineteenth and early twentieth centuries from its origins in the UK (Silver 2003: ch. 3) or the diffusion of mass production of automobiles in the second half of the twentieth century from its origins in the United States (Silver 2003: ch. 2), a recurrent pattern is visible. To put it in a phrase: contrary to the race-to-the-bottom thesis, our counterthesis is that *where capital goes, labor-capital conflict shortly follows.*

WHERE CAPITAL GOES, CONFLICT FOLLOWS

The contemporary Chinese case, we argue, provides empirical evidence in support of this counterthesis. The mass movement of capital into China and the deepening commodification of labor since the mid-1990s have been accompanied by a rising tide of labor unrest in China. According to official Chinese government figures, mass protest increased from ten thousand incidents involving 730,000 protestors in 1993 to sixty thousand incidents involving more than three million protestors in 2003. Moreover, the number of cases brought by workers before the official labor arbitration committees increased steadily from seventy-eight thousand per year in 1994 to more than eight hundred thousand per year in 2003 (White 2007).[1]

The vast majority of the mass labor protests in the second half of the 1990s were carried out by workers being laid off from state-owned enterprises. In 1994, an enterprise restructuring law was passed, allowing state-owned enterprises to carry out mass layoffs as part of an effort to bring production processes in line with international competition. This constituted an attack on established ways of life and livelihood of the urban working class that had been created during the Mao years. The smashing of the "iron rice bowl" livelihood guarantees precipitated a wave of factory occupations and street protests in "China's rustbelt" (Lee 2007). To put it differently, these were protests by workers on the "destructive" end of the Schumpeterian process of "creative destruction," engaged in what we might call Polanyi-type protests as the foundations of their class and their communities were being "unmade" (Silver 2003).

In the second half of the 1990s, there were few signs of open protest by the young migrant factory workers drawn to the coastal areas from the countryside. These migrant workers were generally thought to be part of an inexhaustible supply of cheap labor waiting to be tapped in China's rural areas. As such, most observers predicted that it would be a long time (if ever) before they would be seen openly protesting their wages and working conditions. When an "unprecedented series of [strikes] and walkouts" hit factories in China's booming Pearl River Delta in 2004, it not only "jolted foreign and Chinese factory owners" (Cody 2004), it also constituted a direct challenge to the dominant race-to-the bottom narrative. Indeed, the movement of capital into China has created a new and increasingly militant working class—the outcome of the "creative" side of the process of creative destruction.

While many observers have discounted the mounting labor unrest in China as localized, apolitical, "cellular" activism (Lee 2007), we argue that it is a mistake to underestimate the potential impact of these types of struggles. Indeed, the key theoretical insight of Frances Piven and Richard Cloward in *Poor Peoples' Movements* was precisely that many of the gains made by such movements do not come from the establishment of formal organizations oriented toward the capture of state power. Instead, they are a result of concessions wrung from the powerful in response to widespread, intense, "spontaneous" disruptions from below, in response to the threat of "ungovernability."

Indeed, by the turn of the century, the mounting localized, apolitical, and spontaneous labor struggles emerging out of both sides of the creative-destructive process (together with an escalation in social conflicts over land rights and environmental degradation in rural areas) began to raise the specter of emergent ungovernability if China continued along the same development path it had been taking since the mid-1990s. This fear has been one of the key factors propelling the Chinese central government toward introducing significant changes, first in rhetoric and later in concrete social policies. Between 2003 and 2005, the central government and the Chinese Communist Party began to move away from a single-minded emphasis on attracting foreign capital and fostering economic growth at all costs to promoting the idea of a "new development mode" aimed at reducing inequalities among classes and regions as part of the pursuit of a "harmonious society" (for example, see *People's Daily* 2005). Likewise, concerned about rising unrest and the potential for "social instability," the official trade union, the All-China Federation of Trade Unions (ACFTU), amended its constitution to "make the protection of workers' rights a priority" in 2003 (Chan 2003); by 2007, Hu Jintao was making speeches about the importance of safeguarding "the legitimate rights and interests of workers" (Xinhua 2008).

By 2007, it was also becoming clearer that changes were moving beyond the rhetorical level. The most important concrete manifestation was the new Labor Contract Law that went into effect on January 1, 2008. The new law, among other things, enhances job security, putting significant restrictions on employers' rights to hire and fire workers without cause. It also strengthens the role of trade unions. The new Arbitration Law, which went into effect in May 2008, allows workers to bring cases against their employers to the courts free of charge. And in 2006, the ACFTU, frustrated with Wal-Mart's refusal to allow the official trade unions into its stores in China, initiated an unprecedented grassroots mobilization of workers in Wal-Mart stores—a widely publicized (and eventually successful) campaign that was touted by the ACFTU as a model for bringing effective unions to other recalcitrant workplaces in China (*Business Watch* 2006; see also Chan 2006).

There is also evidence that the new Labor Contract Law is being taken seriously by the central government and, as a consequence, large employers. When Huawei, a large Chinese-owned technology company, called in all workers who had been with the company for more than ten years and asked them to resign voluntarily and then sign new employment contracts as a ploy to evade the law's lifetime employment guarantees for long-time employees, the central government intervened to stop the move, and the company received widespread negative publicity in the mass media (ChinaTechNews.com 2007, *Global Labor Strategies*

2007). In January 2008, when a large automobile assembler sought to use temporary workers to staff an entire plant, the plan was rejected for fear of coming into
conflict with the provisions of the new Labor Contract Law.[2]

In February 2008, the *Wall Street Journal* pointed to the new balance of power
between workers and employers in China. Summing up the judgment of employers, the *WSJ* concluded that the new law "has shifted bargaining power in favor
of employees and raised awareness of rights among workers," ushering in a new
era of higher costs of production (Fong and Canaves 2008).

An analogy between the 2008 Labor Contract Law in China and the 1935 National Labor Relations Act (the Wagner Act) in the United States is instructive. In
both cases, government was responding to the threat of social instability posed by
mounting labor unrest, on the one hand, and the threat of economic instability
posed by a more or less open "underconsumption crisis," on the other hand. In
both cases, the new legislation sought to specify and expand workers' rights while
channeling unrest into formal legal (routine) mechanisms.[3] We know that the
National Labor Relations Act in the United States served as a catalyst for a major
nationwide wave of strikes in 1936–37 and that the strike wave fundamentally
transformed the industrial-relations environment of the United States, as workers
felt encouraged to stand up for their rights in the face of employer intransigence.
It is not implausible to predict that the 2008 Labor Contract Law will likewise
serve as the catalyst for a wave of labor militancy in China—especially if employers (as is likely) attempt to evade the law and if the arbitration system becomes too
burdened with cases to be able to resolve workers' grievances quickly, encouraging them to turn instead to direct action.

In sum, it is not far-fetched to conclude that both in absolute numerical terms
(measurable open unrest) *and* in terms of its impact on the dynamics and future
course of global capitalism, China is becoming the epicenter of world labor unrest and will increasingly be so in the coming decade. Evaluating the likely effects
of this labor unrest on workers inside and outside of China as well as on the trajectory of world capitalism requires that we bring in a further set of analytical
tools, our task in the next section.

SPATIAL "FIXES," PRODUCT CYCLES, AND THE
TRAJECTORY OF GLOBAL CAPITALISM

If an analysis of the dynamics of historical capitalism leads us to predict that
"where capital goes, conflict follows," then this same analysis leads us to look for
a number of predictable capitalist responses to the labor unrest and rising costs in

China. For example, during the past 150 years, capital has responded to labor unrest by geographically relocating production in search of cheaper or more docile labor ("spatial fixes") and by introducing technological/organizational changes in the process of production ("technological fixes"; Silver 2003: chs. 2–3). While these general theoretical insights provide critical analytical tools for understanding contemporary global dynamics, it is also clear that no mechanical application of general theory will suffice. Rather, in this section we must ground (specify) the theory historically/geographically in order to better grasp the current tendencies of global capitalism.

Spatial Fix

There is widespread anecdotal evidence that factory owners in labor-intensive manufacturing are seeking lower-wage sites of production. According to the *Wall Street Journal*, the change in the cost structure in Guangdong and the Pearl River Delta "is sending ripples around the world" as factory owners invest in "new locations deeper inside China" or turn to "poorer countries with lower wage levels" such as Vietnam and Bangladesh (Fong and Canaves 2008; see also Bradsher 2008). In her intensive fieldwork at seven major automobile assembly plants, Zhang (2008) found that although the central government's development plan favored the concentration of automobile production in select cities, auto firms were establishing production units in new regions in response to both competition among local governments to attract auto-industry investment and (real or perceived) differences in the cost and docility of labor forces located in different areas of China.

When strong labor movements emerged in other late industrializers (such as Brazil and South Africa in the 1970s and 1980s), they experienced massive capital flight and deindustrialization. For example, there were massive layoffs in the industrial suburbs of São Paolo (the heart of the Brazilian labor movement) as capital fled to new locations both outside and inside Brazil. One indicator of the impact of these "spatial fixes" on the Brazilian labor movement is the drop in membership in the metalworkers' union in the suburban São Paolo area, from 202,000 in 1987 to 150,000 in 1992 and 130,000 in 1996 (Silver 2003: 57).

Is the Brazilian experience the proper analogy for thinking about likely future dynamics in China? On the one hand, we are already seeing evidence of capital relocation, even though labor unrest in China has not yet reached the scale or intensity seen during the mid-1980s in Brazil. On the other hand, there are good reasons to think that mass capital flight from China is not in the cards. As has been argued elsewhere (see, for example, Arrighi 2007: ch. 11), investment in China is only partly motivated by cheap labor. Rather, economies of agglomeration provided by planned industrial districts and networks, a healthy and educated workforce (in large part the legacy of Mao-era investments in public health and mass literacy), a well-developed transportation and logistics infrastructure, and the size of the internal market are all strong motivations that would remain even if labor costs were to rise substantially. Indeed, if workers' wages rise in China, the size of the market will also increase, making market-oriented investment in China even more attractive.

Of course, access to the Chinese market is not threatened by relocation *within* China (any more than access to the U.S. market was threatened by the large-scale relocation of manufacturing from northern to southern states after the Second World War). Since key Chinese labor legislation is at the national level (rather than the local level), the main outcome of capital relocation internally may be to reduce regional inequalities within China by raising incomes in the new sites of investment, rather than producing a domestic (within China) race to the bottom. Indeed, one of the automobile companies studied by Lu Zhang with production bases in an expensive area of China (where workers have a reputation for being "demanding") set up a new plant in another province with a reputation for cheaper and more docile workers. Shortly after the new factory opened, these allegedly docile workers carried out a strike to protest line speed, arbitrary management decisions, and the fact that their wages were lower than those of workers at the original site of production.[4]

Moreover, the thesis that "where capital goes, conflict follows" is receiving fresh confirmation in the latest favored site for new investment in search of cheap labor—Vietnam. In the Taiwanese press, we find reports of a "strike explosion" hitting foreign-owned businesses in Vietnam in 2007 and 2008. "Anxiety" is reportedly growing among "Taiwanese businessmen" (the largest foreign investors in China) who see the strike situation as getting "worse and worse," with the outcome of strikes strongly favoring the workers (*Lianhe News* 2008).

Technological Fixes

For more than a century, one of the main responses to strong labor movements has been to seek out new forms of labor-saving technology to reduce the total wage bill and reliance on the cooperation of the workforce. Late industrializers tend to introduce the most advanced (labor-saving) technology available even when they are operating in a labor-surplus economy. This mismatch between technology and labor supply weakens workers' marketplace bargaining power.

Modern manufacturing's weak labor absorption capacity is clear in China today. Despite the massive increase in industrial output during the past two decades, employment in manufacturing has essentially stagnated since the mid-1990s. Figure 9.1 illustrates this point with specific reference to the automobile industry in China. While output rose from about one million vehicles in 1992 to more than seven million vehicles in 2006, employment in the automobile industry has remained flat. This outcome was due to the "leaning out" of the state-owned enterprises together with the importation of advanced machinery as well as Taylorist and lean production methods of organizing production (Zhang 2008).

One important question is whether the resulting weak marketplace bargaining power of labor is counterbalanced to any significant extent by strong workplace (structural/disruptive) bargaining power, that is, bargaining power that accrues to workers enmeshed in tightly integrated production processes, where a localized stoppage in one node can cause disruptions on a much wider scale than the stoppage itself. While an in-depth analysis of the workplace bargaining power of Chinese workers is beyond the scope of this chapter, evidence from fieldwork suggests that at least some mass-production workers have significant workplace bargaining power. Take the example of one of the automobile assemblers studied by Zhang, which attempted to introduce "just-in-time" production methods despite a very poor relationship between workers and management. As noted elsewhere (Silver 2003: 67–69), just-in-time production increases the potential workplace bargaining power of labor. It eliminates the buffers built into the traditional Fordist system that had allowed production to proceed in the face of strikes and other events that could cause short-term interruptions in the flow of parts to the assembly line. Relations with management at this particular automobile company were abysmal, reflected among other things in widespread acts of petty sabotage by workers. In the end, in order to keep production flowing smoothly, management felt obliged to eliminate their experiment with just-in-time production methods and return to a system with greater built-in supply buffers.[5]

To be sure, as Evans and Staveteig (2008) point out, only a small percentage of Chinese workers are in manufacturing, and we might add that an even smaller percentage are in capital-intensive industries such as automobile production. To the extent that workplace bargaining power is stronger in capital-intensive manufacturing than in other sectors of the economy and to the extent that the impact of struggles in manufacturing are limited—that is, they don't contribute to "rais-

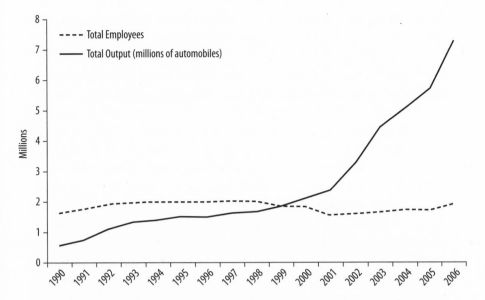

Figure 9.1. Annual Output and Number of Employees in China's Automobile Industry, 1990–2006

ing all workers' boats"—then the fact that a minority of workers have strong workplace bargaining power is not particularly encouraging in relation to the overall project of improving workers' welfare. However, these presumptions (posed by Evans and Staveteig) are debatable. It is not clear that there is a straightforward downward trend in workplace bargaining power as we move from manufacturing to services, and it is not clear that extremely disruptive struggles by a minority of a country's workers have limited social effects (see Silver 2003).

The Product Cycle and Product "Fixes"

What is clear, however, is that China entered the global competition in the mass production of automobiles and other manufacturing activities at a late stage in the "product cycle," that is, in the "standardization" phase when these activities were already subject to intense international competition, that being the period when profit margins are extremely thin. In Vernon's (1966) product-cycle model, newly innovated products tend to get produced in high-income countries, but as products pass through their "life cycle," production facilities are dispersed to increasingly lower-cost (particularly lower-wage) sites of production. In the early "innovative" stage of the product's life cycle, competitive pressures are low, making costs relatively unimportant. But as products reach the stage of "maturity" and finally "standardization," the number of actual and potential competitors grows, as does the pressure to cut costs.

Up until now, we have argued that the geographical relocation of production does not lead to a straightforward race to the bottom in wages and working conditions because new working classes are formed and powerful labor movements tend to emerge in each new favored site of production. However, the product life-cycle theory underscores how each phase of the product cycle takes place in an increasingly competitive environment as production disperses geographically and as the process of production becomes more routinized. In other words, each round of geographical relocation unfolds in a fundamentally different competitive environment. Monopolistic windfall profits—or what Joseph Schumpeter called "spectacular prizes"—accrue to the innovator (1954: 73). But as we move through the stages of the product cycle, there is a decline in an activity's profitability. Moreover, in favoring low-wage sites for new rounds of expansion, production increasingly takes place in sites where the level of national wealth is relatively low. These tendencies, in turn, have important implications for the *outcome* for major waves of labor unrest—especially for the kind of labor-capital accord that labor movements can achieve with a degree of durability for the gains secured (Silver 2003: 77–97).

To clarify this point, let's return for a moment to the analogy (or in this case, the limits of the analogy) with the U.S. post–New Deal era. The strike wave of the Franklin D. Roosevelt years in the United States culminated in a labor-capital-state "social contract" in which employers (especially in mass-production manufacturing) agreed to recognize unions and to steadily increase wages and benefits in step with labor productivity increases. In exchange, workers (and their unions) were to channel grievances through established formal procedures and accept management's right to make decisions about the organization and location of production. The state, in turn, was to promote a macroeconomic environment suitable to this exchange, including keeping unemployment levels low. This social contract remained in effect in the United States for several decades after the Second World War and was openly ruptured only in the 1980s. This relatively durable social contract was in important part underwritten by the "monopoly windfall profits" that accrued to U.S. mass-production employers in the "innovation phase" in the mid–twentieth century.

Clearly, the current competitive environment is less hospitable for most manufacturing activities. Whereas in the United States, autoworkers were able to translate their strong workplace bargaining power into several decades of rising wages and expanding benefits, Chinese autoworkers, with a similar level of workplace bargaining power, have so far experienced stagnating or declining real wages (Zhang 2008: 30). By placing ongoing dynamics in the context of the product cycle, we can also understand better the tensions and contradictions involved at the automobile firm (mentioned above) that, when faced with resistance by workers with strong workplace bargaining power, decided to abandon just-in-time production, that is, it was unable or unwilling to find a way to gain the cooperation of the labor force in its efforts to implement the most advanced organizational forms of production.

We have conceptualized this dynamic in other late industrializers as the social "contradictions of semiperipheral success." From a developmental standpoint, this means that successful late industrializers tend to find themselves "running fast to stay in the same place"—that is, in "the same place" in the global hierarchy of wealth (Silver 1990; Arrighi 1990; cf. chapter 5). However, it is not at all clear that this is the best way to understand contemporary Chinese dynamics.

For one thing, it remains an open question whether China will manage to jump up in the global value-added hierarchy, in which case an analogy with the long-term stable U.S. labor-capital-state social contract of the post–World War II decades may be more relevant than it would seem at first sight. This is a question that we cannot address here, except to point to the massive investments being made by the Chinese central government in the expansion of tertiary education as part of a conscious effort to make the "jump" and capture some of the monopoly windfall profits that accrue to activities in the innovation phase of the product cycle. Yet even if China were able to jump up in the global value-added hierarchy, simple imitation of the wasteful U.S. mass-consumption model would be unsustainable and undesirable on ecological and other grounds.

This brings us to the urgent (but as yet unanswerable) question raised by Giovanni Arrighi (2007) in *Adam Smith in Beijing*: whether China's specific historical legacy—both the revolutionary legacy of the Mao years and the longer-term historical experience of noncapitalist market development—has left open paths for social innovation that depart in fundamental ways from twentieth-century capitalist dynamics.

WORKERS OF THE WORLD AND CHINA

If, as we argued in the first part of this chapter, a major shift in the balance of power between labor and capital is taking place in China, what are the implications for labor and labor movements in other parts of the world? A common storyline in much of the world is that if labor standards were to improve in China, then the attractiveness of China as a site for foreign direct investment would decline dramatically. Global flows of capital would reverse direction, and the problems of labor movements outside of China would be largely solved.

There are problems with this storyline. The first problem has been discussed above. That is, economies of agglomeration provided by planned industrial districts and networks, a healthy and educated workforce, and the size of the internal market are all strong motivations for investment in China that would remain even if labor costs rise substantially. If anything, rising real wages will make China even more attractive as a site of investment as the relative global weight of the Chinese market increases further.[6]

To be sure, some countries of the Global South *may* find themselves in a better position to attract some of the labor-intensive foreign direct investment that might have previously headed to China—although as suggested above, it is not at all clear that the path to "development" in the twenty-first century is through a single-minded pursuit of manufacturing activities in the last stage of the product cycle. Rather, a more likely path might be through the strategic use of the "windfall profits" in commodity prices in support of longer-term investments in development. For one outcome of the rapid economic expansion of China has been an overall secular reversal in the terms of trade between primary and secondary economic activities.

Rising labor costs in China will have a serious impact on workers as consumers outside of China as the foundations of the low-road neoliberal "social compact" pioneered by the United States (and exported elsewhere) begin to crumble. For to the extent that the suppression of real wages in the United States has been socially sustainable, it has been founded on the massive importation of low-cost consumer items from China as well as on a mushrooming current account deficit. This model is in the midst of crumbling—as "stagflation" alarms are sounded—however, it is still unclear in late 2008 whether there will be a "soft landing" or a socially and politically catastrophic collapse.

While the crumbling of this low-road neoliberal social compact is no doubt a good thing for workers around the world, labor academics and activists have not even begun to think through the political dynamics of the emergent new era, much less an overarching vision of the new forms of labor organization. Without such a rethinking, the chances of jumping from the frying pan into the fire are high (cf. Arrighi and Silver 1999: conclusion). At a minimum, such strategies must be prepared to navigate a politically dangerous interregnum between the collapse of the old and the birth of the new—in other words, to be strategically prepared (to the extent that it is possible to be prepared) for the catastrophic collapse scenario. One important place to start is to come to terms with the intimate historical link between the rise of the "welfare state" and the "warfare state" in the West, that is, between the rise of labor power and state power (Silver 2003: ch. 4). Notwithstanding the tensions between states and labor created by the neoliberal turn, this link has never been truly broken. If we are indeed in the midst of a fundamental redistribution of global wealth and power from North to South and from West to East, then a kind of "cultural revolution" in the Global North/West is needed: a cultural struggle in which a more equal world order comes to be seen as a blessing, rather than a threat to be fought off by any means available.

NOTES

1. To be sure, one must use caution in interpreting these figures. Once we adjust for China's population of 1.3 billion, the official figures are less striking. However, the sharp upward trend in the number of incidents is still very dramatic (and the official figures for mass protests are almost certainly an underestimate of the actual number of events).

2. Interview with firm manager by Lu Zhang, Beijing, January 2008.

3. These concerns are made clear in the opening two paragraphs of the National Labor Relations Act. For the text of the law, see www.nlrb.gov/about_us/overview/national_labor_relations_act.aspx, accessed November 12, 2008.

4. Lu Zhang's fieldwork notes, October 2006.

5. Lu Zhang's fieldwork notes, January 2008.

6. A second problem with this storyline, which we will set aside for now, is that it assumes that the problems of labor movements outside China are to a significant degree attributable to competition ("fair" or "unfair") from China. As Ruth Milkman (2006) has shown for the United States, the crisis of the U.S. labor movement in manufacturing preceded the rise of competition from China; moreover, sweatshop conditions emerged in service-sector activities not subject to international competitive pressures such as trucking and janitorial services.

REFERENCES

Arrighi, Giovanni. 1990. "The Developmentalist Illusion: A Reconceptualization of the Semiperiphery." In *Semiperipheral States in the World-Economy*, ed. William G. Martin, 11–42. New York: Greenwood Press.

———. 2007. *Adam Smith in Beijing: Lineages of the Twenty-First Century*. London: Verso.

Arrighi, Giovanni, and Beverly J. Silver. 1999. *Chaos and Governance in the Modern World System*. Minneapolis: University of Minnesota Press.

Bradsher, Keith. 2008. "Investors Seek Asian Options to Costly China." *New York Times*, June 18, 2008.

Business Watch. 2006. "Labour's Breakthrough at Wal-Mart." September 4. English translation.

Chan, Anita. 2006, "Organizing Wal-Mart: The Chinese Trade Union at a Crossroads." *Japan Focus*, September 8.

Chan Siu-sin and Daniel Kwan. 2003. "Union's New Approach Puts Workers' Rights First." *South China Morning Post*, September 12.

China Labour Bulletin. 2007. "Migrant Workers Start to Win Significant Compensation Awards in the Courts." *CLB*, November 23. Available at www.china-labour.org.hk/en/node/50878, accessed November 15, 2008.

ChinaTechNews.com. 2007. "Investigation Arranged for Huawei's Labor." China TechNews.com, November 6. Available at www.chinatechnews.com/2007/11/06/6056-investigation-arranged-for-huaweis-labor-issue, November 15, 2008.

Cody, Edward. 2004. "In China, Workers Turn Tough: Spate of Walkouts May Signal New Era." *Washington Post*, November 27, A1.

Evans, Peter, and Sarah Staveteig. 2008. "The Changing Structure of Employment in Contemporary China." In *Creating Wealth and Poverty in Post-Socialist China*, ed. Deborah Davis and Feng Wang. Stanford, CA: Stanford University Press.

Fong Mei and Sky Canaves. 2008. "Factories on China's South Coast Lose Their Edge: Thousands Close as Increased Costs Alter the Equation." *Wall Street Journal*, February 22, A9.

Global Labor Strategies. 2007. "The Battle for Labor Rights in China: New Developments." Global Labor Strategies, November. Available at http://laborstrategies.blogs.com/global_labor_strategies/2007/11/the-battle-for-.html, accessed November 15, 2008.

Lee Ching Kwan. 2007. *Against the Law: Labor Protests in China's Rustbelt and Sunbelt*. Berkeley: University of California Press.

Lianhe News. 2008. "Strike Explosion in Vietnam. 20 Taiwanese Factories Stop Working." *Lianhe News* (Taipei, Taiwan), April 28.

People's Daily. 2005. "Building Harmonious Society Crucial for China's Progress: Hu." *People's Daily Online*, June 27. Available at http://english.peopledaily.com.cn/200506/27/eng20050627_192495.html, accessed November 15, 2008.

Piven, Frances, and Richard Cloward. 1977. *Poor Peoples' Movements: Why They Succeed, How They Fail*. New York: Vintage Books.

Schumpeter, Joseph. 1954. *Capitalism, Socialism, and Democracy*. London: Allen and Unwin.

Silver, Beverly J. 1990. "The Contradictions of Semiperipheral Success: The Case of Israel." In *Semiperipheral States in the World-Economy*, ed. William G. Martin, 161–81. New York: Greenwood Press.

———. 2003. *Forces of Labor: Workers' Movements and Globalization since 1870*. New York: Cambridge University Press.

Vernon, Raymond. 1966. "International Investment and International Trade in the Product Cycle." *Quarterly Journal of Economics* 80, no. 2: 190–207.

White, Chris. 2007. "China's New Labour Law: The Challenges of Regulating Employment Contracts." Evatt Foundation Papers. Available at http://evatt.org.au/ publications/papers/193.html, accessed November 15, 2008.

Xinhua. 2008. "Hu: China to Promote Sustainable Development, Protect Workers' Rights and Interests." *Xinhua*, January 7.

Zhang Lu. 2008. "Lean Production and Labor Controls in the Chinese Automobile Industry in an Age of Globalization." *International Labor and Working-Class History* 73 (Spring): 24–44.

CHAPTER TEN

A Caveat

Is the Rise of China Sustainable?

HO-FUNG HUNG

In the previous nine chapters, we see the historical origins and contradictory nature of the rapid economic expansion of China and how this expansion has started to shape the global capitalist system. What they present is not a coherent prediction of a unilinear path of global development in the twenty-first century but a cacophony of possible trajectories of global change that the rise of China could bring about—or exacerbate.

The global impacts of the rise of China are threefold. Geoeconomically, it is reshaping the distribution of power and profit along the global value chain, which has been dominated by giant retailers in the core since the inception of the new international division of labor in the 1970s. The thriving and consolidation of giant transnational manufacturing contractors in the Greater China region is shifting the balance of power between periphery manufacturers and core retailer chains, in the former's favor. The increasing organizational strength and bargaining position of these contractors also speed up industrial upgrading in China and other places where these transnational contractors operate (chapter 4).

Geopolitically, the rise of China is creating new sources of conflict between China and core powers. China's increasing weight in the global economy has been at the expense of the relative weight of core powers. In the 1990s, the core's loss of weight was mainly compensated for by its headway into the former Soviet bloc in Eastern Europe and Central Asia. But when the decline of these formerly socialist countries bottomed out at the turn of the twenty-first century, rising China started to find itself in direct conflict with the U.S.-led core powers in a zero-sum competition for global influence (chapter 5). One concrete example of such conflict is the intensifying competition between China and Japan (as well as other core powers) for the allegiance of natural-resources exporters in the periphery (chapter 6). At the same time, China's escalating competition with core powers is tempting it to form alliances with other states aspiring to challenge the existing global order, with Russia, which recently rebounded from its geopolitical and geoeconomic decline, as the most auspicious example. If such geoeconomic and geopolitical integration of China and Russia really materializes, then it could presage the rise of a semiperiphery, Eurasian power bloc that is strong enough to bring about a multipolar world order (chapter 7).

At last, China's economic expansion is also precipitating a prospective revival of the global labor movement. On the one hand, the rapid growth of China's market economy is fomenting an impressive reduction in poverty within China, and it never triggered the massive pauperization that many African and Latin American countries experienced amid their neoliberal reform (this international comparison leads to the characterization of Chinese development as an "accumulation without dispossession" in chapter 2). On the other hand, in the course of market reform, many Chinese workers and peasants are stripped of the collective welfare that they used to enjoy under the state socialist system, and the Chinese population is increasingly polarized into winners and losers in the market economy (this temporal comparison makes Chinese development appear to be an "accumulation with dispossession," as suggested in chapter 3 and chapter 7). The transformation of a vast rural population into nascent proletarians, who become increasingly conscious of their rights and militant in collective action, entails the potential for a new wave of working-class solidarity. The labor movements in the United States and other core states have been attempting to build international solidarity with Chinese workers and to facilitate the rise of a vital labor movement there (chapter 8). Besides this external assistance, indigenous labor activism also emerges in the export-oriented manufacturing zones on its own, despite the draconian repression of the state. The budding labor activism in China, just like the labor movements in previous rising centers of capital accumulation such as the United States in the early twentieth century and South Korea in the late twentieth century, is poised to energize labor movements elsewhere in the global economy (chapter 9).

Most of the above trends are incipient. It is still too early to tell whether they will become sustained processes and realize their full potential in reshaping the global capitalist system in the long run. One necessary condition for the continuation of these trends is the sustained rapid economic expansion of China. In most of this volume, we bracket the discussion about the sustainability of China's developmental miracle and assume that it will continue in the years to come. In what follows, I try to outline the challenges that China must tackle in order to perpetuate its stellar economic performance. I also discuss possible scenarios that could unfold if China's developmental momentum is interrupted by economic crisis.

THE CONTRADICTIONS OF CHINA'S DEVELOPMENTAL MODEL

Amazed by the dazzling economic expansion of China in the last three decades, which confounds any single prediction about a major economic crisis, many of the world's China watchers became convinced that its economic expansion is simply unstoppable. But within China, ironically, the excitement about the prospect of endless economic growth has long been offset by anxiety about a looming economic crisis. In 2007, the Chinese Academy of Social Science warned that China was witnessing an unsustainable expansion of an asset bubble reminiscent of what Japan experienced in the 1980s and the early 1990s. The prolonged economic difficulties that haunted postbubble Japan for a decade and a half, the report warned, may not be far off if timely actions are not taken to rein in the excessive liquidity now threatening China's economy (*People's Daily*, January 13, 2007). At a press conference during the annual plenary session of the National People's Congress in March 2007, Premier Wen Jiabao even characterized the current path of development in China as "unstable, unbalanced, uncoordinated, and unsustainable." In the spring of 2008, he went further, warning that the most difficult times of the Chinese economy in a decade were imminent. The core source of the unsustainability of China's economic expansion is the growing economic imbalance caused by its overinvestment and underconsumption. This imbalance made China dependent on the export market and therefore vulnerable to any contraction in global demand for its product caused either by global economic crisis or by rising protectionism. The stalling of China's economy under the global financial crisis since the fall of 2008 seems to have vindicated these warnings.

The first sociopolitical attribute of China that makes its miracle possible is the salience of local developmental or corporatist states in soliciting foreign investment and promoting local economic growth in a singleminded manner. The second attribute is the vitality of the authoritarian party-state that managed to repress labor's demands and the growth of civil society. While the autonomy and competitive pressure among local states perpetually goad them to increase their individual attractiveness, and hence China's overall attractiveness, to global capital, the authoritarian rule keeps discontent at bay and ensures that the Chinese economy can grow in a breathtaking, polarizing fashion without the need of global capital and other reform's beneficiaries to sacrifice for large-scale income redistribution through taxation and wage increase. These two processes, when unfolding on the vast geographical and demographic scale of China, easily make China the most dynamic center of capital accumulation in the world system. But this same sociopolitical framework is also the root of China's economic imbalance and vulnerability. While the decentralization of economic governance accelerates overinvestment, unchecked social polarization constrains the growth of domestic consumption power. This imbalance seems particularly disturbing when we compare China's pattern of growth with the patterns of other Asian Tigers at their comparable stages of development.

First, the decentralized nature of the Chinese developmental state makes the problem of overinvestment more severe in China than in earlier Asian Tigers. During the initial economic ascendancy of Japan, South Korea, and Taiwan, central governments played a key role in mobilizing and allocating precious financial and other resources to support the growth of strategic industrial sectors. This "pick the winner" process is crucial not only to success in the early stages of industrial takeoff but also to the subsequent industrial upgrading of these economies (Wade 1990; Haggard 1990; Evans 1995). The decentralized economic growth in today's China deviates from the model of a centralized developmental state (So 2003: 18–19). Many local states in China act "developmentally" in that they proactively facilitate growth of selected industrial sectors, and these developmental efforts are often well planned and executed at the local level. The totality of these efforts combined, however, entails anarchic competition among localities, resulting in uncoordinated construction of redundant production capacity and infrastructure. Foreign investors, with the expectation that the Chinese market and world market for Chinese products will grow incessantly, also race with one another to expand their existing industrial capacity in China. Though export-oriented foreign investments yield decent profit so far as the world market, the U.S. market in particular, remains robust, investments made by many state-owned, domestic-market-oriented enterprises are increasingly excessive and unprofitable.

Idle capacity in such key sectors as steel, automobile, cement, aluminum, and real estate has been soaring ever since the mid-1990s (Rawski 2002: 364–65). It is estimated that more than 75 percent of China's industries are currently plagued by overcapacity (Rajun 2006) and that fixed asset investment in industries already experiencing overinvestment accounted for 40 to 50 percent of China's GDP growth in 2005 (Xie 2006, see also Huang 2002; Rawski 2002: 364–65). The State

Development and Reform Commission predicts that output in the automobile industry will be more than double what the market can possibly digest by 2010, if production capacity is not curbed sufficiently (*Xinhuawang*, November 14, 2005). The buildup of excess capacity is exacerbated by the lack of geographical and intersectoral mobility of domestic enterprises, which increases their propensity to invest in already saturating localities and sectors. On the one hand, many provincial or municipal governments have erected protectionist barriers against investment from other provinces or cities. This has fragmented the national economy and constricted the room for virtuous expansion as well as consolidation of domestic capital, creating a "one country, thirty-two economies" malaise (Huang 2003: 140–48). A survey finds that 85.8 percent of state-owned enterprises invested only in the same city and that 91.1 percent invested only in the same province (Kiester and Lu 2001: 26). However, underdevelopment of financial markets makes it difficult for enterprises to divert their savings to invest in underinvested new sectors that yield higher profit, hence restricting their choice to fixed asset investment in their own sectors (Rajun 2006).

To make matters worse, major state-owned banks, rather than discipline enterprises and direct them away from excessive and low-return investments, encourage these investments through lax lending practices. These banks, as the financial arms of the central and local governments, deliver easy credits to insolvent or profligate state-owned industrial enterprises, of which roughly 40 percent incurred losses in 2006, according to government figures (Bank for International Settlement 2007: 56). In contrast, private enterprises, even very successful ones, are at a disadvantageous position in obtaining financial support from major state banks. The irony that losing state enterprises can obtain credit more easily than profitable, promising private enterprises sets China far apart from the developmental experiences of other East Asian developmental states, where state-funded industrial banks efficiently allocate resources to the "winners," not the "losers" (Tsai 2002: 29–35; Shih 2004).

The state banks' motive in extending loans to keep unprofitable state-owned enterprises afloat is to maintain social and political stability by slowing massive layoffs on the part of these units. In addition, these loans are often the result at the behest of local party bosses, who command overwhelming influence over local branches of state banks and are inclined to fuel local investment booms to boost local growth figures and short-term government revenue gain. These loans constitute a channel through which resources are redistributed from the profit-making economic units, which deposit their savings in the banks and pay tax to the government, to the losing ones. This dysfunctional redistribution of financial resources magnifies the sectoral overinvestment into a generalized risk to the economy through the pileup of nonperforming loans in the financial system (Lardy 1998; Rawski 2002; *The Economist*, October 29, 2005). As the Bank for International Settlement remarks, "In China, the principal concern must be that misallocated capital will eventually manifest itself in falling profits, and that this will feed back on the bank system, the fiscal authorities and the prospects for growth more generally. After a long period of credit-fueled expansion, this would be the classic denouement. Indeed, this was very much the path followed [before the prolonged crisis in the 1990s] by Japan" (Bank for International Settlement 2006: 144).

The ratio of nonperforming loans to all outstanding loans has been falling since the late 1990s. But this is largely a result of recurrent governmental overhauls that involve massive government bailouts and transfer of these loans to state-owned asset-management companies, rapid expansion of new loans, and even deliberate underreporting of nonperforming loans (*New York Times*, November 15, 2006; Dobson and Kashyap 2006; Naughton 2007: 460–67). A recent survey shows that after years of bank reform, major state banks continue to lend without taking into account the profitability and risk of their borrowers (Podpiera 2006). As Nicholas Lardy points out, this continuous reckless lending could renew the accumulation of bad debt and "erase some of the very hard-won progress in bank reform in the last eight years" (quoted in *The Economist*, April 8, 2006). Many seemingly "good" loans at times of rapid economic growth could swiftly deteriorate into bad ones when the economy slows, leading to an explosion of nonperforming loans, similar to what Japan underwent in the early 1990s.

The second problem that plagues China's current developmental model is underconsumption. All East Asian Tigers at their initial stage of industrial takeoff were governed by authoritarian regimes. But these regimes were disciplined by Cold War geopolitics. Just next door to Communist China, they were anxious to root out any plausible socialist influence among the lower classes. They achieved this goal through preemptive redistributive policies such as land reform and provision of free education as much as through repression of independent labor and peasant organizations. By letting the fruits of economic expansion trickle down to the lower classes, in particular the rural population, these authoritarian regimes became economically inclusive, even though they were highly exclusive politically (Deyo 1987; Haggard 1990: 223–53). The reduction in income disparity and rising income among the lower classes helped create sizeable domestic markets in these newly industrializing economies. Though the success of these economies is mostly attributable to their export-led growth, domestic consumption also plays an indispensable role in the takeoff process by buffering the economies against the vagaries of the world market, in addition to providing infant industries with sufficient internal demand before they compete internationally (Grabowski 1994).

In contrast, China's party-state in the 1990s singlemindedly pursued rapid economic growth without much success in alleviating the subsequent social polarization, which was aggravated by the government's draconian suppression of dissenting voices from the bottom of the society. Class, urban-rural, and interregional inequalities expanded hand in hand with the economic miracle. Poverty intensified in the rural inland area, and the old bastions of state industry were besieged by extensive unemployment (Wang and Hu 1999; Riskin et al. 2001). As jobs created by export-oriented global capital could not catch up with the jobs disappearing from battered state-owned factories, China appears to have experienced a net loss of manufacturing jobs since the mid-1990s, with the share of manufacturing in total employment never reaching the levels found at the peak of manufacturing employment in the smaller newly industrializing economies (Evans and Staveteig 2008). The peasants-turned-workers in the coastal boom towns are not doing much better. Owing to the colossal size of the pool of surplus labor and the "despotic factory regime" under the auspices of the party-state, manufacturing wage growth amid China's economic miracle is dismal in comparison with the growth in other East Asian newly industrializing economies during their miraculous moments (Lee 1998; Glyn 2005: 22; Hung 2008: 162).

During the most explosive phase of takeoff, South Korea and Taiwan remained modestly equalitarian societies, as their Gini coefficients stayed in the range of 0.3 to 0.4 throughout the 1960s and 1970s (most noteworthy, Taiwan's Gini coefficient declined during its takeoff years from the range of 0.5 to 0.6 in the 1950s to the range of 0.3 to 0.4 in the 1970s). On the contrary, China's Gini coefficient ascended from 0.33 in 1980 to more than 0.45 today. The increasingly skewed distribution of income constrained expansion of the mass-consumption market. Figures from the World Bank suggest that share of wage income in China's GDP declined from 53 percent in 1998 to 41.4 percent in 2005, and that "the declining role of wages and household income in the economy are the key driver behind the declining share of consumption in GDP" (He and Kuijs 2007: 11–12). The growth of consumption in China is hardly stagnant, but it has not kept pace with the exuberant growth in investment, and the consumption-investment gap has been enlarging rapidly ever since 1989 (Hung 2008: 164).

The combination of overinvestment and underconsumption of the Chinese economy makes China increasingly reliant on the global market to export its excess capacity. This in turn makes China very vulnerable to any protracted global economic downturn. At the same time, the long-neglected externalities of development in the form of rapid environmental degradation, which has started to impinge on economic growth, only makes the prospect of China's developmental miracle gloomier.

THE SPECTERS OF OVERACCUMULATION
AND ENVIRONMENTAL CRISES

China's ratio of gross fixed capital formation to final consumption expenditure, which offers us a sense of the imbalance between investment and consumption, has exceeded the level that most other Asian economies reached on the eve of the Asian Financial Crisis (Hung 2008: 165). This escalation of the investment-to-consumption ratio is reminiscent of what the United States and Japan witnessed on the eve of the Great Depression in the 1930s and the "lost decade" of the 1990s, respectively. According to many, these crises, despite unfolding differently and taking place at different junctures in the development of twentieth-century global capitalism, are comparable overaccumulation crises, commonly rooted at a conjuncture of debt-financed expansion of excess industrial capacity, asset inflation, sluggish domestic demand, and falling profitability in the production sectors (Aglietta 1979: 353–79; Devine 1983; Bello 1998; Wade 2000; Murphy 2000; Erturk 2002; Palat 2003).

The accumulation of excess industrial capacity, gluts, and relatively sluggish consumption growth leads to falling prices of finished products in key industrial sectors and falling profit margins in key industries (see also Fan and Felipe 2005; Shan 2006a, 2006b; Islam et al. 2006: 149–54; Hung 2008: 166).The growing economic imbalance and concern about profitless growth lead many to question the sustainability of the current boom and to anticipate an economic crisis to come. This anticipation began to surface among Chinese economists as well as China watchers in the West as early as the aftermath of the Asian Financial Crisis (see, for example, Fernald and Babson 1999; Lin 2000). But this fear was soon allayed by the continuation of robust economic expansion driven by debt-financed investment, FDI inflow, and export growth. These upward trends were not unrelated to the heightened optimism about China's economy at home and abroad, enlivened by China's entry into WTO and its successful bid for hosting the 2008 Olympics in 2001. Ironically, this great expectation among investors further deepens the economy's imbalance, as it intensifies overinvestment without contributing much to the growth of domestic consumption.

While the investment-consumption gap keeps enlarging, China becomes ever more dependent on its booming export sector to neutralize the increasing peril that its excessive capacity in the domestic-market-oriented sector places it in. Ballooning foreign reserve resulting from rapid export growth fuels a credit expansion in the banking sector, boosting debt-financed investment further and in turn exacerbating the buildup of excess production capacity to be countervailed by further export growth. A cycle of surging export and surging investment ensues (see *Washington Post*, January 17, 2006). In sum, China's pattern of economic growth today is marked by a high (and ever-increasing) dependence on export and debt-finance investment, on the one hand, and low domestic consumption, on the other. Although the earlier "East Asian developmental miracles" are known for their high investment and low consumption rates, they are dwarfed by those that China is running. China's current fixed asset investment rate (above 50 percent of GDP) is nearly double Taiwan's and South Korea's rate at their peaks of industrial growth in the 1970s (which was about 25 to 35 percent). Its private consumption rate (below 40 percent), on the other hand, is much lower than Taiwan's and South Korea's rate in the 1970s (about 60 to 70 percent for Korea and 50 to 60 percent for Taiwan).

It is doubtful whether China's formidable export engine, so far the economy's single most profitable component as well as one that neutralizes the risk of an overaccumulation crisis, will last indefinitely. In the three decades following the Second World War, the success of the export-led development strategy of the Asian Tigers rested mainly on the fact that there were so few small developing economies pursuing the strategy. The exports of these economies were easily absorbed in the world market. But when many more developing countries adopted the strategy in the 1980s and 1990s, the world market, flooded with cheap manufactured exports, became ever more volatile. Given how great its economic size and export volume are, China is exceptionally vulnerable (Mead 1999; Palley 2002; Asian Development Bank 2005: 40–62). Worse, China's exporting trade is highly concentrated in the U.S. consumer market, which currently absorbs more than 30 percent of China's total exports (including reexports via Hong Kong; see Roach 2006a, 2006b).

The expansion of the U.S. consumer market has hinged on an unsustainable, debt-financed consumption spree and has created a mega–current account deficit. As has been long anticipated, the U.S. economy has started to readjust via the bursting of its real-estate bubble and collapse of its debt-financed consumerism since 2007. This readjustment of China's main export outlet is occurring alongside a substantial appreciation of the Chinese yuan and the rise of protectionist measures in the U.S. and other economies. This conjuncture of events puts great pressure on the profitability of China's export sector. If the current economic adjustment of the United States escalates into a full-blown and protracted crisis that spreads to the entire global economy, and the gap between domestic production capacity and domestic consumption in China is not sufficiently narrowed in time, the outbreak of an overaccumulation crisis in China is certain.

Just at the moment when an economic slowdown is looming, the environmental cost of three decades of reckless development has begun to exact a toll on the Chinese economy. For example, it is estimated that 40 percent of China's water supply is now so polluted that it is unusable for any purpose, a circumstance that substantially increases the cost of industrial production in many sectors (Economy 2004). Pollution-related diseases are also escalating, and this also diminishes the labor productivity of the country. It is therefore not an exaggeration for a report on the state of the Chinese environment to claim that:

> China's environmental problems are reaching the point where they could constrain its GDP growth. China's State Environmental Protection Administration (SEPA) concluded in June 2006 that environmental degradation and pollution cost the Chinese economy the equivalent of 10% of GDP annually. This figure is echoed in more specific costs reported in the Chinese press: up to $36 billion in lost industrial output from a lack of water to run factories, $13 billion from the degradation and health impact of acid rain, $6 billion from the spread of desert regions, and the list goes on. (Economy and Lieberthal 2007: 90)

In light of these possible constraints on China's economic growth in the future, the prospect for China to perpetuate its rapid economic expansion can no longer be taken for granted.

TOWARD A RESTRUCTURING OF CHINA'S DEVELOPMENTAL MODEL

The highest echelon of China's party-state elite has long been aware of the vulnerability of the economy, and they have been actively devising preemptive policies to redress the economic imbalance. Following the Asian Financial Crisis of 1997–98, China's State Council launched a series of income redistribution programs to boost domestic demand, with an expectation that they could end China's precarious dependence on export and debt-financed investment for economic growth. These initiatives included directing state investment into the impoverished, rural Western interior as well as increasing peasants' disposable income through tax and fee reduction. They aimed to open up China's rural market, a vast and uncharted frontier for many consumer goods, in contrast to the more or less saturated urban markets. They also included the institutionalization of a comprehensive social security system that would encourage urbanites and villagers alike to spend more in the present and save less for future uncertainty. Beginning in late 2003, the central government launched a series of macroeconomic adjustment measures to curb excessive investment via administrative orders and tightening of credit supply to local governments and state-owned enterprises. On the environmental front, the central government strengthened regulations on polluting industrial enterprises, hoping that tougher measures would lead to a phase-out of low-value-added sectors more detrimental to the environment and speed up the rise of cleaner, more technologically intensive industries.

The ambition of these high-sounding measures notwithstanding, the key question is how the central government could ensure their full implementation by local governments. Some optimistically see these measures as the beginning of a great shift in China's developmental model for good, although this shift will take time to unfold (chapter 3). Others pessimistically see them as no more than yet another series of ineffective reforms on paper fiercely resisted by local officials, whose obsession with maximizing their short-term private gains contradicts Beijing's concern about the economy's long-term stability (chapter 7).

Given the strong resistance to these economic and environmental regulations on the part of local vested interests, preventing an overaccumulation crisis through these regulations will inevitably involve more than technical policy change. A restructuring of China's sociopolitical order is necessary. The state could recentralize state power all the way to the central government to strengthen its capacity in coordinating the hitherto anarchic local developments. To break the resistance of the entrenched local interests that frequently hijacked the making or implementation of central government's policy, the party-state could mobilize the support of the downtrodden peasants and workers by installing institutional protection of their rights. There are signs that the current leaders of the CCP have been moving in this direction, as the implementation of the New Labor Contract Law in 2008 suggests (see chapters 8 and 9). On the other hand, it is doubtful whether these sociopolitical restructurings can be accomplished soon, as the sociopolitical order underlining the current economic expansion and its imbalance has taken root during three decades of market transition.

Given the great imbalance of the Chinese economy and the delay in its sociopolitical restructuring, China is increasingly vulnerable to any protracted global economic slump that can curtail China's capability of exporting its excess capacity to the world. On the other hand, we have reason to believe that China is likely to be able to emerge from such a crisis in the long run. Provided with the massive financial resources that the Chinese government has accumulated for the last two decades, it enjoys plentiful leeway to resort to large-scale fiscal stimulus and social spending to shore up consumption demand should the economy run into trouble. If the crisis lingers, the pains of economic collapse and the subsequent sociopolitical conflicts will probably generate an impetus that helps clear the vested interests' resistance to social reform and the restructuring of China's developmental model once and for all, hence accelerating the current half-hearted, incremental restructuring. It is reminiscent of how the Great Depression empowered the progressive reformers in the United States to break the resistance of big business to redistributive and regulatory reforms and introduce the New Deal, which hastened the transition of the economic growth of the United States from a reckless and unstable path dominated by robber barons at the turn of the twentieth century to the more sustainable course of Keynesian-Fordist growth in the mid–twentieth century (Aglietta 1979).

Thus, despite the increasing likelihood of an economic slowdown or contraction in China in the short to medium run due to its overaccumulation tendency and environmental crisis, it is quite possible that the shift of the center of gravity of global capitalism to Asia in general and to China in particular will sustain in the long run, creating a new global order in the twenty-first century. The key determinant of whether this possibility can become reality is whether China can eventually transform its developmental model into a more egalitarian, more coordinated, and less environmentally destructive one.

REFERENCES

Aglietta, Michel. 1979. A Theory of Capitalist Regulation: The U.S. Experience. London: Verso.
Asian Development Bank. 2005. Asian Development Outlook 2005. Manila: Asian Development Bank.
Bank for International Settlement. 2006. 76th Annual Report. Basel: Bank for International Settlement.
———. 2007. 77th Annual Report. Basel: Bank for International Settlement.
Bello, Walden. 1998. "East Asia: On the Eve of the Great Transformation?" Review of International Political Economy 5, no. 3: 424–44.
Devine, James N. 1983. "Underconsumption, Over-Investment, and the Origins of the Great Depression." Journal of Radical Political Economics 15, no. 2: 1–27.

Deyo, Frederic C. 1987. "State and Labor: Modes of Political Exclusion in East Asian Development." In *The Political Economy of the New Asian Industrialism*, ed. F. C. Deyo, 227–48. Ithaca: Cornell University Press.

Dobson, Wendy, and Anil K. Kashyap. 2006. "The Contradiction in China's Gradualist Banking Reforms." *Brookings Papers on Economic Activity*, Fall 2006, 103–48.

Economy, Elizabeth C. 2004. *The River Runs Black: The Environmental Challenge to China's Future*. Ithaca: Cornell University Press.

Economy, Elizabeth C., and Kenneth Lieberthal. 2007. "Scorched Earth: Will Environmental Risks in China Overwhelm its Opportunities?" *Harvard Business Review* 85, no. 6 (June).

Erturk, Korkut A. 2002. "Overcapacity and the East Asian Crisis." *Journal of Post Keynesian Economics* 24, no. 2: 253–75.

Evans, Peter. 1995. *Embedded Autonomy: States and Industrial Transformation*. Princeton: Princeton University Press.

Evans, Peter, and Sarah Staveteig. 2008. "The Changing Structure of Employment in Contemporary China." In *Creating Wealth and Poverty in Post-Socialist China*, ed. Deborah Davis and Feng Wang. Stanford University Press.

Fan, Emma X., and Jesus Felipe. 2005. "The Diverging Patterns of Profitability, Investment, and Growth of China and India, 1980–2003." Center for Applied Macroeconomic Analysis, Australian National University Working Paper.

Fernald, John G., and Oliver D. Babson. 1999. "Why Has China Survived the Asian Crisis So Well? What Risks Remain?" Board of Governors of the Federal Reserve System: International Finance Discussion Paper No. 333.

Glyn, Andrew. 2005. "Imbalances of the Global Economy." *New Left Review* 2, no. 34: 5–37.

Grabowski, Richard. 1994. "The Successful Developmental State: Where Does It Come From?" *World Development* 22, no. 3: 413–22.

Haggard, Stephen. 1990. *Pathways from the Periphery: The Politics of Growth in the Newly Industrializing Countries*. Ithaca: Cornell University Press.

He Jianwu and Louis Kuijs. 2007. "Rebalancing China's Economy—Modeling a Policy Package." World Bank China Research Paper No. 7. Available at www.world bank.org.cn/English/Content/253l63888224.shtml, accessed November 15, 2008.

Huang Yasheng. 2002. "Between Two Coordination Failures: Automotive Industrial Policy in China with a Comparison to Korea." *Review of International Political Economy* 9, no. 3: 538–73.

———. 2003. *Selling China: Foreign Direct Investment during the Reform Era*. Cambridge, UK: Cambridge University Press.

Hung Ho-fung. 2008. "Rise of China and the Global Overaccumulation Crisis." *Review of International Political Economy* 15, no. 2: 149–78.

Islam, Nazrul, Dai Erbiao, and Hiroshi Sakamoto. 2006. "Role of TFP in China's Growth." *Asian Economic Journal* 20, no. 2: 127–59.

Keister, Lisa A., and Jin Lu. 2001. "The Transformation Continues: The Status of Chinese State-Owned Enterprises at the Start of the Millennium." *NBR Analysis* 12, No. 3.

Lardy, Nicholas. 1998. *China's Unfinished Economic Revolution*. Washington, D.C.: Brookings Institution Press.

Lee Ching-kwan. 1998. *Gender and the South China Miracle*. Berkeley: University of California Press.

Lin Justin Y. 2000. "The Current Deflation in China: Causes and Policy Options." *Asian Pacific Journal of Economics and Business* 4, no. 2: 4–21.

Mead, Walter Russell. 1999. "Needed: A New Growth Strategy for the Developing World." *Development Outreach*, World Bank, Summer. Available at http://www.worldbank.org/devoutreach/summer99/article.asp?id=6, accessed November 15, 2008.

Murphy, Taggard R. 2000. "Japan's Economic Crisis." *New Left Review* (January/February): 25–52.

Naughton, Barry. 2007. *The Chinese Economy: Transitions and Growth*. Cambridge, MA: MIT Press.

Palat, Ravi A. 2003. "'Eyes Wide Shut': Reconceptualizing the Asian Crisis." *Review of International Political Economy* Vol. 10, No. 2: 169–95.

Palley, Thomas I. 2002 "A New Development Paradigm: Domestic Demand-Led Growth." *Foreign Policy in Focus*, September.

Podpiera, Richard. 2006. "Progress in China's Banking Sector Reform: Has Bank Behavior Changed?" IMF Working Paper. Available at www.imf.org/external/pubs/ft/wp/2006/wp0671.pdf, accessed November 15, 2008.

Rajan, Raghuram G. 2006. "Financial System Reform and Global Current Account Imbalances." Presentation at the American Economic Association Meeting, January 6, in Boston, Massachusetts. Available at www.imf.org/external/np/speeches/2006/010806.htm, accessed November 15, 2008.

Rawski, Thomas G. 2002. "Will Investment Behavior Constrain China's Growth?" *China Economic Review* 13: 361–72.

Riskin, Carl, Renwei Zhao, and Shi Li, eds. 2001. *China's Retreat from Equality: Income Distribution and Economic Transition*. Armonk, NY: M. E. Sharpe.

Roach, Stephen. 2006a. "The Fallacy of Global Decoupling." Global Economic Forum, Morgan Stanley. Available at www.morganstanley.com/views/gef/archive/2006/20061030-Mon.html, accessed December 11, 2008.

———. 2006b. "China's Rebalancing Imperatives: A Giant Step for Globalization." Morgan Stanley Research Global, December 1.

Shan Weijian. 2006a. "The World Bank's China Delusions." *Far Eastern Economic Review* 169, no. 7: 29–32

———. 2006b. "China's Low-Profit Growth Model." *Far Eastern Economic Review* 169, no. 11.

Shih, Victor. 2004. "Dealing with Non-Performing Loans: Political Constraints and Financial Policies in China." *China Quarterly* 180: 922–44.

So, Alvin Y. 2003. "Rethinking the Chinese Developmental Miracle." In *China's Developmental Miracle: Origins, Transformations, and Challenges*, ed. A. Y. So, 3–28. Armonk, NY: M. E. Sharpe.

Tsai, Kelli S. 2002. *Back-Alley Banking: Private Entrepreneurs in China*. Ithaca: Cornell University Press.

Wade, Robert. 1990. *Governing the Market: Economic Theory and the Role of Government in East Asian Industrialization*. Princeton: Princeton University Press.

———. 2000. "Wheels within Wheels: Rethinking the Asian Crisis and the Asian Model." *American Review of Political Science*, no. 3: 85–115.

Wang Shaogang and Hu Angang. 1999. *The Political Economy of Uneven Development: The Case of China*. Armonk, NY: M. E. Sharpe.

Xie Andy. 2006. "China: What Next?" Global Economic Forum, Morgan Stanley, February 3. Available at http://hk.myblog.yahoo.com/stanley7kim/article?mid=9& fid=-1&action=prev, accessed December 11, 2008.

Contributors

Richard P. Appelbaum, Ph.D., is a professor of sociology and global and international studies at the University of California at Santa Barbara. He currently serves as director of the two-year Masters Degree Program in Global and International Studies that prepares students to work in NGOs, unions, and other social justice organizations. He is also on the Executive Committee of the Center for Nanotechnology in Society, an NSF-funded Nanoscience and Engineering Center. He received his B.A. from Columbia University, M.P.A. from Princeton University's Woodrow Wilson School of Public and International Affairs, and Ph.D. from the University of Chicago. His recent books include *States and Economic Development in the Asian Pacific Rim* (with Jeffrey Henderson; 1992); *Behind the Label: Inequality in the Los Angeles Garment Industry* (with Edna Bonacich; 2000); *Rules and Networks: The Legal Culture of Global Business Transactions* (coedited with William L. F. Felstiner and Volkmar Gessner; 2001), and *Towards a Critical Globalization Studies* (coedited with William I. Robinson; 2005). He chairs the Advisory Council of the Worker Rights Consortium. He is currently engaged in a multidisciplinary study of supply chain networks and nanotechnology in the Asian-Pacific Rim, initially focusing on the development of nanoscience and commercialization in China.

Giovanni Arrighi's main interests are in the fields of long-term, large-scale social change and of inequality within and between nations. The publication of *Adam Smith in Beijing: Lineages of the Twenty-first Century* (2007) completes the investigation of the origins and transformations of the world capitalist system that he initiated with *The Long Twentieth Century: Money, Power, and the Origins of Our Times* (1994) and continued with *Chaos and Governance in the Modern World System* (1999), coauthored with Beverly J. Silver. Dr. Arrighi has taught in Africa, Europe, and North America. His work has been published in more than fifteen languages. His current research focuses on regional differentiation within the Global South with special reference to the contrasting developmental trajectories of Southern Africa and East Asia.

Edna Bonacich is an emeritus professor of sociology and ethnic studies at the University of California, Riverside. Her major research interest is the study of class and race, with special emphasis on racial divisions in the working class. She has studied the garment industry, coauthoring *Behind the Label: Inequality in the Los Angeles Apparel Industry* with Richard Appelbaum. She has recently coauthored, with Jake B. Wilson, a project on the ports of Los Angeles/Long Beach as important (and vulnerable) nodes in the global economy, entitled *Getting the Goods: Ports, Labor, and the Logistics Revolution*. Her current project concerns the Los Angeles African-American community's relationship to the labor movement. By interviewing black labor and community leaders, she is trying to find out what is working, what isn't, and what changes are needed. Edna has tried to link her teaching and research to efforts to produce progressive social change, especially by working with the labor movement.

József Böröcz is an associate professor of sociology at Rutgers University, a faculty associate at the Center for Migration and Development at Princeton University, and a scholarly advisor to the Institute for Political Studies of the Hungarian Academy of Sciences. His current work focuses on the transformation of global structures, the European Union as a geopolitical animal, and the de-colonial critique of the moral geopolitics of "Europe." His website is www .borocz.net.

Paul S. Ciccantell is a professor of sociology at Western Michigan University. His research agenda addresses four linked questions from a comparative, historical, and transnational perspective. What are the characteristics and consequences of the relationship between society and nature? What are the socioeconomic and environmental consequences of state development strategies? How do firms strategize and act in the context of a globalizing world economy? What roles have raw materials and transport industries played in the evolution of the world economy? His publications include two books coauthored with Stephen Bunker, *Globalization and the Race for Resources* (2005) and *East Asia and the Global Economy* (2007). His current research interests focus on Chinese economic development and the role of the coal industry in western Canada.

John Gulick is an associate professor of Sociology at Hanyang University, Ansan Campus, South Korea; he has also taught at universities in California, China, Tennessee, and Japan. His published work appears in *Capitalism Nature Socialism*, *International Journal of Comparative Sociology*, *Journal of World-Systems Research*, and *Peace Review*, among other venues. His research currently focuses on the antinomies of globalism and big power rivalry, the China-Russia-U.S. strategic triangle, the political economy of hydrocarbon extraction and climate change, and the political ecology of the Russian Far East.

Ho-fung Hung is an assistant professor at the Department of Sociology of Indiana University, Bloomington. His research work concentrates on globalization, contentious politics, and nationalism in the Greater China Region from the eighteenth to the twenty-first century. His articles have appeared in such venues as *American Sociological Review, Review of International Political Economy, Social Science History, Asian Perspectives,* and *Sociological Theory,* for which he has won multiple professional awards. He is currently working on a project that looks at how the Confucianist legacy shaped China's trajectories of state formation and social protests from the eighteenth century to the present, in contrast to the Western trajectories. Another project examines the dynamics and limits of the current economic ascent of China as well as its impact on global capitalism.

Stephanie Luce is an associate professor and research director at the Labor Center, University of Massachusetts-Amherst. Her research has focused on low-wage labor markets with an emphasis on living wage campaigns and policies. She is the author of *Fighting for a Living Wage,* and coauthor, with Robert Pollin, of *The Living Wage: Building a Fair Economy.*

Beverly J. Silver is a professor of sociology at the Johns Hopkins University. She is author of *Forces of Labor: Workers' Movements and Globalization since 1870* (2003), which won several awards, including the main Scholarly Publication Award of the American Sociological Association in 2005. She is also coauthor, with Giovanni Arrighi, of *Chaos and Governance in the Modern World System* (1999), which won the 2000 Distinguished Publication Award of the Political Economy of the World System section of the American Sociological Association. Her books have translated for publication in Spanish, Portuguese, Korean, Chinese, Italian, German, and Farsi.

Alvin Y. So is a chair professor at the Hong Kong University of Science and Technology. He received his Ph.D. degree from UCLA and has taught at the University of Hawaii. His research interests include social class, development, and East Asia. His books include: *China's Developmental Miracle* (2003), *War and State Terrorism* (coeditor; 2003), and *Hong Kong's Embattled Democracy* (1999).

Lu Zhang is a Ph.D. candidate in the Department of Sociology at the Johns Hopkins University, where she is completing her dissertation, entitled "Globalization, Market Reform, and the Dynamics of Labor Unrest in China, 1980 to the

Present: A Case Study of the Chinese Automobile Industry." The dissertation is based on twelve months of fieldwork at seven automobile factories in six cities in China with the support of grants from the National Science Foundation and the Social Science Research Council. She is the author of several journal articles appearing in, among other places, *International Labor and Working-Class History, International Journal of Automotive Technology and Management,* and *She Hui Xue (Sociology Quarterly).*

Index